Words Count

Laraine E. Flemming

Houghton Mifflin Company   Boston   New York

Publisher: Patricia A. Coryell
Development Editor: Kellie Cardone
Editorial Assistant: Peter Mooney
Senior Project Editor: Margaret Park Bridges
Senior Manufacturing Coordinator: Marie Barnes
Marketing Manager: Annamarie Rice
Marketing Associate: Laura Hemrika

Cover image: Newspaper Clippings by Don Bishop © 2003 Getty Images

Printed in the U.S.A.

Library of Congress Control Number: 2002109446

Student Text ISBN-13: 978-0-618-25861-1   ISBN-10: 0-618-25861-2

4 5 6 7 GP 10 09

Contents

Preface

To the Instructor

Everyone who has ever decided to consciously enlarge his or her vocabulary has probably had the same experience. We study a list of words and meanings, and think we know them. And, in fact, we do—for a while at least. But as the days go by, the words and their meanings often become a bit muddled. In time, many of the words we thought were firmly anchored in memory have disappeared, and we can no longer recall their meanings.

That's because the human brain has a tough time retaining unconnected or isolated bits of information like individual words on a list. The brain performs much better when there is a larger context, or background, to work with, and it can see relationships and make connections between words and meanings.

It's for precisely this reason that *Words Count*—like its more advanced companion text *Words Matter*—offers a contextual approach to vocabulary building. Each chapter introduces ten words linked by a common theme or thread such as character, crime, friendship, and love. The common thread provides a larger context for word meaning and allows students to mentally group words together while taking note of both similarities and differences. By learning words within the umbrella-like context of a general theme, student readers more readily create the web of connections that ensures long-term remembering.

Features

Multiple-Choice Self-Test: After Chapter 1 sets out the book's basic terminology, each chapter opens with a multiple-choice self-test that students can correct on their own and thereby discover if they have any pre-existing knowledge about the words introduced in the chapter. The self-test also gives them a starting point for evaluating their progress.

Final Mastery Test: At the end of each chapter, students are referred to a mastery test that appears at the back of the book. Intentionally more challenging than the opening self-test, the mastery test presents all ten words in the context of a sentence and asks students to recall rather than simply recognize definitions. However, any student who doesn't pass the mastery test has a chance to review and retest. There are additional exercises both in the instructor's manual and on my personal website. (See Website Instruction below for the URL.) Once students complete their review, they can take a second mastery test, which appears in the Instructor's Manual.

Progress Report: A chart for recording the scores of both the self-test and the mastery test appears on the inside front cover so that students can easily track their progress.

Specific Learning Strategies: A memory peg feature that offers one or more suggestions for remembering word meaning accompanies each new word. Here again, students are encouraged to make connections that ensure both in-depth learning and long-term remembering; for instance, students can remember the meanings of *recluse* and *secluded* by making a mental connection like the following: "A *recluse* is likely to live in a *secluded* location."

Varied Exercises: Each chapter offers four different practice exercises that have been carefully sequenced to slowly increase the level of difficulty. Practice 1 simply requires matching words with their appropriate meanings. Practice 2 tells students to use what they have learned to evaluate statements as true or false, e.g., "The public is likely to pay *homage* to someone who has committed a serious crime."

By practice 3, students fill in the blanks, using two sets of clues, the context of the sentence and the definition in parentheses. Each chapter concludes with a passage or reading that asks students to look beyond individual sentences in order to discover clues to word meaning. After completing the four exercises, most students are well prepared for the mastery test that appears at the end of the book. There are, however, additional exercises available in the instructor's manual and online should any student have difficulty with the mastery test.

Topics of Historical and Cultural Interest: The extended passages in *Words Count* ask students to recall word meaning within a context that is historically or culturally significant. The topics addressed in these passages include the history of the death penalty, the legends surrounding King Arthur, and the abolitionists' fight against slavery. The choice of topics is intentional, since many students who need vocabulary improvement also need to expand their general background knowledge.

Idiom Alerts: Every chapter includes one or two related idioms; for example, "in the red" and "in the black" are introduced in the chapter titled "Money Talk." Unfamiliar idioms can impede comprehension in the same way unfamiliar words do, so including idioms seemed appropriate for a book devoted to vocabulary improvement.

Numerous Chances for Review: Words that have been introduced in a chapter reappear throughout the text. The words are marked with an asterisk so that instructors can engage in ongoing mini-reviews with their students.

Usage Tips: In addition to providing repeated experiences with the same word in different contexts, *Words Count* includes two other features meant to encourage students to make use of their new vocabulary. As its name implies, the *Common Usage* feature indicates how a word is most likely to be used. For example, the phrase "launch into" appears as a likely companion for the word "tirade." The feature titled *Additional Forms* shows students how all the words defined in the chapter are spelled when used as different parts of speech.

Flexible Definitions: Although the number of definitions attributed to a single word is limited by the theme of each chapter, *Words Count* avoids the one word–one meaning approach to vocabulary building. Instead students get specific examples of how context can alter word meaning.

Post-Tests in the Manual: Instructors who want to give their students a straightforward multiple-choice test before requiring the mastery test can turn to the instructor's manual for post-tests that match the chapters' opening self-tests.

Website Instruction: Instructors who want to give their students additional practice on the 250 words introduced in this text can go to http://users.dhp.com/~laflemm for online tutorials.

This book has been percolating in my head for a number of years, ever since I read a wonderful little book called *Teaching Reading Vocabulary* by Dale D. Johnson and P. David Pearson. Johnson and Pearson emphasize the importance of placing new vocabulary in a more general context so that students can more readily store the words in memory. I thought the authors were on to something when I read the book around ten years ago. I still do. An inveterate word lover myself, I have adapted and applied their strategies to my own efforts at vocabulary improvement. In addition to the success I have had with classroom testing, I can also offer a personal testimonial: A contextual approach to vocabulary building really works. Try it in your classroom and see for yourself. I think you will be pleased with the results.

Also Available: *Words Matter* is a more advanced vocabulary book that follows the same format as *Words Count*. *Reading Keys* (1st edition) and *Reading for Results* (9th edition) are the ideal companion texts for students using *Words Count,* while *Reading for Thinking* (4th edition) would be a good companion text to *Words Matter.*

Words of Thanks: Dawn Sedik of Valencia Community College classroom-tested *Words Count,* and the suggestions she and her students made proved invaluable. Much of the book's sequence is based on Dawn's suggestions about the original order of both the explanations and exercises. Joan Hellman of Community College of Baltimore County–Catonsville reviewed the manuscript in its earliest form. With her usual directness, Joan told me to stop elaborating on all the possible nuances of word meaning and give students what she termed a "back-pocket definition," a brief definition that would be of practical value to student readers struggling with their textbooks. This was a very smart suggestion, and I cannot thank her enough.

As she has in the past, Ann Marie Radaskiewicz helped me enormously in the writing of this book, and she is responsible for many clever sentences and paragraphs. I don't know what I would do without her.

And finally, thanks to my two editors, Kellie Cardone and Mary Jo Southern. Kellie remains the most efficient and most supportive editor I have ever had. She also has a gifted eye for design and knows how to make the format highlight rather than obscure the text. To good effect, she has sensibly reined in my fancier notions about design. Mary Jo has moved on, but in my mind, she remains the Maxwell Perkins of college publishing. There is no one like her, and her influence on both me and my books has been enormous. Typically, it was she who gave my two vocabulary books their snappy titles. She is a genius at every aspect of textbook publishing, and I shall not find her like again. For that reason, I'm dedicating the book to her, still my friend even if she is no longer my editor.

Best wishes and good luck,
Laraine Flemming

Chapter 1

Setting the Stage for Vocabulary Building

Chapter by chapter, *Words Count* will introduce you to 250 words that need to be part of your reading vocabulary. Before you turn to the lists of words and meanings that make up each chapter, however, let's go over some terms and concepts that are essential to using this book successfully.

Two Keys to Remembering

Learning the meanings of new words is not difficult. What *can* be tricky is remembering what those words mean as time passes. For precisely that reason, *Words Count* includes two features that will help you remember both words and meanings.

The Common Thread

The words in every chapter of *Words Count* revolve around a common theme or thread like "money matters" or "character comments." The common thread places the individual words in some larger context, or category, making them easier to remember. They are easier to remember because the mind has a hard time remembering disconnected pieces of information. It does much better with facts, figures, or terms that appear in some larger web of connections. Say, for example, you encounter a group of words united around the theme "errors and mistakes." That theme gives you a mental category in which you can store the new words.

Within the category "errors and mistakes," you can also make connections between words based on what kinds of errors they represent. For instance, a *fallacy* is an error in reasoning that carries no legal penalty. The same cannot be said of a *felony*, a word that refers to a major crime that can land you in jail. It is precisely those kinds of mental activities—categorizing, analyzing, comparing and contrasting of words—that will help you retain both words and meanings.

Memory Pegs

Each of the words introduced in this book is accompanied by something called a *memory peg*. Memory pegs are tips that will help you store new words in long-term memory. The memory pegs range from discussions of word origins to images for visualization. But their purpose remains the same. They make new words more meaningful and therefore more memorable.

Whatever you do, don't breeze through the Memory Peg sections thinking, "I know the meaning. What do I need this for?" Memory pegs will give you additional ways to anchor new words in your mind.

Context Defines Meaning

You may already know this, but it's worth repeating: Where word meaning is concerned, context or setting is key. For example, a common meaning for the

1

word *game* is "an activity done for entertainment." That meaning fits nicely with the following sentence:

> To pass the time, they played one game after another.

However, what happens to the meaning of *game* in this context?

> When it came to sports, one of the twins was more *game* than the other; no matter how badly she was losing, she would not give up.

In this context, the word *game* means "unyielding," "competitive," or "spirited."

Understanding the importance of context is essential to using *Words Count* because the common thread of every chapter identifies and limits each word's context. For example, if there were a chapter in this book titled "Mood Words," you might discover this definition for *sanguine:* "cheerful and good-tempered." What you wouldn't find is the definition "red or blood colored," since that definition does not fit the chapter's theme. In other words, each chapter in this book gives you definitions that fit a specific context. Once you learn the words, you may occasionally encounter them in a completely different context. If you do and the meaning you know doesn't fit, see if you can figure out a meaning that does, or else look the word up. Then make it a point to add the new meaning to the one you already know.

Common Context Clues

1. Contrast *antonym*	The sentence or passage mentions a word that is the exact opposite in meaning: "Usually he had a *terse*, straightforward style that was easy to read, but his new novel was <u>wordy</u> to a fault." Based on the contrast clue, you can assume that *terse* means a. witty. <u>b. brief.</u> c. colorful.
2. Restatement *definition* *synonym*	The sentence or passage includes a simpler version of the word you don't know: "Her *loquacious* style made her easy to talk to, but after a while, her <u>chattiness</u> was irritating." Based on the restatement clue, you can assume that *loquacious* means a. gentle. b. good humored. <u>c. talkative.</u>
3. Example *memory* *Pegs*	The sentence or passage offers an illustration of behavior or events associated with the word in question: "She was exhausted from studying and needed to do something *frivolous* to relax, <u>like watch a sitcom or give herself a pedicure.</u>" Based on the example, you can assume that *frivolous* means a. self-destructive. b. important. <u>c. unimportant.</u>
4. General knowledge *background* *Prior* *knowledge*	The sentence or passage describes an experience or an event you know about. Thus, your own background knowledge provides a clue to word meaning: "The *clamor* in the concert hall only increased as Jennifer Lopez walked onstage." Based on your general knowledge, you can assume that *clamor* means <u>a. noise.</u> b. quiet. c. complaining.

Synonyms and Antonyms

Throughout the chapters that follow, you will repeatedly see the words *synonyms* and *antonyms*. Synonyms are words that have similar meanings; antonyms are words with opposite meanings. Often, you can use synonyms or antonyms as memory pegs. For example, having learned the meaning of *loquacious*, you might well tell yourself that *loquacious* is an antonym for *silent* and a synonym for *chatty*. It's connections like these that encourage remembering.

Similar Doesn't Mean Identical

When you learn synonyms for new words, keep in mind that "synonyms are words that have similar though not identical meanings."[1] For example, *denounce* and *castigate* are often called synonyms. And, indeed, they are. Yet that doesn't mean they are completely interchangeable. *Denounce* and *castigate* both mean "to criticize harshly." However, *denounce* implies that the criticism was made in a public place. Now that you are aware of the subtle difference between the two synonyms, how would you fill in the blanks below?

1. In Britain's parliament, members of the opposing parties are always quick

   to _____ one another's policies.

2. Afraid his child would get in an accident, the father was quick to

   _____ the teenager for racing on the neighborhood streets.

In sentence 1, *denounce* is the better choice because the context suggests that the criticism was made in public. In sentence 2, *castigate* is the better choice because the sentence does not suggest that an audience was present.

Literal and Figurative Meanings

Throughout this text you'll see statements like this one that opens Chapter 25: "Whether it's the literal heat of a blazing fire or the figurative warmth of a heated argument, the words in this chapter have something to do with heat." As you can probably tell from this example, something "literal" takes place in the real world. Fires do generate heat measurable by thermometers. Something that happens figuratively, however, is real only in imaginative terms. So an argument doesn't *literally* give off heat. You can't go into a room where two people are arguing and measure the room's temperature to see if it's increased by twenty degrees. However, you can imagine that arguments, particularly angry ones, require so much energy it's as if the participants were heating up a room.

Here's an example of the word *inflammable*, meaning "capable of causing fire," used literally and figuratively. In the blank that follows each sentence, indicate which is which by writing *L* or *F*.

1. The truck was carrying an *inflammable* liquid so dangerous that the driver

   was afraid of going over bumps. _____

2. The president of the company had a highly *inflammable* temper, and her

   employees treated her with kid gloves. _____

Dale D. Johnson and P. David Pearson, *Teaching Reading Vocabulary* (New York: Holt, Rinehart, and Winston, 1984), p. 2.

In sentence 1, the liquid really can cause fire, so you are correct to put an *L* in the blank. In sentence 2, the word *inflammable* is used figuratively. The woman is certainly not going to go up in flames, but she can get fired up and lose her temper very quickly.

Words and Connotations

Sometimes in the memory pegs, you'll see the word *connotations* used to help you distinguish between two similar meanings. Here's an illustration of what you might find in a memory peg passage: "The words *thrifty* and *stingy* are synonyms. Both words mean 'careful with money.' However, the connotations of *thrifty* are positive whereas the connotations of *stingy* are negative."

Connotations are the associations some words acquire in addition to their denotation, or dictionary meaning. Most people, for example, rather like being told they are *thrifty*. The word connotes, or suggests, being careful with money in a smart or thoughtful way. Thrifty people look for sales, don't get taken in by misleading ads, and make it a point to comparison shop. The word *stingy*, in contrast, suggests that someone is excessively concerned about saving money and quite reluctant to spend it even when spending is necessary. The stingy person might suffer ninety-degree heat rather than buy an air conditioner, even one that's used or on sale. Above all, he or she will try hard to have someone else pay for a meal or a movie. For the thrifty person, spending money requires effort and thought. For the stingy, spending money is almost painful and they try to avoid it if possible.

While some words are neutral and carry with them no connotations of any kind—the words *chair*, *table*, *eye*, and *curtain*, for example, probably don't arouse any emotion or feeling in you—other words are heavily connotated. Thus when learning new words, it pays to think about the associations connected to their use.

Context Counts

When learning the connotations of a word, you need to remember that context can alter both meaning and connotation. For example, what are the connotations of the word *stories* in the following sentence: "The teacher delighted the youngsters with her *stories* about talking animals." In this context, the word *stories* has positive associations. It refers to tales or fables that give pleasure. The stories are something to be proud of or pleased with. But what about the word *stories* in this sentence: "To get back at the manager who fired him, the ex-employee spread *stories* about a romance between the manager and her secretary." In this context, the word *stories* has negative connotations. The word is now a synonym for *lies* and has taken on a whole new set of negative associations.

Practice 1

Directions: Read each sentence and look carefully at the italicized word. Then write *positive*, *negative*, or *neutral* in the blank at the end of the sentence to describe the connotations of the word.

1.   The two men sat over a glass of beer and *gossiped* about work, friends,

and family. _____

2. It was two in the morning, but the two were in deep *discussion* and didn't realize the time. _____

3. After *gobbling* his food, the child was covered in syrup. _____

4. The food critic *ate* quickly, letting nothing show on his face.

_____

5. The *slender* gymnast seemed to soar into the air. _____

6. *Scrawny* for his age, Timmy was still desperate to play football.

_____

7. The two brothers *glared* at one another throughout dinner, and when the bill came, neither one reached for it. _____

8. Expectantly, the instructor *looked* at the class and waited for an answer.

_____

9. The wind *whipped* through the trees. _____

10. The warm breeze *fluttered* the papers on the table. _____

Practice 2

Directions: For each sentence, put an *L* or an *F* in the blank to indicate if the italicized word is used literally or figuratively.

1. After the game, Denise tried to *unwind* by watching an old movie. ____

2. He couldn't *unwind* the telephone cord. ____

3. She asked her father to write her a *blank* check, but he only laughed. ____

4. When he was asked the first question, the poor contestant went *blank* from anxiety. ____

Terms for Word Analysis

Many of the memory pegs in this book will suggest you divide words into parts as a way of remembering their meanings. To use these suggestions, you'll need to know the terms *roots*, *prefixes*, and *suffixes*.

Roots

Roots are the word parts that give words their core meaning. For example, the words *prescribe, scribble,* and *scripture* all come from the Latin root *scrip* or *scrib*, meaning "write." Because the words stem from the same root, they all have something to do with writing.

Once you can identify the common root in several different words, you have a key to their meanings. However, you also have a chance to use their common relationship as a way of storing the words in memory. You can do so by creating a word map, which looks like this:

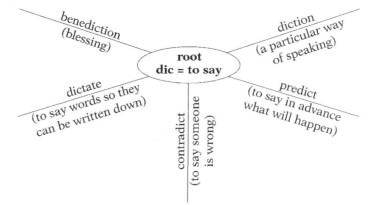

Making a word map forces you to think about the meanings of words as well as their relationship to one another. That kind of in-depth thinking encourages long-term remembering.

Prefixes

Prefixes are word parts that appear at the beginning of words and modify word meaning. Thus, for example, the root *gress* means "to step or go." Put the prefix *re-*, meaning "back" or "backward," in front of it, and you have the word *regress*, meaning "to go backward." Change the prefix and you change the meaning. If you put *pro-*, meaning "forward," in front of *gress*, you have the word *progress*, meaning "go forward."

Suffixes

Suffixes are word parts that appear at the end of words. While some suffixes (see box below) do affect word meaning, they are more likely to reveal how the word functions as a part of speech.

Speech Part	Meaning	Example
Suffix (*n.*) *-an, -ian* *-ant, -ent* *-ar, -er, -or* *-eer, -ier*	someone who does or is what's described in the word	American, physician servant, agent bursar, farmer, mayor engineer, cashier
Suffix (*n.*) *-ette* *-ule, -cule*	something small	statuette, kitchenette capsule, molecule
Suffix (*adj.*) *-ful* *-ous*	having the quality of full of	beautiful, merciful famous, gracious
Suffix (*adj.* and *adv.*) *-less*	without	hopeless, brainless
Suffix (*n.*) *-ism*	state or condition; practice or belief	hypnotism, communism

Idioms

Every chapter in this textbook includes one or two idioms. **Idioms** are phrases that say something different from the actual literal meanings of the words. For example, if you call someone a "babe in arms," you're not talking about his or her age. Rather, you are talking about that person's attitude, and you are suggesting that he or she is extremely innocent—as innocent, in fact, as a "babe (or baby) in arms."

The Secret of Vocabulary Building: Active Review

Reviewing the words and meanings in this book is absolutely essential. But so, too, is your method of review. *Active* review will produce better and faster results than passive review.

Active Reviews

Active reviews force your mind into action. They make you dig in and search your memory until you arrive at the appropriate meaning. That's the basic principle of active reviewing. However, there are different ways to put that principle into practice.

You can, for example, put the words on index cards, with the word on one side and the definition on the other. Off and on throughout the week, take out the cards and arrange them with the words showing. As you look at each word, try to remember the meaning. If you can't, try to call up the memory peg provided with the word. Then, turn the card over to check the definition you either came up with or couldn't recall.

You can also start a vocabulary notebook. Make sure to put the words on one side of the page and the meanings on the other so you can hide the definitions as you try to recall them. Or, try working on vocabulary with a friend so you can quiz each other. You may even use the words in sentences, sometimes incorrectly, and ask each other to determine if word and context match. The point is simple: Use a method of review that forces you to think.

Passive Reviews

As you probably have guessed by now, passive reviews don't require much effort. All you have to do is look at the word, then look at the meaning. Just keep doing this until your eyes glaze over. But don't be surprised if (1) it takes a while for word and meaning to sink in, and (2) the words and meanings don't seem to stay with you. Because they don't really engage the mind, passive reviews are just not as effective as active ones.

Checking Out

Directions: Check your understanding of the chapter by circling the letter of the correct response to each question.

1. Words and meanings are easier to remember if
   a. you learn them in order.
   b. they have a context.
   c. the definitions are short.

2. The mind has a hard time remembering
   a. disconnected pieces of information.
   b. words that rhyme.
   c. words in context.

3. Synonyms are words
   a. opposite in meaning.
   b. similar in meaning.
   c. that sound the same but have different meanings.

4. Antonyms are words
   a. opposite in meaning.
   b. similar in meaning.
   c. that sound the same but have different meanings.

5. Literal meanings of words
   a. refer to activities that can be carried out in the real world.
   b. make sense only in imaginative terms.
   c. cannot be translated into other languages.

6. Figurative meanings of words
   a. make sense only in imaginative terms.
   b. don't make realistic sense.
   c. are restricted to poetry.

7. Roots
   a. modify the core meanings of words.
   b. identify the part of speech.
   c. give words their core meaning.

8. Prefixes
   a. give words their core meaning.
   b. appear at the end of words and indicate function.
   c. appear at the beginning of words and modify word meaning.

9. Idioms are examples of
   a. literal language.
   b. figurative language.
   c. synonyms.

10. Active reviews
    a. rely mainly on repetition.
    b. cannot be done alone.
    c. force the mind to search for meaning.

Pronunciation Key

Words Count uses the same symbols and sound relationships that appear in the *American Heritage Dictionary*. Those symbols and sounds appear below. *Note: Words Count* does not use stress marks to indicate which syllable is emphasized when the word is spoken. Instead, the syllable receiving the strongest emphasis is printed in capitals.

Symbol	Sound	Symbol	Sound
ă	pat	ô	caught, paw, for, horrid, hoarse
ā	pay		
â	care	oi	noise
ä	father	ŏŏ	took
b	**bib**	ōō	**boot**
ch	**ch**ur**ch**	ou	**out**
d	**deed**	p	**pop**
ĕ	pet	r	**r**oar
ē	bee	s	**s**auce
f	**f**i**fe**, **ph**ase, rou**gh**	sh	**sh**ip, di**sh**
g	**g**a**g**	t	**t**ight, stop**ped**
h	**h**at	th	**th**in
hw	**wh**ich	*th*	**th**is
ĭ	pit	ŭ	cut
ī	pie, by	ûr	urge, term, firm, word, heard
îr	pier		
j	**j**u**dge**	v	**v**alve
k	**k**ick, **c**at, pi**que**	w	**w**ith
l	**l**id, need**l**e	y	**y**es
m	**mum**	z	**z**ebra
n	**n**o, sud**den**	zh	vi**s**ion, plea**s**ure, gara**ge**
ng	thi**ng**	ə	**a**bout, **i**tem, edibl**e**, gall**o**p, circ**u**s
ŏ	pot		
ō	t**o**e	ər	butt**er**

Chapter 2

Character Comments

The Common Thread

The words in this chapter are all adjectives used mainly to describe character or behavior. As you learn them, try to think of people or incidents that illustrate the character or behavior described.

obstinate	altruistic
assiduous	lethargic
intrepid	introverted
extroverted	insolent
callous	blasé

Self-Test — Character Comments

Directions: For each italicized word, circle the letter of what you think is the correct definition.

1. *Obstinate* means
   a. impolite.
   b. critical.
   c. stubborn.

2. *Assiduous* means
   a. persistent.
   b. outgoing.
   c. dishonest.

3. *Intrepid* means
   a. brave.
   b. lazy.
   c. careful.

4. *Extroverted* means
   a. shy.
   b. outgoing.
   c. careful.

5. *Callous* means
   a. colorful.
   b. excitable.
   c. uncaring.

6. *Altruistic* means
   a. selfish.
   b. unselfish.
   c. clever.

7. *Lethargic* means
   a. busy.
   b. talkative.
   c. tired.

8. *Introverted* means
   a. rude.
   b. hard-working.
   c. withdrawn.

9. *Insolent* means
   a. rude.
   b. charming.
   c. angry.

10. *Blasé* means
    a. hot-headed.
    b. sophisticated.
    c. selfish.

Turn to page 241 to correct your test. Record your grade in the self-test column on the inside front cover of your textbook. Then go on to **Words and Meanings** on pages 11–13.

Words and Meanings

Here again are the words from the self-test. Only this time, they are accompanied by their most common meanings and pointers on pronunciation.

1. **obstinate (ŎB-stə-nĭt) *adj.***   excessively stubborn, difficult to manage or move

   Sample Sentence   The *obstinate* donkey sat in the road and refused to move.

   > **MEMORY PEG** The root of obstinate, *obstin*, means "persist." It's no surprise, then, that someone who is obstinate "persistently" sticks to a position, an opinion, or behavior no matter what the consequences or criticism. If knowing something about the root is not enough of a memory aid, visualize that stubborn donkey refusing to move from the middle of the road.

   Additional Forms† obstinacy, obstinateness

2. **assiduous (ə-SĬJ-ōō-əs) *adj.***   persistent, determined, hard-working, thorough

   Sample Sentence   *Assiduous* by nature, she could not give up on a task once she had begun it.

   > **MEMORY PEG** Tie this word to a visual image of bees working in a hive or ants carrying off crumbs of bread. Both insects exemplify what it means to be *assiduous*. They work hard, and they don't give up. You can also think of *assiduous* as a positive way of saying someone is *obstinate*. Like the *obstinate*, the assiduous don't give up. But they are persistent for a purpose, rather than just being pigheaded.

   Additional Form   assiduousness

3. **intrepid (ĭn-TRĔP-ĭd) *adj.***   brave, fearless, bold

   Sample Sentence   George Mallory was an *intrepid* climber who died trying to conquer Mount Everest.

   > **MEMORY PEG** In *intrepid*, the prefix *in-* means "not," while *trep* means "alarm." Remember, then, that people who are *intrepid* are not easily alarmed. If that doesn't fix the word in your memory, think of somebody involved in a pastime or profession that requires real nerve—say, a trapeze artist or a tightrope walker. You have to be *intrepid* to swing on a trapeze or walk a tightrope.

4. **extroverted (ĔK-strə-vûr-tĭd) *adj.***   friendly, sociable, outgoing

   Sample Sentence   An extremely *extroverted* person, President Bill Clinton was a nightmare for his Secret Service agents: Clinton couldn't resist plunging into a crowd in order to greet well-wishers.

   > **MEMORY PEG** The prefix *extro-*, like *extra-*, means "outside," whereas the root *vert* means "turn." Think of *extroverts* as people turned outward rather than inward. And if you need an image of an *extrovert*, that of former president Bill Clinton will do just fine.

   Additional Forms   extrovert, extroversion

---

†   There may be other forms of the word, but *Words Count* introduces *only* the ones you are most likely to encounter. Please note as well that the text does not include additional forms that are obvious, for example, a plural form created by adding the letter *s*.

5. callous (KĂL-əs) adj.   unfeeling

Sample Sentence   Some people are so *callous* to suffering they won't even stop to help a person hurt and in need of assistance.

> **MEMORY PEG**   Many years ago, people watched through their apartment windows as a young woman named Kitty Genovese was stabbed to death. This tragic incident illustrates perfectly the meaning of *callous*.

Additional Form   callousness

6. altruistic (al-trōō-ĬS-tĭk) adj.   unselfish, charitable, always thinking of others

Sample Sentence   Dorothy Day's† *altruistic* character is an inspiration for us all: She devoted her life to caring for those less fortunate than she.

> **MEMORY PEG**   *Altruistic* comes from the Latin word *alter*, meaning "other." Those who are *altruistic* think of others before themselves. Need an image? Think of Mother Teresa, who lived in poverty and tended the poor for most of her life.

Additional Forms   altruism, altruistically

7. lethargic (lə-THÄR-jĭk) adj.   slow, tired, lacking in energy

Sample Sentence   People suffering from Lyme disease feel extremely *lethargic;* even the simplest activity brings on exhaustion.

> **MEMORY PEG**   It will help to remember that the word *lethargy* comes from the river Lethe of Greek mythology. According to myth, the dead would drink the river's water to forget their past lives and prepare themselves for the afterlife. Eventually, *lethargic* became associated with the feeling of being dead tired.

Additional Form   lethargy

8. introverted (ĬN-trə-vûr-tĭd) adj.   timid, shy, self-absorbed

Sample Sentence   *Introverted* as a child because she was blind and deaf, Helen Keller grew up to be a lively, extroverted adult.

> **MEMORY PEG**   Link *introverted* to *extroverted*, telling yourself that one is the antonym for the other. If you need an image, picture a party where everyone is laughing and talking except for one lone soul standing in a corner. That person is a definite *introvert*.

Additional Forms   introvert, introversion

9. insolent (ĬN-sə-lənt) adj.   rude, insulting

Sample Sentence   Union leader Jimmy Hoffa was *insolent* when questioned by Attorney General Robert Kennedy, and Kennedy never forgave Hoffa's rudeness.

---

†   Dorothy Day (1897–1980): American reformer who founded a newspaper, *The Catholic Worker,* which was committed to peace and social justice.

MEMORY PEG Suppose your instructor asked you why your term paper was late and you responded by saying, "What's it to you?" That response would be a perfect example of *insolent* behavior.

Additional Form insolence

10. **blasé (blä-ZĀ)** *adj.*   cool, sophisticated, not easily impressed; disinterested because of frequent exposure

Sample Sentence When he approached the young woman to ask for a date, he tried hard to seem cool and *blasé*.

MEMORY PEG To remember the meaning of *blasé*, think of someone you know who never seems to be anxious or ill-at-ease, no matter what the circumstances. If you don't know anyone like that, visualize secret agent James Bond of movie and novel fame. He's the perfect example of a *blasé* individual. Imagine growing up as the child of a Hollywood star and seeing famous people all the time. The children of Hollywood are bound to be *blasé* around movie stars.

Idiom Alert

In character: If someone tells you your behavior is *in character*, he or she is saying that what you've done fits your personality, for example: "His willingness to work harder than anybody else was *in character*."

Practice 1   Matching Words and Meanings

Directions: To match word and meaning, fill in the blanks with the appropriate letters.

1. obstinate	_____	a. unfeeling
2. assiduous	_____	b. unselfish
3. intrepid	_____	c. shy and withdrawn
4. extroverted	_____	d. stubborn
5. callous	_____	e. brave
6. altruistic	_____	f. persistent
7. lethargic	_____	g. outgoing
8. introverted	_____	h. rude
9. insolent	_____	i. cool and sophisticated
10. blasé	_____	j. tired

Practice 2   Answering True or False

Directions: To indicate if a statement is *true* or *false,* circle the correct answer.

True   False   1. People who are *obstinate* give up too easily.

True   False   2. Employers like *assiduous* workers.

True   False   3. The most *intrepid* surfers like riding the waves when the ocean is really rough.

True   False   4. The *extroverted* usually avoid parties.

True   False   5. You can depend on the *callous* to aid the needy.

True   False   6. People who are *altruistic* usually promote their own interests.

True   False   7. Being *lethargic* is a big advantage for people involved in competitive sports.

True   False   8. The *introverted* are comfortable only in a group.

True   False   9. *Insolent* waiters usually earn big tips.

True   False   10. The *blasé* are easily impressed.

Practice 3   Making Sentence Sense

Directions: Fill in the blanks with the word that fits both the context and the definition in parentheses.

callous	obstinate	assiduous	blasé	altruistic
introverted	insolent	lethargic	intrepid	extroverted

1. The student knew she was losing the argument, but she was too _____ to give up. (excessively stubborn)

2. Of the tennis-playing Williams sisters, Serena and Venus, Serena is the more _____. (outgoing)

3. When several famous actors walked into the restaurant, the reporter tried to act _____, but she couldn't keep from staring. (sophisticated)

4. _____ to a fault, the minister gave all his money to the poor and left his family penniless. (unselfish)

5. The student was so _____ the young substitute teacher burst into tears. (rude)

6. _____ from childhood on, Beryl Markham† never seemed to know the meaning of fear. Certainly her memoir *West with the Night* suggests a woman not easily frightened. (fearless)

† Beryl Markham (1903–1986): British writer and pilot who was the first person to fly solo across the Atlantic Ocean from east to west.

7. The patient's _____ manner suggested that he was being treated with the drug Librium, which is known to cause fatigue. (tired, lacking in energy)

8. After years of _____ research, he was finally able to write a biography of Cuban dictator Fidel Castro. (persistent)

9. Andrew Jackson's† _____ treatment of Native Americans made his name hated and feared throughout the Indian nations. (unfeeling)

10. Pat Nixon's† _____ personality made her uncomfortable in the public spotlight. (shy, withdrawn)

Practice 4   Filling in the Gaps

Directions: Fill in the blanks with one of the words from the chapter. If two words seem equally right, study the context. One word will be better than the other.

assiduously	**lethargic**	**insolence**
introverted	**extroverted**	**obstinate**

1. **Coming into the Light**

   When teacher Anne Mansfield Sullivan entered Helen Keller's life in 1887, Keller was only seven years old. However, she was also blind, deaf, and unable to speak, the results of an illness that struck her in early childhood at the age of two. Cut off from the world, Keller was an _____ child. Not surprisingly, she resented Sullivan's attempts to make her more _____ . Every time Sullivan tried to teach Keller how to use sign language, the girl reacted like a wild animal. Lacking language, she still managed to be rude and insulting. Keller apparently hoped her _____ would discourage Sullivan's efforts. Sullivan, however, quickly realized that Keller really wanted to learn. The little girl was just terrified of trying and failing. _____ in her determination to brighten Keller's dark world, Sullivan refused to quit. Battle by battle, letter by letter, she _____ chipped away at the child's emotional armor until she taught Keller how to sign, read Braille, and even speak. Over time, little Helen Keller went from

† Andrew Jackson (1767–1845): seventh president of the United States (1829–1837).
† Thelma Catherine "Pat" Nixon (1912–1993): first lady of the United States (1969–1974), who apparently hated being in the public spotlight.

being sickly and _____ to become outgoing and even adventurous. Thanks to Sullivan's determination and Keller's own lively intelligence, Keller went on to become world famous as a writer and lecturer.

blasé	**intrepid**
altruistic	**callous**

2. Amelia Earhart's Soaring Life

At age twenty-three, Amelia Earhart flew in an airplane for the first time. Never _____ when something really interested her, Earhart immediately began taking flying lessons, applying herself with her typical enthusiasm. By 1921, she had earned her pilot's license. But Amelia Earhart was not content to simply soar through the skies above her home. Instead, she began setting records. In 1922, she set the altitude record for women and went on to win air races. In time, Earhart became the first woman to fly solo across the Atlantic Ocean, the first person (male or female) to fly across the Pacific from Hawaii to the U.S. mainland, and the first woman to fly across the transcontinental United States.

Famous for her achievements, Earhart traveled across America giving lectures. Women were drawn to Earhart. She inspired them in an era when women had few career opportunities. In addition, the daring adventurer was not _____ or uncaring on the subject of women's issues. On the contrary, she was _____ enough to encourage other women to pursue their dreams in the same determined way she had pursued hers. Again and again, she urged women to dedicate themselves to their goals with energy and passion. To be sure, Earhart was following her own advice when she decided to become the first person to go around the globe in an airplane. Although such a trip could be dangerous, the _____ pilot set out in June 1937. On July 2, though, after having completed almost two-thirds of her journey, her plane vanished somewhere over the Pacific Ocean. To this day, the mystery of her disappearance has never been solved.

To test your mastery of the words introduced in this chapter, turn to page 191 in the back of the book.

Chapter 3

More Character Comments

The Common Thread

This chapter focuses on more adjectives used to describe character. Each time you learn a new word, consider how it does or does not match up with other words on the list. And, again, think of people or situations that give the words a personal meaning and anchor them in your memory.

staunch	pretentious
avid	staid
credulous	pious
proficient	reticent
morose	convivial

Self-Test   More Character Comments

Directions: For each italicized word, circle the letter of what you think is the correct definition.

1. *Staunch* means
   a. loyal.
   b. religious.
   c. outgoing.

2. *Avid* means
   a. annoying.
   b. confident.
   c. enthusiastic.

3. *Credulous* means
   a. not sociable.
   b. easily deceived.
   c. snobbish.

4. *Proficient* means
   a. very capable.
   b. extremely happy.
   c. greedy.

5. *Morose* means
   a. moody.
   b. alert.
   c. arrogant.

6. *Pretentious* means
   a. fashionable.
   b. honest.
   c. self-important.

7. *Staid* means
   a. lively.
   b. serious.
   c. self-centered.

8. *Pious* means
   a. dishonest.
   b. religious.
   c. demanding perfection.

9. *Reticent* means
   a. shy.
   b. educated.
   c. dull and boring.

10. *Convivial* means
    a. good at one's work.
    b. dedicated.
    c. social.

Turn to page 241 to correct your test. Record your grade in the self-test column on the inside front cover of your textbook. Then go on to **Words and Meanings** on pages 18–20.

Words and Meanings

Here again are the words from the self-test. Only this time, they are accompanied by their most common meanings and pointers on pronunciation.

1. staunch (stônch) *adj.*   devoted or dedicated to a person, organization, or set of beliefs or opinions; loyal

Sample Sentence   A long-time dog lover, he was a *staunch* supporter of animal rights.

> **MEMORY PEG**   The word *staunch* comes from a Latin word that means "to stand." Use this clue to help you remember that *staunch* people stand firm in their beliefs; they are fiercely loyal to another person or to a cause.

Additional Form   staunchness

2. avid (ĂV-ĭd) *adj.*   enthusiastic about, having a craving or desire for

Sample Sentence   *Avid* golfers will play even if it's cold or raining.

> **MEMORY PEG**   *Avid* comes from the Latin word *avere*, meaning "to desire." Thus, people who are *avid* desire a lot of something.

Additional Form   avidity

Common Usage   avid *about;* avid *for*

3. credulous (KRĔJ-ə-ləs) *adj.*   easily tricked or deceived

Sample Sentence   Victims of get-rich-quick schemes are often too *credulous* for their own good.

> **MEMORY PEG**   Like the word *incredible*, the word *credulous* is based on the Latin root *cred*, meaning "belief." Thus someone who is *credulous* is "full of belief." If knowing the meaning of the root doesn't help, imagine someone who believes that he can lose weight without exercising or counting calories. After all, there are *credulous* people who believe the diet ads that make that claim.

Additional Forms   credulousness, credulity

4. proficient (prə-FĬSH-ənt) *adj.*   very qualified, having a high degree of competence

Sample Sentence   The computer courses at our school are designed to make students *proficient* users of popular software programs.

> **MEMORY PEG**   Link the word *proficient* to the word *professional*. Tell yourself that athletes who become very "proficient" at a sport sometimes turn "professional."

Additional Form   proficiency

Common Usage   proficient *in*

5. morose (mə-RŌS) *adj.*   gloomy, ill-tempered, depressed

Sample Sentence   Winston Churchill, Britain's prime minister during World War II, suffered from depression; thus he was often moody and *morose*.

> **MEMORY PEG**   Link the word *morose* to the word *mope* because someone who is "morose" is also likely to "mope" around and complain about the world and its ills. In fact, *mopey*, an informal way of saying *depressed*, is a good synonym for *morose*.

Additional Form   moroseness

6. pretentious (pri-TĔN-shəs) *adj.*   giving the impression of importance by showing off or bragging

Sample Sentence   A writer who uses long, difficult vocabulary words where smaller, simpler ones will do risks coming across as a *pretentious* showoff.

> **MEMORY PEG**   When you see the word *pretentious*, think of the word *pretend*. To pretend means to "put on a false appearance." Not surprisingly, that's exactly what *pretentious* people do. They like to exaggerate or emphasize their own worth or position in order to impress others.

Additional Forms   pretension, pretentiousness

7. staid (stād) *adj.*   serious, sober, and dignified; old-fashioned

Sample Sentence   A funeral director is expected to be *staid* in appearance and manner.

> **MEMORY PEG**   When you see the word *staid*, think of the word *stay*, along with several other words that begin with the letter *s*. *Staid* people solemnly stay the same. They are steady and serious, but also a bit stiff, and they are usually uncomfortable with change.

Additional Form   staidness

8. pious (PĪ-əs) *adj.*   having or showing religious devotion

Sample Sentence   *Pious* Muslims face toward Mecca, Islam's holiest city, and pray five times a day.

> **MEMORY PEG**   *Pious* comes from the Latin word *pius*, meaning "dutiful." *Pious* people are dutiful in their religious practices. They go to a church, synagogue, or mosque regularly. They do not take their faith or its practice lightly.

Additional Forms   piousness, piety

9. reticent (RĔT-ĭ-sənt) *adj.*   reserved; keeping one's thoughts and feelings to oneself; shy

Sample Sentence   People who go on television talk shows are not particularly *reticent* when it comes to revealing the most intimate details of their private lives.

MEMORY PEG   *Reticent* comes from the Latin word *reticens*, which means "keeping silent." Remember that *reticent* people "keep silent" about what they're thinking and feeling. The *reticent* are reserved, restrained, and reluctant to reveal any information about themselves. If you are thinking that introverted* might be a synonym for *reticent*, you are absolutely right.

Additional Form   reticence

10. **convivial (kən-VĬV-ē-əl)** *adj.*   merry and fond of company; sociable

Sample Sentence   *Convivial* people love the holiday season because it is filled with parties and get-togethers.

MEMORY PEG   At the root of *convivial* is the Latin word *vivere*, meaning "to live." The prefix *con-*, in turn, means "together" or "with." So remember that *convivial* people like to live it up with their friends. Unlike those who are *reticent*, *convivial* people delight in social occasions like parties. And, yes, extroverted* is an excellent synonym for *convivial*. Similarly, introverted* would be an antonym.

Additional Form   conviviality

Idiom Alert

Out of character: As you might expect, behavior *out of character* doesn't fit what people know of your personality, for example, "For her to pick up a check was very *out of character*."

Practice 1   Matching Words and Meanings

Directions: To match word and meaning, fill in the blanks with the appropriate letters.

1. staunch	_____	a. shy
2. avid	_____	b. moody
3. credulous	_____	c. serious
4. proficient	_____	d. showing religious devotion
5. morose	_____	e. given to bragging
6. pretentious	_____	f. sociable
7. staid	_____	g. loyal
8. pious	_____	h. enthusiastic
9. reticent	_____	i. extremely capable
10. convivial	_____	j. easily tricked

*   Words marked with an asterisk have been introduced in previous chapters.

Practice 2   Answering True or False

Directions: To indicate if a statement is *true* or *false,* circle the correct answer.

True   False   1. A *staunch* friend is someone who is only pretending to like you.

True   False   2. Someone who is *avid* about football would probably attend football games regularly.

True   False   3. People who are *credulous* won't accept anything on faith; they need solid proof to be convinced.

True   False   4. A highly *proficient* surgeon is likely to make careless mistakes.

True   False   5. People who are *morose* by nature don't necessarily want to be cheered up.

True   False   6. If a *pretentious* individual got a promotion, he would not tell anyone.

True   False   7. Men and women who are *staid* are likely to spend a lot of money on fashionable and trendy clothing.

True   False   8. A nun is a *pious* person.

True   False   9. A *reticent* student may have some difficulty participating in class discussions.

True   False   10. A *convivial* person is usually ill at ease in large groups.

Practice 3   Making Sentence Sense

Directions: Fill in the blanks with the word that fits both the context and the definition in parentheses.

staunch	staid	convivial	pretentious	credulous
morose	pious	avid	reticent	proficient

1. Truly _____ church members sometimes attend services three times a week. (having or showing religious devotion)

2. _____ believers in free speech generally oppose attempts to censor the Internet. (firmly loyal to a person, organization, or set of beliefs or opinions)

3. By all accounts, first lady Martha Washington was somewhat _____ in both manner and dress, and many complained that Martha liked to show off. (giving the impression of importance by showing off or bragging)

4. Naturally _____, he had a hard time getting used to his wife's sunny and extroverted* temperament. (gloomy, moody)

5. _____ college students often spend too much time socializing, and their grades suffer as a result. (merry and fond of company)

6. Only the most _____ mountain climbers try to ascend Mount Everest. (interested and enthusiastic)

7. The queen of England is a _____ woman, whose old-fashioned suits and hats are often the source of British humor. (serious, sober, and dignified)

8. Because he was so _____ about his past, she knew very little about his child-hood. (reserved; keeping one's thoughts and feelings to oneself)

9. He was a highly _____ chef but so ill-tempered he couldn't get anyone to work in his kitchen. (very qualified and skillful)

10. Only the very _____ believe stories about humans being kidnapped by aliens from outer space. (easily fooled)

Practice 4   Filling in the Gaps

Directions: Fill in the blanks with one of the words from the chapter. If two words seem equally right, study the context. One word will be better than the other.

reticent	morose	pretentious	credulous	convivial
staunch	avidly	pious	staid	proficient

First Ladies Aren't Cut to a Pattern

Just as the American public has liked some presidents more than others, it has favored some first ladies more than others. The extroverted* fourth first lady, Dolley Madison, had a _____ nature. Her love of parties and social occasions made her extraordinarily well liked. Sarah Polk, our country's eleventh first lady, was also a popular hostess. She was a _____ woman whose religious beliefs led her to ban dancing, drinking, and card playing from the White House. But she was such a good conversationalist that her guests did not mind the absence of liquor at her parties. Jacqueline Kennedy, wife of thirty-fifth president John F. Kennedy, was wildly popular, and she managed to impress even the normally blasé* French, mainly because of her beauty and style. Barbara Bush, wife of forty-first president George H. W. Bush, was beloved, too. Proper and _____ rather than glamorous, Barbara Bush appealed to Americans, who liked her sensible, down-to-earth personality.

Other first ladies have been deeply admired for their contributions. Many of them _____ supported various social causes. The often _____ and moody Mary Todd Lincoln, for example, still found the time to be a _____ opponent of slavery. Eleanor Roosevelt won the country's admiration for her assiduous* support of causes like child welfare, civil rights, and equal rights for women. The American people also admired "Lady Bird" Johnson, wife of thirty-sixth president Lyndon Johnson. Because she did not want her family's income to depend on politics, she bought a struggling radio station and built it into a multimillion-dollar communications company. Women, in particular, admired Mrs. Johnson for being a smart and very _____ businesswoman, clever and competent enough to create her own fortune.

Other first ladies, however, have not fared well in the court of public opinion. Hillary Clinton was an extremely accomplished lawyer in her own right. Still, many Americans disliked her. They considered Mrs. Clinton a bit too ambitious. Nancy Reagan, wife of president Ronald Reagan, was harshly criticized for being both vain and _____. While many Americans were having trouble making ends meet, she spent large sums of money buying designer fashions and throwing dinner parties for the rich and famous. Mrs. Reagan was also considered by some to be foolishly _____ once it was discovered that she consulted astrologers in order to help her husband's career. The public has also been critical of _____ first ladies like fifth first lady Elizabeth Monroe and thirty-third first lady Bess Truman. Because they liked to keep to themselves, both were often targets of public scorn.

(*Sources of information:* Janet L. Smith, "First Ladies Have Long Been a White House Force," James Madison University, November 8, 2000; www.jmu/jmuweb/general/news/general_20001185815.shtml; "First Ladies," The American Presidency, http://gi.grolier.com/presidents/nbk/first/firstlady.html.)

To test your mastery of the words introduced in this chapter, turn to page 193 in the back of the book.

Chapter 4

Words for Thought

The Common Thread

Different kinds of activities call for different kinds of thinking. It's no surprise, then, that our language contains a number of words that refer to or describe the way we think. Chapter 4 introduces ten such words. As you learn them, try to imagine the kind of task or situation where each word might apply.

synthesize	hypothesis
apprehensive	conjecture
engrossed	delusion
rational	concept
ponder	introspection

Self-Test   Words for Thought

Directions: For each italicized word, circle the letter of what you think is the correct definition.

1. *Synthesize* means
   a. combine.
   b. divide.
   c. guess.

2. *Apprehensive* means
   a. forgetful.
   b. anxious.
   c. thoughtful.

3. *Engrossed* means
   a. sensitive.
   b. absorbed.
   c. serious.

4. *Rational* means
   a. absorbing.
   b. investigating.
   c. logical.

5. *Ponder* means
   a. consider carefully.
   b. misunderstand.
   c. remember.

6. *Hypothesis* means
   a. unproven theory.
   b. proven theory.
   c. unsolved puzzle.

7. *Conjecture* means
   a. opinion.
   b. proven theory.
   c. memory.

8. *Delusion* means
   a. false belief.
   b. fake logic.
   c. idea.

9. *Concept* means
   a. image.
   b. idea.
   c. memory.

10. *Introspection* means
    a. looking inward.
    b. imaginary.
    c. feeling.

Turn to page 241 to correct your test. Record your grade in the self-test column on the inside front cover of your textbook. Then go on to **Words and Meanings** on pages 25–27.

Words and Meanings

Here again are the words from the self-test. Only this time, they are accompanied by their most common meanings and pointers on pronunciation.

1. **synthesize (SĬN-thǐ-sīz)** *v.*   combine, blend, or unify into a new, more complex idea or creation.

   Sample Sentence   While writing his history paper, Kevin found it hard to *synthesize* the opposing points of view concerning anti-Communism in the fifties.

   MEMORY PEG   To remember this word, think of the prefix *syn-*, which means "together." So, to *synthesize* means to put things together or combine them to form a new whole.

   Additional Forms   synthesis, synthesizer

2. **apprehensive (ăp-rǐ-HĔN-sǐv)** *adj.*   anxious or fearful about future events, filled with dread

   Sample Sentence   With each passing day, she grew more *apprehensive* about her son's fate.

   MEMORY PEG   To remember the meaning of *apprehensive*, imagine this scene. It's your turn to give a speech before the members of a community group. Suddenly you realize that you've lost your notes. Now you'll have to give the speech from memory. What you are feeling at that moment is anxiety about how the speech will turn out. In a word, you are *apprehensive*.

   Additional Form   apprehension

3. **engrossed (ĕn-GRŌST)** *adj.*   absorbed, deeply involved

   Sample Sentence   Kristin was so *engrossed* in the fairy tale she didn't hear her name called.

   MEMORY PEG   Link this word to the best movie you've ever seen or the best book you've ever read. Then make up a sentence like the following, only substitute your own experience: "I was so *engrossed* by *The Lovely Bones* I couldn't put it down."

   Additional Form   engrossing
   Common Usage   engrossed *in*

4. **rational (RĂSH-ə-nəl)** *adj.*   **a.** having the ability to reason

   Sample Sentence   In contrast to animals, humans are *rational* beings.

   b. sane

   Sample Sentence   She was so upset that she was no longer capable of *rational* thought.

   MEMORY PEG   Relate the word *rational* to the word *reason*. A rational individual is one who has the power of reason, and a rational explanation is one that is reasonable. To form this word's antonym, simply add the prefix *ir-*, meaning "not" (*irrational*).

   Additional Forms   rationalize, rationally, rationalist

5. ponder (PŎN-dər) v.   to carefully weigh or consider

Sample Sentence   He didn't want to make a quick decision; he needed more time to *ponder* the idea of quitting a business he had built from scratch.

> **MEMORY PEG**   The word *ponder* comes from a Latin root meaning "weight." It follows, then, that people are likely to *ponder* decisions that are "weighty" or important.

6. hypothesis (hĭ-PŎTH-ĭ-sĭs) n.   **a.** a possible but still unproven theory or explanation of events

Sample Sentence   One *hypothesis* about the disappearance of dinosaurs is that they died after a large meteor hit Earth.

b. an idea assumed to be true for the purpose of an argument or investigation

Sample Sentence   For the sake of argument, let's accept Jack's *hypothesis* that a marriage should be based on friendship rather than passion.

> **MEMORY PEG**   To remember the meaning of *hypothesis*, note that it contains the word *thesis*, which means "idea." In meaning *a*, the hypothesis is an "idea" that is yet to be proven. In meaning *b*, the "idea" is just assumed to be true. No further proof is expected. In other words, in meaning *a*, proof is expected to be forthcoming. In meaning *b*, no further proof is required.

Additional Forms   hypothesize, hypothetical

7. conjecture (kən-JĔK-chər)   **a.** an opinion or judgment based on incomplete evidence, a guess (*n.*)

Sample Sentence   On camera, the journalist acted as if she knew how the election would turn out, but her comments were pure *conjecture*.

b. to infer or guess (*v.*)

Sample Sentence   The secretary of defense was unwilling to *conjecture* about the outcome of the war.

> **MEMORY PEG**   For meaning *a*, try linking *conjecture* to *hypothesis*. Both words refer to ideas or opinions yet to be proven. Keep in mind, however, that the word *conjecture* refers to an opinion that is and may always be based on incomplete evidence. The word *hypothesis*, in contrast, is often used in a scientific context to suggest that proof will be forthcoming. For meaning *b*, tell yourself that people like to *conjecture* about the reality of flying saucers. Yet, in fact, they are only guessing since there is no real proof that they exist.

Common Usage   *sheer* conjecture, *pure* conjecture, *empty* conjecture, conjecture *about*

8. delusion (dĭ-LOO-zhən) n.   false belief or opinion

Sample Sentence   The supporters of Evita Perón† labored under the *delusion* that she had their best interests at heart, but their beloved "Evita" cared only about herself.

† Eva Duarte de Perón (1919–1952): The wife of Argentinean dictator Juan Perón, "Evita" had her own personal following.

> **MEMORY PEG**   A *delusion* is a mistaken idea or a false belief. But it has strong negative connotations. It suggests not just a misunderstanding, but the mind's failure to function rationally. Someone who thinks the evening news begins at seven when it starts at six-thirty is mistaken. Someone who believes that cats are in league with the devil is delusional.

Additional Forms   delude, delusional

Common Usage   *under* the delusion

9. **concept (KŎN-sĕpt)** *n.*   general idea, scheme, or plan of organization

Sample Sentence   The speaker's paper lacked a unifying *concept,* and he seemed to ramble from one unconnected thought to another.

> **MEMORY PEG**   Relate the word *concept* to composition. When you write a paper, you need a general idea or *concept* to organize your thoughts. But *concepts* aren't restricted to writing. They are everywhere. They are the general ideas that organize how we think and behave.

Additional Form   conception, conceptual

10. **introspection (ĭn-trə-SPĔK-shən)** *n.*   self-examination, looking inward

Sample Sentence   Most psychotherapy requires patients to engage in serious *introspection.*

> **MEMORY PEG**   The word parts will help you recall the meaning of *introspection.* The prefix *intro-* means "within," and the Latin root *spec* means "to look." So the word *introspection* means "to look within" at one's own thoughts and feelings. Since you already know the word *introvert,** think of an *introvert* as someone likely to engage in *introspection.*

Additional Form   introspective

Idiom Alert

Think tank: Used to refer to the brain, the phrase turned up around 1900. Over time, it began to refer to a group or an organization devoted to problem solving or research, for example, "Never known for original thought, the senator gets most of his ideas from the Harrison *think tank.*"

Practice 1   Matching Words and Meanings

Directions: To match word and meaning, fill in the blanks with the appropriate letters.

1. synthesize   _____   a. reasonable and logical

2. apprehensive   _____   b. to consider in depth

3. engrossed   _____   c. general idea, scheme, or plan

4. rational   _____   d. anxious about the future

5. ponder   _____   e. opinion based on incomplete evidence

6. hypothesis   _____   f. combine, blend, or integrate

7. conjecture   _____   g. a possible but as yet unproven explanation

8. delusion   _____   h. a false belief that is not based on reality

9. concept   _____   i. self-examination

10. introspection   _____   j. deeply absorbed or concentrated

Practice 2   Answering True or False

Directions: To indicate if a statement is *true* or *false*, circle the correct answer.

True   **False**   1. To write a good research paper, you need to *synthesize* several sources on the same subject.

True   **False**   2. These days many people are *apprehensive* about flying.

True   **False**   3. Someone who is *engrossed* by a mathematical problem usually finds it hard to concentrate.

True   **False**   4. Superstitions are the product of *rational* thought.

True   **False**   5. People who don't *ponder* the decision to marry are likely to regret it.

True   **False**   6. A good *hypothesis* has to be proven before it's presented to the public.

True   **False**   7. The word *fact* is a synonym for *conjecture*.

True   **False**   8. Someone who believes that airplanes can fly is *delusional*.

True   **False**   9. Some new parents have no *concept* of what it means to raise a child.

True   **False**   10. Parties are perfect for *introspection*.

Practice 3   Making Sentence Sense

Directions: Fill in the blanks with the word that fits both the context and the definition in parentheses.

| conjecture | hypothesis | synthesize | delusional | concept |
| introspection | ponder | rational | engrossed | apprehensive |

1. People who believe in fairies are said to be _____ . (holding false beliefs that aren't supported by reality)

2. Rock operas like Queen's *Bohemian Rhapsody* and The Who's *Tommy* manage to cleverly _____ elements of rock and roll with opera. (combine, blend)

3. Writing in a diary or a journal tends to encourage _____ . (self-examination)

4. The journalists reported that the battle was over, but their reports were based only on _____ . (opinion based on incomplete evidence)

5. The conflict between reality and appearance was the play's organizing _____ . (general idea or plan of organization)

6. A few scientists argue that global warming is still just a _____ rather than a proven fact, but most argue that global warming is a very real danger. (a theory or possible explanation)

7. In general, there aren't too many Americans who can _____ death without anxiety. (carefully consider)

8. Someone who is under the influence of drugs may not be capable of _____ behavior. (reasonable and logical)

9. Computer scientists often get so _____ in their work they forget about time. (deeply absorbed)

10. Everyone was becoming _____ about the new disease that was spreading so rapidly. (anxious)

Practice 4   Filling in the Gaps

Directions: Fill in the blanks with one of the words from the chapter. If two words seem equally right, study the context. One word will be better than the other.

synthesize	engrossed	pondering	conjecture	concept
apprehensive	rational	hypothesis	delusion	introspection

Writing a Research Paper

Many students mistakenly assume that writing a research paper is an extraordinarily difficult task.

They are _____ even before they start writing. Since research papers generally require students to come up with an original idea or _____ , only the most

intrepid* student writers feel up to the task. Yet while it's true that _____ the topic

for your research paper the night before it's due *is* a recipe for failure, there's no reason for that to

happen. Instead, as soon as you hear that a research paper is due, start thinking about a working

_____ or _____ that you can eventually argue or prove through

research.

Now some students have the mistaken notion that an idea for a paper will come to them only

if they engage in deep _____ . Then by a mixture of inspiration and luck, they will

mysteriously come up with something to write about. But finding an idea to explore in writing

can be much easier than that. One way to come up with a thesis for your paper is to read several

writers on the same topic and then _____ their various ideas into a statement you

can research. For example, you might read three different articles on President John F. Kennedy's

role in the civil rights movement and come up with three different opinions: (1) Kennedy was

a great champion of civil rights. (2) Kennedy would have ignored civil rights if he could have.

(3) Kennedy was forced to champion civil rights, but what he did was still important. Once you

combine those three points of view into a statement—"Although John F. Kennedy tried to avoid

the civil rights issue, he was forced to confront it and ended up advancing the cause of civil

rights"—you're ready to start your research.

If you pick a topic you are really interested in, you may be surprised by how _____

you become in your work. You may even discover that you like doing research and in no time at

all, you will be ready to make a rough draft of your thoughts. However, don't labor under the

_____ that your first draft is your best work. Instead, give that first draft a full day

to sit. When you look at it again, you'll have a clearer sense of what to add or subtract.

Of course, if you want to, you can just continue to be afraid of research papers and avoid

thinking about them until the night before they are due. But that's not a _____

way to handle your fears. Instead, plan your paper, day by day and piece by piece. Then when the

time comes to turn the paper in, you will be ready.

> To test your mastery of the words introduced in this chapter, turn to page 195 in the back of the book.

Chapter 5

Honorable and Dishonorable Mention

The Common Thread

All the words in this chapter can label behavior or character as either worthy of great respect or deserving of harsh criticism. Use that common thread to make as many connections as you possibly can among the ten words included in the chapter.

revere	notorious
homage	reprehensible
stalwart	disreputable
notable	lewd
integrity	devious

Self-Test | Honorable and Dishonorable Mention

Directions: For each italicized word, circle the letter of what you think is the correct definition.

1. *Revere* means
   a. love.
   b. honor.
   c. obey.

2. *Homage* means
   a. character.
   b. devotion.
   c. respect.

3. *Stalwart* means
   a. firm of purpose.
   b. big of heart.
   c. wise.

4. *Notable* means
   a. wise.
   b. strong-willed.
   c. remarkable.

5. *Integrity* means
   a. living by a strict ethical code.
   b. the ability to tell the truth.
   c. the willingness to change.

6. *Notorious* means
   a. known far and wide.
   b. widely known for good reasons.
   c. famous for the wrong reason.

7. *Reprehensible* means
   a. celebrated by the public.
   b. excessively spoiled.
   c. deserving of blame.

8. *Disreputable* means
   a. widely known for public service.
   b. remarkable in action.
   c. shameful in behavior.

9. *Lewd* means
   a. famous.
   b. obscene.
   c. lovable.

10. *Devious* means
    a. honest and open.
    b. not straightforward.
    c. courageous.

Turn to page 241 to correct your test. Record your grade in the self-test column on the inside front cover of your textbook. Then go on to **Words and Meanings** on pages 32–34.

Words and Meanings

Here again are the words from the self-test. Only this time, they are accompanied by their most common meanings and pointers on pronunciation.

1. revere (rī-VÎR) v.   to honor; to regard with great admiration or devotion

Sample Sentence   Mahatma Gandhi (1869–1948), the Indian leader who used peaceful means to win his country's independence from Britain, is still *revered* by people all over the world.

> **MEMORY PEG**   Think of Paul Revere, who is *revered* for having the courage and daring to jump on his horse and sound the alarm that the British were coming. Typically, *revere* is used to express admiration for (a) religious figures, (b) great heroes, and (c) people who have strongly influenced our lives.

Additional Forms   reverence, reverential

2. homage (HŎM-ĭj, ŎM-ĭj) n.   great honor or respect shown publicly

Sample Sentence   When president John F. Kennedy was laid to rest, the nation and the world paid *homage* to his memory.

> **MEMORY PEG**   Link this word to a specific image. For example, think of how the British pay *homage* to their queen—they bow or curtsy. That specific example of paying *homage* should anchor the meaning in your memory.

Common Usage   *pay* or *give* homage *to*

3. stalwart (STÔL-wərt) adj.   **a.** having impressive strength of body or spirit

Sample Sentence   Vin Diesel has just the right *stalwart* presence to be an action hero.

b. firm of purpose

Sample Sentence   *Stalwart* in his determination to win control of the situation, Captain Chamberlain repeated his order to march until the soldiers obeyed.

> **MEMORY PEG**   Link *stalwart* to "stall" and tell yourself that someone who is *stalwart* does not get "stalled" in pursuit of a goal. He or she has the physical presence or mental toughness to keep going. Sometimes the context will tell you exactly which of the two meanings applies. However, frequently the word is used in a way that suggests both, for example, "Unquestionably *stalwart* in battle, Ulysses S. Grant was not a particularly effective president." *Stalwart* can also be used as a noun to identify people who show great strength or great devotion: (1) "There were only a few *stalwarts* in the combat division, but when it came to survival, they made all the difference." (2) "Party *stalwarts* refused to listen to any criticism of their candidate's position."

Additional Form   stalwartness

4. notable (NŌT-tuh-bəl)   **a.** striking, worthy of notice (*adj.*)

Sample Sentence   Even as a child, Beryl Markham was *notable* for her courage.

b. important, famous, well-known (*adj.*)

Sample Sentence   The *notable* author was not pleased to see so many empty seats in the audience.

c. famous person (*n.*)

Sample Sentence   The local *notables* don't consider community affairs important enough to attend town meetings.

| MEMORY PEG | Link *notable* to the word "notice." Someone *notable* gets "noticed" for being unusual, gifted, or famous. Keep in mind that *notable* can be applied to things and events as well as to people: "The room was *notable* for its lack of charm." |

Additional Form   notability

5. **integrity (ĭn-TĔG-rĭ-tē)** *n.*   dedication to high moral, ethical, or professional standards

Sample Sentence   Bob Dylan has too much *integrity* to let his music be used in commercials.

| MEMORY PEG | Do you know someone who is honest and fair in every situation? Link the word *integrity* to an image of that person. |

6. **notorious (nō-TÔR-ē-əs)** *adj.*   famous or well known for being bad or evil

Sample Sentence   *Notorious* for his mindless cruelty, the Cambodian dictator Pol Pot murdered thousands of innocent people.

| MEMORY PEG | To remember the word *notorious*, link it to someone who really was *notorious*, like gangster Al Capone or serial killer Ted Bundy. Keep in mind, however, that you can also attach the word to places and events, as in the following sentence: "That region is *notorious* for its freezing winters." |

Additional Forms   notoriety, notoriousness

7. **reprehensible (rĕp-rĭ-HĔN-sə-bəl)** *adj.*   deserving blame or criticism

Sample Sentence   The child molester's *reprehensible* crimes made him hated even in prison.

| MEMORY PEG | Link the word *reprehensible* to the word *notorious* by telling yourself that people often become *notorious* if their behavior is consistently *reprehensible* or "blameworthy." You can also link *reprehensible* to three other words that start with the same two or three letters: *rebuke*, *reproach*, and *reprimand*. All three are synonyms for *blame* or *criticize*, which is what people usually do in response to *reprehensible* behavior. |

Additional Forms   reprehend, reprehension

8. **disreputable (dĭs-RĔP-ye-tə-bəl)** *adj.*   shameful in character, behavior, or appearance; lacking in respectability

Sample Sentence   When the talk show host's *disreputable* behavior toward his family came to light, his audience began tuning him out.

| MEMORY PEG | Keep in mind that *dis-* is a prefix meaning "without" and *reputable* is a word on its own that means "having a good reputation." So someone *disreputable* is "without a good reputation because of actions, behavior, or appearance." If you are thinking that *reprehensible* is very close in meaning to *disreputable*, you are right. *Reprehensible*, however, refers more to behavior and actions than to appearance. |

Additional Forms   disrepute, disreputability

9. lewd (lo͞od) *adj.*   focused on sex; obscene

Sample Sentence   The accountant never knew what to say when her boss launched into one of his *lewd* stories.

> **MEMORY PEG**   Think of shock jocks like Howard Stern. They make a living from being *lewd*. You can also keep in mind that *lewd* rhymes with *crude*.

Additional Form   lewdness

10. devious (DĒ-vē-əs) *adj.*   tricky, not straightforward

Sample Sentence   In his novel *The Songs of the Kings*, writer Barry Unsworth portrays the famed Greek hero Ulysses as a *devious* character propelled solely by self interest.

> **MEMORY PEG**   It helps to remember that *devious*, like *deviate*, is based on the word parts *de-* (from) plus *via* (road). People who are *devious* figuratively get off the straight road and end up on a crooked one. Although one can talk about taking a *devious* route to a real location, the word usually refers to a mode of behavior. Someone with *devious* ways is unlikely to play by the accepted rules of any game. And yes, he or she probably would not mind cheating if it meant winning.

Additional Form   deviousness

Idiom Alert

Aboveboard: This expression comes from the late sixteenth century, when card players were warned to keep their hands above the playing board as a sign of playing fair. Today when we say people's actions are strictly *aboveboard*, we mean they are honest. Similarly, if someone is doing something *under the table*, that person is behaving in an illegal or unethical fashion.

Practice 1   Matching Words and Meanings

Directions: To match word and meaning, fill in the blanks with the appropriate letters.

1. revere	_____	a. remarkable or excellent
2. homage	_____	b. dedication to high ethical, moral, or professional standards
3. stalwart	_____	c. shifty
4. notable	_____	d. to regard with admiration
5. integrity	_____	e. infamous
6. notorious	_____	f. publicly show honor or respect
7. reprehensible	_____	g. obscene
8. disreputable	_____	h. strong or firm
9. lewd	_____	i. worthy of blame or criticism
10. devious	_____	j. lacking respectability

Practice 2   Answering True or False

Directions: To indicate if a statement is *true* or *false*, circle the correct answer.

True   False   ·1. Americans who *revere* their country are proud to display its symbol, the Stars and Stripes.

True   False   2. A curtsy is a form of *homage* expected of those who meet the queen of England.

True   False   3. It's possible to be *stalwart* in mind but weak in body.

True   False   4. Unfortunately, *notable* achievements sometimes go unrecognized.

True   False   5. A lack of *integrity* is a virtue.

True   False   6. *Notorious* individuals are often rewarded with medals and trophies from their government.

True   False   7. Acceptance of a bribe is an example of *reprehensible* behavior.

True   False   8. Teens who behave *disreputably* will be rewarded by their parents.

True   False   9. Comedians are never *lewd*.

True   False   10. Landlords like to rent to *devious* people.

Practice 3   Making Sentence Sense

Directions: Fill in the blanks with the word that fits both the context and the definition in parentheses.

disreputable	**reprehensible**	**integrity**	**revere**	**homage**
lewd	**stalwart**	**devious**	**notorious**	**notable**

1. E-mailing a _____ photograph to a coworker can be cause for dismissal. (crudely sexual)

2. Many Britons _____ the royal family in a way that is hard for Americans to understand. (to regard with respect)

3. The _____ fortune hunter convinced the wealthy woman that he loved her. (not straightforward; shifty)

4. The football player's _____ actions got him kicked off the team. (worthy of blame)

5. The young actor had too much _____ to sell his talent to the highest bidder. (high moral standards)

6. Jesse James, who robbed banks and trains for more than fifteen years, was one of the nineteenth century's most _____ outlaws. (widely known for evil or bad actions)

7. The annual Pulitzer Prizes recognize the contributions of _____ writers, journalists, and composers. (worthy of note or notice)

8. The _____ pioneers who settled the American West did not let hardship interfere with their plans. (strong and firm)

9. Since Russian leader Vladimir Lenin died in 1924, his preserved body has been on display so that Russians and tourists can pay _____ to him. (special honor or respect shown publicly)

10. Writing novels was once considered a _____ activity for ladies, so great authors like Mary Ann Evans†, Jane Austen, and Charlotte Brontë wrote under pen names. (lacking respectability)

Practice 4   Filling in the Gaps

Directions: Fill in the blanks with one of the words from the chapter. *Note:* In this case, some of the words may be interchangeable. Just make sure to use a word that fits the context.

notorious	lewd	reprehensible
integrity	disreputable	devious

1. **Theaters and Sin**

   In the sixteenth century, when Shakespeare was just beginning his career, playwrights were not considered people of _____. By the same token, theaters were considered places of sin. Religious leaders openly condemned theatergoing as a _____ pursuit, guaranteed to corrupt the innocent and lead them into _____ and _____ behavior. As a matter of fact, in 1594, the lord mayor of London asked Queen Elizabeth I of England to demolish all the theaters in the city. He claimed that public theaters were becoming _____ as places of prostitution. According to the good mayor, con men and thieves were also flocking to the theater to ply their _____ trades. Fortunately for Shakespeare and the other playwrights of the time, not to mention theatergoers, the queen did not agree, and the theaters survived.

† Mary Ann Evans (1819–1880) is the pen name of George Eliot, the author of *Middlemarch* and many other novels.

stalwart	homage	notable	revere

2. **Religion Among Native Americans**

Religious beliefs obviously vary among individual Native American tribes. However, certain general tendencies can be identified. One _____ feature is the lack of a central holy book—for example, the Bible for Christians, the Koran for Muslims, or the Torah for Jews—that is found in many other religions. The teachings of prophets are also not central to Native American religions as they are in Judaism, Christianity, and Islam. However, many tribes do _____ two key spirits or gods. One is the creator of the world, to whom various tribes pay _____ through rituals, ceremonies, and prayers. The other is a guiding spirit who bestows the gift of character and provides the tribes with the models of _____ behavior necessary for survival. While the spirit responsible for creation is a major god, the spirit responsible for character is more minor.

To test your mastery of the words introduced in this chapter, turn to page 197 in the back of the book.

Chapter 6

Money Talk

The Common Thread

In this chapter, all the words revolve around money and finance. There are words like *revenue* to describe money made, and words like *deficit* to describe money lost. As you learn each of the ten words, look for similarities or differences among them to help you remember word meaning.

frugal	prosper
extravagant	compensation
lucrative	deficit
entrepreneur	cartel
revenue	endow

Self-Test   Money Talk

Directions: For each italicized word, circle the letter of what you think is the correct definition.

1. *Frugal* means
   a. good at accounting.
   b. careful with money.
   c. wasteful with money.

2. *Extravagant* means
   a. spending money thoughtlessly.
   b. saving every penny.
   c. charitable.

3. *Lucrative* means
   a. profitable.
   b. losing money.
   c. wasteful.

4. *Entrepreneur* means
   a. someone who is bankrupt.
   b. someone who is wealthy.
   c. someone who owns and operates a business.

5. *Revenue* means
   a. finances.
   b. earnings.
   c. taxes.

6. *Prosper* means
   a. fail.
   b. succeed.
   c. spend.

7. *Compensation* means
   a. charges.
   b. payment.
   c. withdrawal.

8. *Deficit* means
   a. credit.
   b. shortage.
   c. payment.

9. *Cartel* means
   a. organizational fraud.
   b. individuals organized in a group for shared benefit.
   c. special tax.

10. *Endow* means
    a. give a gift.
    b. spend a fortune.
    c. pay as you go.

Turn to page 241 to correct your test. Record your grade in the self-test column on the inside front cover of your textbook. Then go on to **Words and Meanings** on pages 39–41.

Words and Meanings

Here again are the words from the self-test. Only this time, they are accompanied by their most common meanings and pointers on pronunciation.

1. **frugal (FRŌŌ-gəl) *adj.*** **a.** marked by the careful management of money or material resources

   Sample Sentence   Now that she was rich, the singer was no longer concerned with being *frugal.*

   b. costing little, inexpensive

   Sample Sentence   The nineteenth-century writer Henry David Thoreau encouraged his readers to lead a *frugal* life.

   MEMORY PEG   Remember the meaning of *frugal* by tying it to its much less positive synonym, "stingy." Being *frugal* is considered a positive characteristic; being stingy is not.

   Additional Forms   frugality, frugalness

2. **extravagant (ĭk-STRĂV-ə-gənt) *adj.*** **a.** given to spending large sums of money, often unwisely

   Sample Sentence   The American public loved Jackie Kennedy for her beauty and grace, and forgave the first lady her *extravagant* ways.

   b. more than is typical, excessive

   Sample Sentence   The critic, who was also a personal friend of the director, gave the movie *extravagant* praise.

   MEMORY PEG   Think of *extravagant* as an antonym for *frugal*. And, like *frugal*, the word *extravagant* doesn't apply just to money. You also can talk about someone's *extravagant* demands. It's in this context that the meaning "excessive" comes into play.

   Additional Form   extravagance

   Common Usage   extravagant *with, about*

3. **lucrative (LŌŌ-krə-tĭv) *adj.*** profitable, producing wealth

   Sample Sentence   The famous director said she would never direct a video for MTV, but she gave in when Madonna's agent made an extremely *lucrative* offer.

   MEMORY PEG   *Lucre* is an old-fashioned word for money. Like *lucrative, lucre* comes from the Latin word *lucrum,* meaning "profit." Thus, you can tell yourself that a *lucrative* investment guarantees plenty of *lucre.*

4. **entrepreneur (ŏn-trə-prə-NÛR) *n.*** a person who organizes, operates, and assumes the risk of a business venture

   Sample Sentence   The owner of Mary Kay Cosmetics was one of the first female *entrepreneurs* to become successful.

| MEMORY PEG | The word *entrepreneur* comes from a French word, *entreprendre*, meaning "to undertake." *Entrepreneurs* are those people who have the nerve to undertake business ownership despite the risks it involves. |

5. revenue (RĔV-ə-noo) *n.*   income, profit

Sample Sentence   The owner of the video store was jailed for failing to report all *revenue* from the business.

| MEMORY PEG | To remember the meaning of *revenue*, think of the Internal Revenue Service, a government agency very interested in an accurate report of each citizen's or corporation's *revenue*. |

Common Usage   revenue *from*

6. prosper (PRŎS-pər) *v.*   to do well, particularly in financial terms; to thrive

Sample Sentence   In the 1990s, people invested in Internet stocks, expecting to *prosper*, but investors were badly disappointed.

| MEMORY PEG | The English word *prosper* comes from the Latin word *prosperare*, meaning "to make fortunate." And someone who *prospers* in life has, indeed, been made fortunate. Keep in mind, too, that people who *prosper* in life are often *extravagant*, spending money freely. Of course, they are just as likely to be *frugal*, not wishing to see their *prosperity* vanish. |

Additional Forms   prosperous, prosperity

7. compensation (kŏm-pən-SĀ-shən) *n.*   payment, frequently to offset a favor or injury

Sample Sentence   Despite how essential they are, hospital nurses don't receive adequate *compensation*.

| MEMORY PEG | Try linking the word to the phrase "workers' compensation." This is a payment made to workers who get hurt on the job, and it exactly illustrates the word *compensation* when it refers to a payment made to offset suffering. To recall the more general meaning of *compensation* illustrated in the sentence above, tell yourself that simply getting paid is another form of "workers' compensation." |

Additional Forms   compensate, compensatory

Common Usage   compensate or compensation *for*

8. deficit (DĔF-ĭ-sĭt) *n.*   shortage or loss, often in the form of money; debt

Sample Sentence   In the years following the Revolutionary War, the new American government was faced with a serious *deficit*.

| MEMORY PEG | The word *deficit* comes from the Latin word *deficere*, which means "to be lacking." Keep the word *lack* in mind when you think of a *deficit* because that's what a *deficit* always amounts to—a lack of something that is needed. That's why some people describe a lack of sleep as a sleep *deficit*. |

9. cartel (kär-TĔL) *n.* nations, companies, or parties that unite to become more powerful as a group, often by controlling production of goods

Sample Sentence   Until the United States becomes less dependent on oil, we will worry every winter that the Middle Eastern oil *cartel* will cut supplies.

> **MEMORY PEG** The word *cartel* was used in the seventeenth century to refer to a written agreement among nations concerning the exchange and treatment of prisoners. Although the wartime context eventually disappeared from the meaning of *cartel*, the idea of an agreement has remained. Thus, *agreement* is the word you need to focus on. A *cartel* is an agreement among independent individuals or groups that band together for their common good.

10. endow (ĕn-DOU) *v.* **a.** to provide an institution or individual with financial aid without expectation of return

Sample Sentence   The board members were thrilled to learn that a local millionaire was going to *endow* the museum with the funds needed to build a new wing.

b. to supply with talent, beauty, or intelligence

Sample Sentence   Nature had *endowed* the comic with a quick wit that made her a spectacularly successful performer.

> **MEMORY PEG** Link the word *endow* to nineteenth-century industrialists like Andrew Carnegie and John D. Rockefeller. Having made millions, they—particularly Carnegie—*endowed*, or gave financial gifts to, a number of museums, schools, and libraries.

Additional Form   endowment

 Idiom Alert

In the red: It's a common bookkeeping practice to put debts in red ink. Thus, to be *in the red* is to be financially in trouble, as in, "The owner of the new hardware store was discouraged because he was once again *in the red*."

In the black: In contrast to debts, profits are usually entered in black ink. Thus, to be *in the black* is to be "out of debt," for example, "After the Revolutionary War ended, many believed that the government was so in debt it would never be *in the black* unless drastic action was taken."

Practice 1   Matching Words and Meanings

Directions: To match word and meaning, fill in the blanks with the appropriate letters.

1. frugal   _____   a. profitable

2. extravagant   _____   b. a shortage

3. lucrative   _____   c. earnings

4. entrepreneur   _____   d. a person who owns and operates a business

5. revenue   _____   e. individuals, companies, or institutions that unite for a common benefit

6. prosper   _____   f. payment, often to offset injury

7. compensation   _____   g. spending money freely

8. deficit   _____   h. to do well, often financially

9. cartel   _____   i. to provide with money

10. endow   _____   j. thrifty

Practice 2   Answering True or False

Directions: To indicate if a statement is *true* or *false*, circle the correct answer.

True   **False**   1. A *frugal* person would toss an item into his shopping cart without even checking the price.

True   **False**   2. An *extravagant* person might well shop without looking at price tags.

True   **False**   3. Most people want *lucrative* investments.

True   **False**   4. Teachers, nurses, and firefighters are *entrepreneurs*.

True   **False**   5. A cash register usually contains a drugstore's daily *revenues*.

True   **False**   6. A person who *prospers* is likely to resent it.

True   **False**   7. People who work expect *compensation*.

True   **False**   8. When government spending exceeds its tax income, a budget *deficit* is the result.

True   **False**   9. When businesses decide not to compete and work together to fix prices, they have formed a *cartel*.

True   **False**   10. People who *endow* organizations or institutions expect to get their money back.

Practice 3   Making Sentence Sense

Directions: Fill in the blanks with the word that fits both the context and the definition in parentheses.

lucrative	compensation	revenue	frugal	cartel
extravagant	entrepreneur	prosperous	deficit	endowed

1. The plastic surgeon was so _____ that he could afford to send all five of his children to expensive private colleges. (well-off financially)

2. Much of the government's _____ is in the form of taxes. (income)

3. The band's _____ for the night's music was free beer and all the food the band members could eat. (payment)

4. After her real estate firm failed, she became far less _____. (spending money freely)

5. The Rockefellers have _____ a number of cultural institutions. (to provide with money or talent)

6. The writer Mark Twain had a second career as an inventor, but none of his inventions proved _____. (financially successful)

7. People who are _____ don't buy a new toaster when it breaks down; they get the old one fixed. (thrifty in the management of money)

8. Noticing that the town had no laundromat, the college senior decided to become an _____ and open one. (a person who assumes the risk for a business venture)

9. Independent mom-and-pop farms find it difficult to compete against a _____ of larger industries that can sell fruits and vegetables at lower prices. (independent business organizations that combine to become more powerful as a group)

10. When the store owner's expenses exceeded his profits, he was forced to get a loan to cover the _____. (shortage or loss of money)

Practice 4   Filling in the Gaps

Directions: Fill in the blanks with one of the words from the chapter. If two words seem equally right, study the context. One word will be better than the other.

entrepreneurs	endowments	lucrative	revenues
frugal	deficit	extravagant	

1. The Self-Made Millionaire

Thomas J. Stanley and William D. Danko, authors of the book *The Millionaire Next Door,* have identified several characteristics typical of self-made millionaires. In general, those who make rather than inherit their millions are _____ who saw a _____ opportunity and took it. Having made their fortunes, they are not about to squander them by being _____ . If anything, they are _____ and avoid _____ spending by not buying on credit. Most of the millionaires studied by Stanley and Danko increased their _____ to the point where they could invest their profits on a yearly basis and amass small fortunes. Surprisingly, many self-made millionaires don't plan on leaving their children huge _____ . They expect their children to make their own fortunes.

prosperous	compensation	cartel

2. Business as Usual

In 1998, several once-competitive tobacco companies, among them Philip Morris and R. J. Reynolds, transformed themselves into a _____ . They banded together in order to fight off a lawsuit brought by forty-six states determined to be reimbursed for Medicaid payments made to ailing smokers. When the smoke cleared, both sides had signed an agreement that gave the states trillions of dollars in _____ , to be invested in anti-smoking campaigns. Now this may sound like a great victory to those of us longing for a smoke-free world, but, in fact, the tobacco companies involved are as _____ as ever. The lawsuit did not destroy their ability to do business. And the states? They seem to be using the settlement money for everything but smoking-related issues.

> To test your mastery of the words introduced in this chapter, turn to page 199 in the back of the book.

Chapter 7

Timely Words

The Common Thread

In this chapter, some of the words describe the order of events. Others enable us to talk about the past or consider the present. As you learn each new word, see if you can connect it to one or more of the others.

retrospect	interim
precedent	subsequent
imminent	procrastinate
synchronize	sporadic
perennial	concurrent

Self-Test   Timely Words

Directions: For each italicized word, circle the letter of what you think is the correct definition.

1. *Retrospect* means
   a. going away.
   b. looking back.
   c. returning.

2. *Precedent* means
   a. influential example.
   b. form.
   c. ancient system of time.

3. *Imminent* means
   a. later.
   b. long ago.
   c. quickly approaching.

4. *Synchronize* means
   a. repeat
   b. bring together in time.
   c. occur separately.

5. *Perennial* means
   a. following in time.
   b. historically inaccurate.
   c. continuing indefinitely.

6. *Interim* means
   a. meantime.
   b. beginning.
   c. ending.

7. *Subsequent* means
   a. last.
   b. original.
   c. following.

8. *Procrastinate* means
   a. schedule.
   b. postpone.
   c. push ahead.

9. *Sporadic* means
   a. occasional.
   b. forever.
   c. regularly.

10. *Concurrent* means
    a. at the beginning.
    b. at the end.
    c. at the same time.

Turn to page 241 to correct your test. Record your grade in the self-test column on the inside front cover of your textbook. Then go on to **Words and Meanings** on pages 46–48.

Words and Meanings

Here again are the words from the self-test. Only this time, they are accompanied by their most common meanings and pointers on pronunciation.

1. retrospect (RĔT-rə-spĕkt) *n.*   looking back, remembering

Sample Sentence   In *retrospect*, the setbacks of high school usually don't seem very important; but at the time, they often feel like matters of life and death.

> **MEMORY PEG**   The meaning of *retrospect* will stay with you if you remember that *retro* means "backwards" and *spec* means "look." You might even circle the prefix and root and write the meanings over each word part.

Additional Form   retrospection

Common Usage   in *retrospect*

2. precedent (PRĔS-ĭ-dənt) *n.*   influential example that affects future events

Sample Sentence   George Washington set a *precedent* for future presidents when he delivered the first inaugural address on April 30, 1789.

> **MEMORY PEG**   The prefix *pre-* means "before" or "in front of." The root *cede* means "to go." Remember that a *precedent* goes before and influences what happens afterward. Keep in mind, too, that lawyers often look for a *precedent* when trying a case. That is, they want to know how the courts have ruled in similar situations.

Additional Form   precedence

Common Usage   *set* a precedent

3. imminent (ĬM-ə-nənt) *adj.*   speedily approaching, about to happen

Sample Sentence   It hasn't rained for two months, so a serious drought is *imminent*.

> **MEMORY PEG**   Link *imminent* to the word *immediately*, which starts with the same three letters. Then remember that something *imminent* is about to happen immediately.

Additional Form   imminence

4. synchronize (SĬNG-krə-nīz) *v.*   to make events or movements happen at the same time or closely in time

Sample Sentence   In order to *synchronize* their movements, the swimmers practiced their routine two hours per day.

> **MEMORY PEG**   The prefix *syn-* means "together." The root *chron* means "time." It follows, then, that to *synchronize* means "to bring together in time."

Additional Form   synchronization

5. perennial (pə-RĔN-ē-əl)   **a.** lasting an indefinitely long time, enduring, constant (*adj.*)

Sample Sentence   The *perennial* optimist, he insisted that getting fired would change his life for the better.

> **b.** something that occurs or recurs on a consistent basis (*n.*)

Sample Sentence   Television shows about cops and robbers are a hardy *perennial*.

> **MEMORY PEG**   The prefix *per-* means "through" or "throughout." This fact should help you remember that something *perennial* lasts through time.

6. interim (ĬN-tər-ĭm) *n.*   meantime; the time between one time and another

Sample Sentence   In the *interim* between governments, there was widespread anxiety as people wondered when the new leadership would be in place.

> **MEMORY PEG**   Like the word *intermission*, the word *interim* uses the prefix *inter-*, meaning "between." Thus, both words suggest a time "between" other events.

7. subsequent (SŬB-sĭ-kwĕnt) *adj.*   following in time, following in order

Sample Sentence   Franklin D. Roosevelt was the only U.S. president to serve three terms in office; previous and *subsequent* presidents served only one or two terms.

> **MEMORY PEG**   The root *sequi*, meaning "to follow," is at the center of *subsequent*. Circle and label it. You can use it as an aid to remembering that *subsequent* events "follow" others in time.

Common Usage   subsequent *to*

8. procrastinate (prō-KRĂS-tə-nāt) *v.*   to postpone, put off, or delay

Sample Sentence   People who *procrastinate* are often plagued by fear of failure.

> **MEMORY PEG**   *Cras* is the Latin word for "tomorrow." Remember that people who *procrastinate* think that everything can be put off until later.

Additional Forms   procrastination, procrastinator

9. sporadic (spə-RĂD-ĭk) *adj.*   irregular, occasional, lacking in pattern

Sample Sentence   The signs of the disease were so *sporadic* no one realized how far her illness had progressed until it was too late.

> **MEMORY PEG**   *Sporadic* comes from a Latin word meaning "scattered," so *sporadic* events are scattered in time. You can't predict their occurrence.

Additional Form   sporadically

10. concurrent (kən-KÛR-ənt) *adj.*   happening at the same time as something else

Sample Sentence   It was impossible for him to be at *concurrent* events unless, of course, his fairy godmother made him twins.

> **MEMORY PEG**   In criminal trials, judges often hand out *concurrent* sentences for different crimes. In other words, all of the sentences are served at the same time. Think of *concurrent* sentences to remember that *concurrent* means happening at the same time.

Idiom Alert

Time and tide wait for no one: This saying warns against procrastination. Time and the tide ignore human concerns; while we delay, life is rushing on and passing us by.

Practice 1   Matching Words and Meanings

Directions: To match word and meaning, fill in the blanks with the appropriate letters.

1. retrospect	_____	a.	succeeding or following in time
2. precedent	_____	b.	postpone
3. imminent	_____	c.	remembering
4. synchronize	_____	d.	an act, event, or decision that sets an example
5. perennial	_____	e.	occurring without pattern
6. interim	_____	f.	about to occur any moment
7. subsequent	_____	g.	a period of time between two events
8. procrastinate	_____	h.	to make events occur together in time
9. sporadic	_____	i.	continual
10. concurrent	_____	j.	happening at the same time.

Practice 2   Answering True or False

Directions: To indicate if a statement is *true* or *false*, circle the correct answer.

True   False   1. When you look at events in *retrospect*, you imagine how they will turn out in the future.

True   False   2. A legal *precedent* may help rewrite existing laws, but it has no effect on future cases.

True   False   3. When a tornado strikes, people, animals, and property are in *imminent* danger.

True   False   4. *Synchronized* dancers are usually out of step, but the effect is intended.

True   False   5. A *perennial* annoyance is constantly irritating.

True   False   6. In athletic competition, an *interim* event occurs when all the other events are over.

True   False   7. One earns a high school diploma *subsequent* to completing grammar school.

True   False   8. People who *procrastinate* never do today what they can put off till tomorrow.

True   False   9. *Sporadic* crimes don't have a pattern.

True   False   10. When events are *concurrent*, one always follows the other.

Practice 3   Making Sentence Sense

Directions: Fill in the blanks with the word that fits both the context and the definition in parentheses.

subsequent	synchronized	precedent	procrastinate	sporadic
concurrently	retrospect	interim	perennial	imminent

1. For an unfortunate few, acne is a _____ problem that persists into adulthood long after the teen years have come and gone. (lasting an indefinitely long time)

2. If the sentences run _____ , he will be out of prison in ten years. (happening at the same time)

3. Her first child was a redhead, but all of her _____ children were brunettes. (following in time or order)

4. In _____ , some fashion fads, like the Nehru jacket† for men, seem ridiculous.

5. The length of the commercial actors' walkout in 2001 set a union _____: It lasted six months. (an influential example)

6. All too often, students _____ about writing term papers. (delay)

7. In the foreign film, the words were poorly _____ with the movements of the actors' lips. (brought together in time)

8. Thanks to budget cuts, there would be no school lunches until spring, so in the _____ the kids had to bring their lunch from home. (period of time between events)

9. At horror movies, the music usually signals when a character is in _____ danger. (about to occur very soon)

10. Although peace has come to Guatemala, the country is still plagued by _____ violence. (lacking a pattern)

† Nehru jacket: Named after India's prime minister Jawaharlal Nehru (1889–1964), this traditional Indian jacket was known for its banded collar.

Practice 4   Filling in the Gaps

Directions: Fill in the blanks with one of the words from the chapter. If two words seem equally right, study the context. One word will be better than the other.

subsequent	sporadic	retrospect
imminent	perennially	synchronized

1. **The Eruption of Mount St. Helens**

   In March of 1980, a Washington volcano called Mount St. Helens began rumbling. But residents didn't worry too much, even though scientists had warned that an explosion might well be

   _____ . Although in _____ the residents' casual attitude toward

   such obvious danger might seem foolhardy, it's not that surprising. From the standpoint of

   many residents, the volcano had been _____ rumbling without ever really

   producing a full-scale explosion. Thus some were surprised when on May 18 Mount St.

   Helens produced a series of explosions that happened one right after the other, as if

   _____ , sending streams of burning ash and steam into the air. A gigantic explo-

   sion killed fifty-seven humans and thousands of animals. It also destroyed 232 square miles of

   forest. Today, Mount St. Helens is relatively quiet, but it still has _____ flare-

   ups. Obviously, there's no guarantee that _____ explosions won't be as or even

   more devastating.

interim	procrastinated	precedent	concurrent

2. **Brown v. Board of Education**

   Around 1900, several court cases set an unfortunate _____ . They legally affirmed

   the practice of segregation in public schools. While numerous legal attempts were made to set

   aside these decisions throughout the 1940s, it wasn't until 1954 that the Supreme Court finally

   ruled in *Brown v. Board of Education* that "separate but equal" schools were unacceptable and,

   more to the point, unconstitutional. Unfortunately, social change was not _____ with changes in the legal system. In the _____ between the Supreme Court's decision and full desegregation, many school districts _____ about ending segregation. Some even encouraged violent protests and threats in hope that African Americans would be too afraid to enter previously all-white schools. But, in the end, even the schools that were most intent on dragging their feet had to give in. Desegregation was the law of the land.

To test your mastery of the words introduced in this chapter, turn to page 201 in the back of the book.

Chapter 8

More Timely Words

The Common Thread

Here are ten more words that describe our relationship to time. As you learn them, think about their relationship not just to one another but also to the words in the previous chapter.

passé	sequential
millennium	contemporary
impending	provisional
circa	consecutive
archaic	habitual

Self-Test   More Timely Words

Directions: For each italicized word, circle the letter of what you think is the correct definition.

1. *Passé* means
   a. in fashion.
   b. out of fashion.
   c. ahead of one's time.

2. *Millennium* means
   a. one hundred years.
   b. a period lasting one thousand years.
   c. a two-hundred-year span.

3. *Impending* means
   a. already occurred.
   b. arriving in the far-off future.
   c. about to happen.

4. *Circa* means
   a. before.
   b. after.
   c. around.

5. *Archaic* means
   a. modern.
   b. ancient.
   c. happening soon.

6. *Sequential* means
   a. late.
   b. in a series.
   c. after the fact.

7. *Contemporary* means
   a. having an immediate effect.
   b. born too late.
   c. belonging to the same time period.

8. *Provisional* means
   a. temporary.
   b. long-term.
   c. over quickly.

9. *Consecutive* means
   a. coming at the right time.
   b. newly discovered.
   c. following one after the other.

10. *Habitual* means
    a. happening frequently.
    b. ending abruptly.
    c. going backward in time.

Turn to page 241 to correct your test. Record your grade in the self-test column on the inside front cover of your textbook. Then go on to **Words and Meanings** on pages 53–55.

Words and Meanings

Here again are the words from the self-test. Only this time, they are accompanied by their most common meanings and pointers on pronunciation.

1. **passé (pă-SĀ) *adj.***   no longer current or in fashion

   Sample Sentence   Bell-bottom pants have been *passé* for at least thirty years, but they seem to be coming back in style.

   > **MEMORY PEG**   Underline the word *pass* in *passé*, and remember that a fashion that's *passé* has passed its peak.

2. **millennium (mə-LĔN-ē-əm) *n.***   a span of one thousand years

   Sample Sentence   With the arrival of the *millennium*, there were extravagant* predictions about computer problems, but the predictions proved wrong.

   > **MEMORY PEG**   Remember that *mille* means "thousand" in Latin, and that's just how long a *millennium* lasts.

   Additional Form   millennial

3. **impending (ĭm-PĔN-dĭng) *adj.***   about to happen

   Sample Sentence   The accountant tried to be relaxed, but the *impending* interview with the FBI had clearly unsettled her nerves.

   > **MEMORY PEG**   *Impending* can be usefully broken down into its parts. *Im-* means "over," and *pend* means "hang." In other words, if something is *impending*, it's hanging over you.

4. **circa (SÛR-kə) *prep.***   around, in approximately

   Sample Sentence   It's impossible to date the discovery of milk with any degree of exactness, although *circa* 6000 B.C. is a common guess.

   > **MEMORY PEG**   At the heart of *circa* is the root *circ*, meaning "around." So if something happened *circa* 1920, it probably didn't happen on that date, but somewhere "around" that time.

5. **archaic (är-KĀ-ĭk) *adj.***   ancient, no longer current or applicable

   Sample Sentence   Those laws are *archaic*, more appropriate to the pioneer days than to the present.

   > **MEMORY PEG**   *Archaic*—like *archaeology*—comes from the Greek word *archaios*, meaning "ancient." Thus, an *arch*aeologist would be interested in finding the *archaic* structures of a long-lost civilization.

   Additional Form   archaically

6. sequential (sĭ-KWĔN-shəl) adj.   occurring in an order or series

Sample Sentence   To put the watch back together, you have to follow a series of *sequential* steps; otherwise it won't work right.

> **MEMORY PEG**   *Sequential*, like *sequel* and *sequence*, is one of a number of English words based on the Latin root *sequi*, meaning "to follow." You might also tell yourself that reciting the alphabet requires you to say the letters in *sequential* order.

Additional Form   sequentially

7. contemporary (kən-TĔM-pə-rer-ē)   **a.** modern, current (*adj.*)

Sample Sentence   He likes furniture that has a *contemporary* look.

b. one born in the same time or age (*n.*)

Sample Sentence   Benjamin Franklin and John Quincy Adams were not *contemporaries*, but Adams's father, John, was Franklin's *contemporary*.

> **MEMORY PEG**   To remember meaning *a*, keep in mind that *contemporary* furniture, if well designed, will never become *passé*. It will always seem modern. To remember meaning *b*, use word analysis. *Con* means "together" or "with," and *temp* means "time." *Contemporaries*, then, are together in time.

Additional Forms   contemporaneous, contemporarily

8. provisional (prə-VĬZH-ə-nəl) adj.   temporary, of limited time

Sample Sentence   Because of fighting among the warlords, no one believed that Afghanistan's *provisional* government could last more than a month or two.

> **MEMORY PEG**   Remember the word *perennial* from the previous chapter? Whereas *perennial* suggests an indefinite span of time, *provisional* suggests the exact opposite. The situation so described is definitely temporary.

9. consecutive (kən-SĔK-yə-tĭv) adj.   following one after the other without interruption

Sample Sentence   After it rained for five *consecutive* days, those families living by the river became apprehensive* about a flood.

> **MEMORY PEG**   In criminal trials, judges don't have to assign the concurrent* sentences discussed in the previous chapter. They can, if they choose, hand out *consecutive* sentences that run one after the other without interruption. To link and remember the meanings of both words, tell yourself that anyone going to prison would prefer *concurrent* rather than *consecutive* sentences. And, yes, *sequential* and *consecutive* are synonyms.

10. habitual (hə-BĬCH-ōō-əl) adj.   happening frequently, established by long use or persistent recurrence, constant

Sample Sentence   Almost without his notice, he had become a *habitual* gambler.

> **MEMORY PEG**   At the core of the word *habitual* is the word *habit*, and that's your clue to meaning. Like a habit, *habitual* actions, thoughts, or events have been "established by long use."

Additional Form   habituate

Idiom Alert

Time was: This idiom offers you another way to say "in the past," as in: "Time was, teachers in the classroom were all-powerful rulers, but things have changed."

Practice 1   Matching Words and Meanings

Directions: To match word and meaning, fill in the blanks with the appropriate letters.

1. passé	———	a. approximately or around
2. millennium	———	b. current or modern
3. impending	———	c. a span of one thousand years
4. circa	———	d. likely or expected to happen
5. archaic	———	e. following one after the other without interruption
6. sequential	———	f. no longer current or in fashion
7. contemporary	———	g. happening frequently
8. provisional	———	h. very old; ancient
9. consecutive	———	i. temporary
10. habitual	———	j. in a particular order or series

Practice 2   Answering True or False

Directions: To indicate if a statement is *true* or *false*, circle the correct answer.

True   False   1. The expression "You're the cat's meow," popular in the 1930s, is definitely *passé*.

True   False   2. A person who reaches the age of 100 has arrived at his or her second *millennium*.

True   False   3. People often evacuate beaches before an *impending* hurricane.

True   False   4. We use the word *circa* to identify a specific date in time.

True   False   5. Kids who call their parents' thinking *archaic* are complimenting the parents on being up-to-date.

True   False   6. When you follow a recipe, adding the ingredients *sequentially* is never important.

True   False   7. William Shakespeare is a *contemporary* of Stephen King.

True   False   8. An employee with *provisional* status can count on working for the company for a long time.

True   False   9. A *habitual* liar fibs only rarely.

True   False   10. If the weather is dark and gloomy for several *consecutive* days, many people start feeling depressed and morose.*

Practice 3   Making Sentence Sense

Directions: Fill in the blanks with the word that fits both the context and the definition in parentheses.

passé	**archaic**	**consecutive**	**millennium**	**provisional**
circa	**impending**	**contemporary**	**sequential**	**habitual**

1. The archaeologist was upset to see tourists clambering over the _____ temple of Venus. (very old; ancient)

2. Her license was _____; she needed more hours in the air to be a fully licensed pilot. (temporary)

3. The "big hair" styles of the 1980s are now considered _____ . (no longer current or in fashion)

4. Although the antiques expert could not tell the exact age of the bracelet, he believed it had been made _____ 1880. (around)

5. On the eve of January 1, 2000, Americans celebrated not only the beginning of what they hoped would be a prosperous* new year but also the start of the third _____ . (period of one thousand years)

6. Solving an algebra problem involves the completion of several _____ steps. (following in a particular order)

7. Among the young, tattoos and body piercings are _____ fashions. (current or modern)

8. Anytime she went without breakfast for two or three _____ days, she started to feel lethargic* and crabby. (following one after the other without interruption)

9. Intrepid* in all other aspects of his life, the young man was apprehensive* about his _____ marriage. (expected to happen soon)

10. His _____ tendency to make lewd* comments earned him the dislike of co-workers. (established by frequent use)

Practice 4   Filling in the Gaps

Direction: Fill in the blanks with one of the words from the chapter. If two words seem equally right, study the context. One word will be better than the other.

passé	**circa**	**sequential**	**millennium**
contemporary	**consecutive**	**archaic**	

1. Time and Fashion

In his book *Taste and Fashion*, Professor James Laver claims that fashion fads generally follow a

_____ pattern. Around a year before a fashion really becomes popular, it's con-

sidered slightly daring. When it does become truly popular, that same fashion becomes essential

to looking fresh and _____ . A year later—it's rare for a fashion trend to stay

on top for two _____ years—that very same fashion starts to seem just a bit

_____ . Within ten years, it is often considered downright _____ ,

an antique ready for the museums. But thirty years later, the very same fashion becomes ripe for

a comeback and renewed popularity.

Initially, Professor Laver's hypothesis* may seem a bit too pat. But it's not pure conjecture.*

There is some evidence to support it. At the start of the new _____ in 2001, young

people were sporting bell-bottoms, tie-dyed t-shirts, and platform shoes. These fashions had been

popular _____ 1970, but by the 1980s they were considered totally out-of-date.

If Professor Laver's interpretation is correct, come 2010, those very same articles of clothing will

be viewed as unwearable, suitable only for the showcase of a museum devoted to past fads and

fashions. But by 2030, they just might make a come-back.

(*Source of information:* Martin S. Remland, *Nonverbal Communication in Everyday Life*. Boston: Houghton Mifflin, 2000, p. 123.)

impending	habitual	provisional

2. Confronting the Nursing Shortage

According to the U.S. Department of Health and Human Services, an aging population has created a demand for more nurses. Yet currently at least, the number of men and women entering the nursing profession does not meet the demand. Making matters worse is the fact that older nurses are retiring and younger nurses are not taking their place. As a result, the nursing shortage is becoming a _____ problem for states like California and New York among others.

Experts warn that if these twin trends continue, hospitals could lack as many as 500,000 nurses by the year 2020. This _____ crisis will certainly cause the quality of health care to decline, while risks to patients will increase. To meet the shortage, some states are allowing nurses with only a _____ status to begin working, even though they have not yet completed the required licensing and screening procedures. To further reduce the threat of a shortage, hospitals, nurses' organizations, and colleges are trying hard to attract more nurses to the field.

(*Sources of information:* "Government Projects Shortage of Nurses," CNN.com, February 14, 2001, www.cnn.com/2001/ HEALTH/02/14/nurse.shortage.02/ and "Some Worry Nursing Shortage Could Put Patients at Risk,"CNN.com, January 12, 2001, www.cnn.com/2001/HEALTH/01/12/nursing.shortage/index.html.)

To test your mastery of the words introduced in this chapter, turn to page 203 in the back of the book.

Chapter 9

Keeping Secrets

The Common Thread

In the best of all possible worlds, people would always tell the truth and avoid secrecy. But that's not always possible. The following words are likely to turn up at those times when people are not direct with one another.

espionage	furtive
intrigue	cache
covert	dissemble
guise	stealth
pseudonym	cryptic

Self-Test Keeping Secrets

Directions: For each italicized word, circle the letter of what you think is the correct definition.

1. *Espionage* means
   a. disguise.
   b. spying.
   c. deviousness.*

2. *Intrigue* means
   a. secret plot.
   b. code.
   c. detective work.

3. *Covert* means
   a. illegal.
   b. concealed.
   c. dishonest.

4. *Guise* means
   a. puzzle.
   b. false appearance.
   c. mystery.

5. *Pseudonym* means
   a. false-hearted.
   b. false name.
   c. false address.

6. *Furtive* means
   a. secretive.
   b. pretending.
   c. disguise.

7. *Cache* means
   a. a secret hiding place.
   b. an illegal act committed by a group.
   c. blackmail.

8. *Dissemble* means
   a. take apart.
   b. use a false name.
   c. pretend.

9. *Stealth* means
   a. hiding place.
   b. a secretive manner.
   c. a secret message.

10. *Cryptic* means
    a. in hiding.
    b. coded or secret.
    c. silent.

Turn to page 241 to correct your test. Record your grade in the self-test column on the inside front cover of your textbook. Then go on to **Words and Meanings** on pages 60–62.

Words and Meanings

Here again are the words from the self-test. Only this time, they are accompanied by their most common meanings and pointers on pronunciation.

1. **espionage (ĔS-pē-ə-näzh) *n.***   the art or practice of using spies to obtain secret information about another government or organization

    Sample Sentence   When it comes to *espionage*, no one was better at it than double agent Kim Philby.†

    > **MEMORY PEG**   To commit the word to memory, circle the letters *espion* and write "spy" over them because that's what they mean in French. You can also remember that the letters *spion* in *espionage* add up to the word *spy* in German. In other words, there are at least two spies in the word *espionage*.

2. **intrigue (ĬN-trēg, ĭn-TRĒG)**   **a.** secret plot or scheme (*n.*)

    Sample Sentence   When the palace *intrigue* to overthrow the king was discovered, the participants were beheaded.

    b. to plot or scheme (*v.*)

    Sample Sentence   Julius and Ethel Rosenberg were believed to have *intrigued* against the United States; for that reason, both were executed.

    > **MEMORY PEG**   Appropriately enough, the word *intrigue* comes from the Italian word *intrigare*, which means "to plot." Thus, people given to *intrigue* are always plotting something. However, you should also be aware that *intrigue* can have a more harmless meaning, "to arouse interest," as in: "The researchers were *intrigued* by the speaker's description of how the virus was spread."

    Additional Form   intriguingly

3. **covert (KŬV-ərt, KŌ-vərt, kō-VÛRT) *adj.***   secret, covered, or concealed

    Sample Sentence   The woman in charge of *covert* operations for the CIA spent many years in the Middle East.

    > **MEMORY PEG**   Remember that the word *covert* includes the word *cover*, and any *covert* activity is performed undercover or in secret.

    Additional Form   covertness

4. **guise (gīz) *n.***   **a.** false appearance, pretense

    Sample Sentence   Under the *guise* of a friend, she convinced the young girl to reveal everything she knew about the theft of the jewelry.

    b. outward appearance

    Sample Sentence   She appeared in the *guise* of a fairy godmother.

---

†   Harold (Kim) Philby (1912–1988): While working for British intelligence, he also spied for the Russians.

> **MEMORY PEG** To remember this word, you should know that it comes from the French word for "manner." Thus, a person's *guise*, or "manner," can create a false identity (meaning *a*) or reveal a true one (meaning *b*).

5. **pseudonym (SŌŌD-n-ĭm)** *n.*   false name, pen name

   Sample Sentence Anne Rice, author of several best-selling novels, also writes softcore pornography under two *pseudonyms*, Anne Rampling and A. N. Rocquelaure.

   > **MEMORY PEG** The meaning of this word is easy to remember if you know its parts. *Pseudo* means "false," and *nym* means "name."

   Common Usage   *under a* pseudonym

6. **furtive (FŪR-tĭv)** *adj.*   underhanded, not open, sly

   Sample Sentence The uniformed man said he wanted to read the gas meter, but his *furtive* manner made her suspicious.

   > **MEMORY PEG** Remember that thieves who aren't *furtive* usually end up in jail. And yes, *covert* and *furtive* are synonyms, but of the two, *furtive* is the more negative. It suggests that the person so described is up to no good.

   Additional Form   furtiveness

7. **cache (kăsh)** *n.*   a hiding place for food, valuables, or weapons; a store or collection of goods kept hidden

   Sample Sentence When the soldiers searched the house, they found a *cache* of weapons hidden beneath the floorboards.

   > **MEMORY PEG** Since the word *cache* refers to a hiding place, try telling yourself that a *cache* is the place to keep large sums of cash.

   Common Usage   *a* cache *of*

8. **dissemble (dĭ-SĔM-bəl)** *v.*   to disguise or conceal behind a false appearance

   Sample Sentence As a member of the French underground during World War II, she had to *dissemble* whenever she came face-to-face with a German soldier.

   > **MEMORY PEG** The word *dissemble* comes from the Latin word *sembler*, meaning "to appear." Remember that people who *dissemble* try to "appear" other than they are.

   Additional Forms   dissemblance, dissembler

9. **stealth (stĕlth)** *n.*   secrecy; moving or acting so as not to be seen or heard

   Sample Sentence She had acquired the papers in *stealth*, never letting her husband know she was investigating his past.

   > **MEMORY PEG** To remember this word, think of the *stealth* bomber, an airplane that cannot be detected by radar and therefore can go on "secret" missions.

Additional Forms   stealthy, stealthily

Common Usage   *in, with, by* stealth

10. **cryptic (KRĬP-tĭk)** *adj.*   coded, hidden, mysterious; difficult to understand

Sample Sentence   The letter in the bottle contained a *cryptic* message that warned of an unnamed but devastating disaster.

> **MEMORY PEG**   Remember that *cryptic* comes from the Greek word for "hidden." Something that is *cryptic*, like a secret code, cannot be understood by anyone who doesn't have the key. In other words, it remains hidden or mysterious.

Additional Forms   cryptical, cryptically

Idiom Alert

Cold war: First used in 1947 in a book called *The Cold War*, about the hostility shared by then-Communist Russia and the United States. The term refers to a constant state of mistrust and military alert. Although weapons were seldom used, spying was a constant activity on both sides. "When Gary Powers's spy plane went down in Russia during the cold war, the U.S. was reticent* to admit that Powers was engaged in espionage,* even though Powers himself admitted it."

Practice 1   Matching Words and Meanings

Directions: To match word and meaning, fill in the blanks with the appropriate letters.

1. espionage   _____   a. secrecy

2. intrigue   _____   b. sly or underhanded

3. covert   _____   c. coded or hidden

4. guise   _____   d. false name

5. pseudonym   _____   e. spying

6. furtive   _____   f. a false appearance

7. cache   _____   g. secret plot or scheme

8. dissemble   _____   h. a hiding place

9. stealth   _____   i. to disguise or conceal behind a false appearance

10. cryptic   _____   j. concealed

Practice 2   Answering True or False

Directions: To indicate if a statement is *true* or *false*, circle the correct answer.

True   False   1. Most nations are proud about engaging in *espionage*.

True   False   2. People who can't keep secrets shouldn't engage in *intrigue*.

True   False   3. If you are planning a surprise party, you shouldn't be *covert* about your intentions.

True   False   4. A fake I.D. can be part of a *guise*.

True   False   5. Priests and doctors are likely to use a *pseudonym* in their work.

True   False   6. People with something to hide are likely to be *furtive*.

True   False   7. A *cache* is unlikely to hold anything of value.

True   False   8. It's probably not a good idea to trust anyone who is given to *dissembling*.

True   False   9. The words *stealth* and *disguise* are synonyms.

True   False   10. A good code needs to be *cryptic* or it's worthless.

Practice 3   Making Sentence Sense

Directions: Fill in the blanks with the word that fits both the context and the definition in parentheses.

guise	cache	covert	cryptic	intrigues
furtive	pseudonyms	espionage	dissembling	stealth

1. The kidnapper called himself Paul Morrow, but that was just one of his _____. (false names)

2. The bears broke into the cabin and stole the campers' _____ of food. (a collection of hidden goods)

3. For years, FBI agent Robert Hanssen engaged in _____ without being caught. (spying)

4. The young French queen Marie Antoinette† was constantly the object of palace _____ meant to damage her reputation. (plots or schemes)

5. Bad at _____, she couldn't disguise her contempt for a man who sold his vote to the highest bidder. (assuming a false appearance)

† **Marie Antoinette** (1755–1793): the much despised wife of Louis XVI; both rulers were beheaded during the French Revolution.

6. In the 1920s, Prohibition did not stop the manufacture of alcohol; it simply turned the process into a _____ operation. (hidden)

7. Superman moves among ordinary people in the _____ of Clark Kent, a newspaper reporter. (false appearance; pretense)

8. The shoplifter's _____ behavior alerted the store detective to what was going on. (underhanded, sly)

9. The thief warned his partner to proceed with _____ because there were alarms everywhere. (secrecy)

10. The _____ message was discovered by the enemy, but it could not be interpreted because it was written in Navajo. (coded)

Practice 4   Filling in the Gaps

Directions: Fill in the blanks with one of the words from the chapter. *Note:* In this case, some of the words may be interchangeable. Just make sure to use a word that fits the context.

cryptic	dissemble	stealth	covert	caches

1. **Special Forces**

    The United States military includes several groups of all-male special operations soldiers who go on particularly dangerous or difficult missions. Like traditional soldiers, these special forces are trained in hand-to-hand combat and _____ maneuvers. The members of these groups receive additional training that provides them with the knowledge and skills they need to conduct their operations in _____. The dangerous nature of their assignments often requires them to _____ about their goals and activities. Their assignments often include secretly gathering classified information, uncoding _____ messages, searching for _____ of weapons, and entering enemy territory to clear the way for regular ground troops. For example, the U.S. Army Special Forces, better known as the Green Berets, are called the "eyes and ears" of regular forces because of their ability to gather critical information completely undercover and pave the way for the troops' arrival.

espionage   intrigue   guises   pseudonyms   furtive

2.   After Forty Years, James Bond Lives On

One of the most enduring characters in motion picture history has been that master of

_____ , James Bond, also known as Agent 007. Since the first film, based on Ian

Fleming's novel *Dr. No,* was released in 1962, audiences have flocked to theaters in order to see

Bond's _____ and action-packed films. Bond has been portrayed over the years by

five different actors, including Sean Connery, Roger Moore, and Pierce Brosnan. Regardless of

who plays him, Bond is always handsome and charming but also dangerously clever. He uses his

wits, his fists, and his high-tech gadgets to defeat the plans of even the most well-planned criminal

conspiracy. Bond also excels at using _____ and _____ to hunt

down criminal masterminds engaged in _____ and usually deadly plotting. In a

Bond film, it doesn't matter how well hidden or well guarded the villains' hideout is. James Bond

will always find it and interrupt the evildoers' villainous plans.

To test your mastery of the words introduced in this chapter, turn to page 205 in the back of the book.

Hiding Out

The Common Thread

Like Chapter 9, Chapter 10 focuses on secrecy and concealment. The ten words in this chapter revolve around hiding or concealing one's identity, motives, or appearance. For each of the words, try to imagine a setting or scene where it might apply.

skulk	clandestine
incognito	lair
duplicity	secluded
sham	recluse
ruse	feign

Self-Test | Hiding Out

Directions: For each italicized word, circle the letter of what you think is the correct definition.

1. *Skulk* means
   a. to keep a secret.
   b. to hide from people.
   c. to move in a stealthy* fashion.

2. *Incognito* means
   a. in disguise.
   b. of Italian descent.
   c. overexposed.

3. *Duplicity* means
   a. double trouble.
   b. double-dealing.
   c. mysterious.

4. *Sham* means
   a. a magician.
   b. a cache.*
   c. a pretense.

5. *Ruse* means
   a. spy.
   b. puzzle.
   c. trick.

6. *Clandestine* means
   a. in code.
   b. not telling the truth.
   c. done in secret.

7. *Lair* means
   a. an open platform.
   b. loot from a crime spree.
   c. a hideaway.

8. *Secluded* means
   a. open to inspection.
   b. remote from others.
   c. in disguise.

9. *Recluse* means
   a. a homeless person.
   b. someone who loves attention.
   c. someone who withdraws from the world.

10. *Feign* means
    a. to disappear.
    b. to arrive secretly.
    c. to pretend.

Turn to page 241 to correct your test. Record your grade in the self-test column on the inside front cover of your textbook. Then go on to **Words and Meanings** on pages 67–69.

Words and Meanings

Here again are the words from the self-test. Only this time, they are accompanied by their most common meanings and pointers on pronunciation.

1. skulk (skŭlk) *v.*   to move around as if trying not to be seen

Sample Sentence   When the soldiers found the man *skulking* in the bushes, they immediately took him to their commanding officer.

> **MEMORY PEG**   The word *skulk* is of Scandinavian origin. It described someone who didn't want to work and hid out to avoid it. Although that meaning occasionally still turns up, the far more common one describes someone going undercover because he or she is up to no good. To remember that meaning, try imagining someone dressed in black, sneaking from bush to bush to avoid being seen.

2. incognito (ĭn-kŏg-NĒ-to) *adj.* or *adv.*   with identity concealed; in disguise

Sample Sentence   The undercover police officers were *incognito* while on the trail of drug dealers. (*adj.*)

Sample Sentence   The escaped convict managed to live *incognito* for two years before his neighbors discovered who he really was. (*adv.*)

> **MEMORY PEG**   The word *incognito* comes from an Italian word meaning "unknown." People who are *incognito* are unknown because they have made it a point to conceal their identity. Thus, you can remember the word by associating it with celebrities who need to go places *incognito* to avoid being mobbed.

Common Usage   to *be* or *go* incognito.

3. duplicity (dōō-PLĬS-ĭ-tē) *n.*   deliberate deviousness* or deception

Sample Sentence   It was hard to say what made the swindler more dangerous, his *duplicity* or his charm.

> **MEMORY PEG**   Connect the *d* in *duplicity* to the *d* in double. Tell yourself that *duplicity* is the art of double-dealing. And, yes, do link *duplicity* to *deviousness,** a word you already know from Chapter 5.

Additional Form   duplicitous

4. sham (shăm)   **a.** something false or empty that is presented as genuine; a pretense (*n.*)

Sample Sentence   Her claim to being a military hero is a complete *sham*.

                                                              b. a person who assumes a false character, an imposter (*n.*)

Sample Sentence   The man is not a millionaire; he's a total *sham*.

                                                              c. false or fake (*adj.*)

Sample Sentence   Don't be fooled by her *sham* meekness; she's a tough and successful trial lawyer.

| MEMORY PEG | Link *sham* to what many consider its point of origin, the word *shame.* Someone who is or uses a *sham* should be ashamed of being an imposter or using pretense and fakery. |

5. ruse (rōōs, rōōz) *n.*   an action or device meant to confuse or mislead

Sample Sentence   The clever swindler seemed to have a new *ruse* for every victim.

| MEMORY PEG | Tell yourself that *ruse* is a fancy way of saying "trick" or scheme. Or try placing the word in a rhyming context that reveals its meaning, e.g., "Celebrities sometimes choose to use a *ruse* to avoid getting their picture in the news." |

Common Usage   *use a* ruse

6. clandestine (klăn-DĔS-tĭn) *adj.*   done in secret, or stealth,* frequently for evil purposes

Sample Sentence   When Benedict Arnold's† *clandestine* meetings with a British officer were discovered, Arnold's reputation as a military hero was destroyed, and he was no longer revered* as a hero.

| MEMORY PEG | Espionage,* adultery, and planning a surprise party are all examples of *clandestine* activities. Think of those examples to remember that *clandestine* means "done in secret." |

Additional Form   clandestineness

7. lair (lâr) *n.*   a hideaway, especially for criminals

Sample Sentence   The thieves stashed the stolen goods in their *lair,* an abandoned factory outside the city limits.

| MEMORY PEG | To remember the meaning of *lair,* keep in mind that it can also mean "the den of a wild animal." Like wild animals, criminals who prey on society need someplace to hide. The place they hide in is often referred to as a *lair.* |

8. secluded (sĭ-KLŌŌ-dĭd) *adj.*   removed or remote from others; isolated

Sample Sentence   Surrounded by trees, the house was so *secluded* no one knew it was there.

| MEMORY PEG | The word *seclude* comes from a Middle English word that meant "to shut off." Remember, then, that something *secluded* is shut off from everyone and everything. It might be far away, or it might be hidden. For example, criminals usually like to hide out in *secluded lairs* to avoid being discovered. |

Additional Forms   seclude, secludedness, seclusion

9. recluse (RĔK-lōōs, rĭ-KLŌŌS) *n.*   a person who withdraws from the world to live apart from everyone else

Sample Sentence   The famous author lived as a *recluse* and refused to grant interviews.

†   Benedict Arnold (1741–1801): Revolutionary War general who was first a great military hero and later on a traitor to his country.

> **MEMORY PEG**   The word *recluse* comes from a Latin word that means "to shut up." People who choose to be *recluses*, then, shut themselves up from the rest of the world. Remember that *recluses* retreat and retire from society and rarely, if ever, go out in public. They usually live in *secluded* places where they won't be bothered by others.

Additional Form   reclusive

10. feign (fān) *v.*   to give a false appearance

Sample Sentence   She tried to *feign* deafness in order to avoid answering any questions, but the sheriff saw through her ruse.*

> **MEMORY PEG**   As kids, almost everyone tries at least once to *feign* illness in order to avoid school. To remember the meaning of *feign*, then, think of yourself as a child trying to convince one or both of your parents that you were too ill to go to school.

Idiom Alert

Open secret: This idiom started out as the title of a Spanish play called "The Noisy Secret." It made its way into Italian, where it became the "public secret," and finally turned up in English, in the 1800s, as the "open secret," meaning that something supposedly hidden is really quite public, e.g., "It's an open secret that the network is not happy with the new anchorman."

Practice 1   Matching Words and Meanings

Directions: To match word and meaning, fill in the blanks with the appropriate letters.

1. skulk	_____	a. a person who lives apart from everyone else
2. incognito	_____	b. trick
3. duplicity	_____	c. something false that is presented as genuine
4. sham	_____	d. to move around as if trying not to be seen
5. ruse	_____	e. with identity concealed or in disguise
6. clandestine	_____	f. pretend
7. lair	_____	g. removed or remote from others
8. secluded	_____	h. secret, stealthy
9. recluse	_____	i. double-dealing
10. feign	_____	j. a hideaway, especially for criminals

Practice 2   Answering True or False

Directions: To indicate if a statement is *true* or *false*, circle the correct answer.

True   False   1. The term *skulking* refers to military maneuvers carried out in secret.

True   False   2. On Halloween, lots of people go out *incognito*.

True   False   3. A bank robber with a mask over his face is the perfect illustration of *duplicity*.

True   False   4. Mob boss John Gotti was a *sham* gangster.

True   False   5. Only magicians use *ruses*.

True   False   6. *Clandestine* meetings are usually kept secret.

True   False   7. A drug dealer is likely to have a *lair*.

True   False   8. People who want privacy usually vacation in *secluded* locations.

True   False   9. A *recluse* fears being alone.

True   False   10. Someone *feigning* a heart attack needs immediate medical attention.

Practice 3   Making Sentence Sense

Directions: Fill in the blanks with the word that fits both the context and the definition in parentheses.

ruse	clandestinely	incognito	duplicity	feigned
secluded	recluse	lair	sham	skulking

1. The candidate's claim to be a family man turned out to be a _____ ; he had actually carried on several affairs while he was married. (something false presented as genuine)

2. If the surprise party was to be a success, they needed a _____ to get their mother
   home before nine. (trick or scheme)

3. The suspect had been seen _____ around campus, and police wanted to talk to
   him. (sneaking around)

4. The kidnappers blindfolded their captive so that later she would not know the location of their
   _____ . (a hideaway, especially for criminals)

5. The homeowners surrounded the backyard with a high fence that made the area more
   _____ . (removed or remote from others)

6. Before becoming president, Harry Truman _____ a lack of ambition by insist-
   ing that he wasn't qualified for such a high office. (pretended)

7. Gossip columnist Hedda Hopper was famous for her _____ ; to get a story, she would pretend a motherly affection for the celebrity she planned to destroy in her column. (double-dealing)

8. Alone on the deserted island, the castaway was forced to live as a _____ for two years until rescue arrived. (a person who withdraws from the world to live apart from everyone else)

9. The movie star preferred to travel _____ , hiding her distinctive hair under a wig and using a fake name. (with identity concealed or in disguise)

10. Because the two lovers came from feuding families, Romeo and Juliet had to meet _____ . (in secret)

Practice 4   Filling in the Gaps

Directions: Fill in the blanks with one of the words from the chapter. *Note:* In this case, some of the words may be interchangeable. Just make sure to use a word that fits the context.

secluded	skulk	feigned	lair	duplicity
recluses	ruse	clandestine	sham	incognito

The Real Bonnie and Clyde

In the 1930s, Bonnie Parker and Clyde Barrow were two of America's most notorious* criminals. In part, at least, they are famous even today because their two-year crime spree was the subject of a now classic 1967 film, *Bonnie and Clyde.* But their fame has also lasted because the two were very, very good at public relations. Throughout their short and bloody career, they _____ a devotion to the poor and portrayed themselves as modern-day Robin Hoods. The two didn't _____ around or live like _____ in an attempt to avoid attention. On the contrary, they seemed avid* for it. Instead of traveling _____ and keeping a low profile, they kept a little Kodak camera in the car and would occasionally snap pictures of themselves toting guns. Some of the pictures they auto-graphed and distributed to friends. Others they left in abandoned cars, where the police could find them and the photos could make their way to the press.

In a long and truly awful poem, "The Story of Bonnie and Clyde," Bonnie Parker summed up the _____ image she was determined to leave behind. The poem paints her and Clyde as intrepid* and altruistic* young people fighting a corrupt social system that favors the rich over the poor. Bonnie's poem, however, is a rhymed exercise in _____ . During their crime spree, in which at least thirteen people died, Bonnie and Clyde didn't just rob banks. In pursuit of cold cash rather than social justice, the couple robbed hardware stores and grocery markets. In other words, they robbed and killed the very working people they claimed to champion.

But in addition to killing grocery and sales clerks, Bonnie and Clyde murdered policemen, a mistake that sealed their doom. The police became the couple's staunch* enemies and were determined to hunt the twosome down no matter how _____ their _____ . Aware that the police were intent on capturing them, Bonnie and Clyde became a bit more stealthy.* Yet even as their behavior and hiding places became more _____ , a traitor in their midst tipped off the police to their whereabouts.

On the morning of May 23, 1934, the two were driving down a narrow dirt road near Sailes, Louisiana, when they saw an abandoned pickup truck. Failing to recognize the _____ intended to trap them, Clyde slowed down and peered around. At precisely that moment, the sheriff told his posse to shoot. In a matter of minutes, both Bonnie and Clyde were dead from multiple gunshot wounds.

> To test your mastery of the words introduced in this chapter, turn to page 207 in the back of the book.

Chapter 11

Expressions of Approval and Disapproval

The Common Thread

Sometimes approval can be a formal matter, so much so that a word acquires legal status, for example, *ratify*. But there are other times when words for approval or disapproval have no legal meaning. We use them just to indicate something is good or bad. That's when we turn to words like *commemorate* and *denounce*.

reproach	sanction
denounce	proponent
chide	advocate
disdain	ratify
aversion	commemorate

Self-Test — Expressions of Approval and Disapproval

Directions: For each italicized word, circle the letter of what you think is the correct definition.

1. *Reproach* means
   a. praise.
   b. criticize.
   c. accept.

2. *Denounce* means
   a. accuse in public.
   b. agree with.
   c. plead with.

3. *Chide* means
   a. accept with qualifications.
   b. applaud in public.
   c. scold mildly.

4. *Disdain* means
   a. despise.
   b. admire.
   c. accept.

5. *Aversion* means
   a. dislike.
   b. favor.
   c. insult.

6. *Sanction* means
   a. discourage.
   b. reject.
   c. encourage.

7. *Proponent* means
   a. enemy.
   b. supporter.
   c. model.

8. *Advocate* means
   a. argue against.
   b. plead in favor of.
   c. agree with.

9. *Ratify* means
   a. silently accept.
   b. argue against.
   c. formally approve.

10. *Commemorate* means
    a. disagree with someone.
    b. design a monument.
    c. honor the memory of someone.

Turn to page 241 to correct your test. Record your grade in the self-test column on the inside front cover of your textbook. Then go on to **Words and Meanings** on pages 74–76.

Words and Meanings

Here again are the words from the self-test. Only this time, they are accompanied by their most common meanings and pointers on pronunciation.

1. reproach (rĭ-PRŌCH)   **a.** disappointment, disapproval (*n.*)

Sample Sentence The state government's decision to raise gasoline taxes met with *reproach* by some commentators.

b. to find fault with or criticize (*v.*)

Sample Sentence Some commentators *reproached* the state government for its decision to raise gasoline taxes.

MEMORY PEG To remember the meaning of *reproach*, keep in mind the expression "to be above reproach." People above (or beyond) *reproach* are so good that they never become the subject of criticism.

Additional Forms reproachful, reproachfulness

2. denounce (dĭ-NOUNS) *v.*   to criticize openly as evil; to publicly accuse or criticize

Sample Sentence The leaders of many countries *denounced* the president of North Korea's decision to produce nuclear weapons.

MEMORY PEG To remember the meaning of *denounce*, link it to *announce*. When you *denounce* someone, you announce to the world that the person has done something shameful.

Additional Forms denunciation, denouncer, denouncement

3. chide (chīd) *v.*   to state disapproval in order to bring about improvement; scold

Sample Sentence Although I don't want to, I'll have to *chide* my soft-hearted son for bringing home so many stray cats.

MEMORY PEG Link the *ch* in <u>*chide*</u> to the *ch* in the word <u>*children*</u>. It is children who are likely to be *chided* by parents hoping for better behavior.

4. disdain (dĭs-DĀN)   **a.** to view with contempt; to despise (*v.*)

Sample Sentence General George Patton *disdained* those soldiers who applied for a leave of absence from the frontlines.

b. a feeling or show of contempt or disgust (*n.*)

Sample Sentence When the reporter disapproved of the actions he described, he tended to curl his upper lip in *disdain*.

MEMORY PEG To remember the meaning of *disdain*, visualize someone curling his or her lip to show obvious *disdain* or disgust.

Additional Form disdainful

5. aversion (ə-VÛR-zhən, shən) n.   a very strong dislike

Sample Sentence   President George H. W. Bush became known for his *aversion* to broccoli.

> **MEMORY PEG**   It may help your memory to know that *ver* means "turn," and the prefix *a-*, in this case, means "away." When you have an *aversion* to someone or something, you are likely to turn away in disgust.

Additional Form   averse

Common Usage   *have an* aversion *to*

6. sanction (SĂNGK-shən)   **a.** to encourage or approve, sometimes as an official act (*v.*)

Sample Sentence   The Constitution once *sanctioned* the treatment of slaves as property.

> **b.** to punish as a way of changing behavior, particularly that of governments (*v.*)

Sample Sentence   At one time, South Africa was *sanctioned* for the racist policies known as apartheid.†

> **c.** a punishment designed to change behavior, particularly behavior of governments (*n.*)

Sample Sentence   The *sanctions* imposed on Iraq have led to much hardship for its citizens.

> **MEMORY PEG**   As the two sample sentences under *a* and *b* show, to sanction may mean one thing in one context and almost its opposite in another context. The reason is that the word comes from the Latin word *sanctio*, meaning "law." Remember, then, that *sanctions*, like laws, permit some actions and punish others. That way you will remember the opposing definitions of the word *sanction*.

7. proponent (prə-PŌ-nənt) n.   someone who argues in favor of something; a strong supporter

Sample Sentence   During the debate, stalwart* *proponents* of strict environmental controls clashed with those who wanted to weaken environmental restrictions.

> **MEMORY PEG**   Keep in mind the expression "pro and con." Someone on the *pro* side is "in favor" in the same way that a *proponent* is a supporter of a theory, event, or idea.

Common Usage   proponent *of*

8. advocate (ĂD-və-kāt)   **a.** to speak, plead, or argue in favor of something (*v.*)

Sample Sentence   Vegetarians *advocate* meatless diets.

(ĂD-və-kət)   **b.** a supporter, someone who speaks in favor (*n.*)

† Apartheid: an official policy of racial separation.

Sample Sentence   Sarah Brady† is a staunch* *advocate* of gun control.

> MEMORY PEG   If you are a proponent* of a cause, it's very likely that you will *advocate* that cause to others. It will help, too, to know that *voc* means "call." That way you can tell yourself that an *advocate* is likely to "call" in favor of a cause or person.

Additional Forms   advocacy, advocator

9. **ratify (RĂT-ə-fī) v.**   to formally approve or give permission

Sample Sentence   The much-debated amendments to the Constitution were finally *ratified* in 1791.

> MEMORY PEG   Think of the Equal Rights Amendment,† which has been waiting for *ratification* by some states for more than a decade; or think of the treaty against the spreading of nuclear weapons that has been *ratified* or formally approved by most countries.

Additional Forms   ratification, ratifier

10. **commemorate (kə-MĔM-ə-rāt) v.**   a. to honor or pay homage* to the memory of someone or something, often with a ceremony

Sample Sentence   The mayor spoke at the event *commemorating* the bravery of the firefighters who lost their lives on September 11, 2001, while attempting to rescue others.

b. to serve as a memorial to

Sample Sentence   Martin Luther King Day *commemorates* Dr. King's role in the struggle for civil rights during the 1960s.

> MEMORY PEG   Focus on the two middle syllables in *commemorate*. Link them to the opening syllables of *memory*. That way you will remember that *commemorate* means "to honor the memory of someone or something."

Additional Forms   commemorative, commemoration

Common Usage   *in* commemoration

 Idiom Alert

Damn with faint praise: This expression refers to a compliment so weak it amounts to an insult, as in "The critic damned the movie with faint praise by suggesting that the best thing about it was the spectacular cinematography."

---

†   Sarah Brady is the wife of James Brady, who was shot and left paralyzed after a 1981 assassination attempt on President Ronald Reagan.

†   Equal Rights Amendment: a constitutional change that would guarantee women's rights.

Practice 1   Matching Words and Meanings

Directions: To match word and meaning, fill in the blanks with the appropriate letters.

1. reproach	_____	a. formally approve
2. denounce	_____	b. disapproval
3. chide	_____	c. scold
4. disdain	_____	d. strong supporter
5. aversion	_____	e. honor the memory
6. sanction	_____	f. despise
7. proponent	_____	g. strong dislike
8. advocate	_____	h. punishment meant to change behavior
9. ratify	_____	i. plead or argue in favor of
10. commemorate	_____	j. criticize publicly

Practice 2   Answering True or False

Directions: To indicate if a statement is *true* or *false*, circle the correct answer.

True   False   1. A *reproach* is an expression of disapproval.

True   False   2. People who *denounce* others have only praise for them.

True   False   3. Dogs are usually *chided* for being good watchdogs.

True   False   4. People who *disdain* rap music are likely to be big fans of Planet Asia, Perverted Monks, and Eminem.

True   False   5. An *aversion* is an extravagant* form of affection.

True   False   6. A *sanction* can be a sign of either agreement or disagreement.

True   False   7. A *proponent* of animal rights will most likely wear a fur coat in winter.

True   False   8. Heavy smokers are not likely to *advocate* no-smoking laws.

True   False   9. *Ratification* is a form of approval.

True   False   10. Notable* people are likely to be *commemorated*.

Practice 3   Making Sentence Sense

Directions: Fill in the blanks with the word that fits both the context and the definition in parentheses.

ratify	chided	aversion	proponent	reproach
denouncing	commemorates	sanctioned	advocated	disdain

1. As a _____ of peace with the communists, Vice President Henry Wallace was outnumbered by those who thought the United States and Russia had to be perennial* enemies. (supporter)

2. The look of _____ on the defendant's face indicated what she thought of her defense attorney. (disappointment)

3. Even after he was publicly _____ by the other members of Congress, the representative refused to admit any wrongdoing. (scolded)

4. Tenants upset by the large increase in their rent wrote angry letters _____ the city council's decision. (criticize publicly)

5. The "Wall" in Washington _____ those who died serving their country during the Vietnam War. (to serve as a memorial to)

6. The queen barely concealed her_____ for the nobles who came to pay homage* to the throne. (contempt)

7. The senator_____ replacing the current graduated income tax rate with a flat tax rate. (to speak in favor of)

8. There's not a school in the world where cheating is _____ . (officially approved)

9. Japan has decided to _____ the international agreement that requires each participating country to reduce its output of harmful carbon dioxide gases. (to approve formally)

10. She has such an _____ to snakes that she becomes agitated if she even sees one on television. (intense dislike)

Practice 4   Filling in the Gaps

Directions: Fill in the blanks with one of the words from the chapter. If two words seem equally right, study the context. One word will be better than the other.

reproaches	**denounced**	**advocate**
proponents	**aversion**	

1. The Fight Against Slavery

As early as 1786, Americans protested the practice of slavery in the United States. George Washington, Benjamin Franklin, and Thomas Paine, for example, were all notable* members of the Pennsylvania Abolition Society, a group that assisted runaway slaves escaping to freedom. For several decades, until the Thirteenth Amendment to the Constitution finally put a stop to slavery in 1865, more and more people became abolitionists, who _____ slavery as a disreputable* institution that should be immediately abandoned. Many in the abolitionist movement considered themselves pious* Christians, who had a moral _____ to treating other human beings as if they were beasts of burden. In addition, abolitionists worried that enslaving others was a deeply reprehensible* act that would earn them God's _____ , perhaps even eternal damnation. Driven by their need to right a moral wrong, _____ of abolition argued for their cause in newspapers, pamphlets, speeches, and sermons. By the 1830s, the abolition movement had become a crusade as more and more Americans began to _____ an end to the buying and selling of human beings. By 1838, there were more than 1,350 antislavery societies with almost 250,000 members.

(*Sources of information:* "The Freedom Sympathizers and Fighters," http://education.ucdavis.edu/NEW/STO/lesson/ socstud/railroad/Abolit.htm; "Abolitionists," *The Columbia Electronic Encyclopedia*, 2000, http://www.infoplease.com/ ce6/history/A0802190.html; Mary Beth Norton et al., *A People and a Nation*, vol. 1, 5th ed., Boston: Houghton Mifflin, 354–357.)

sanction	ratification	commemorated
disdain	chide	

2. Prohibition in America

Prohibition, a ban on the manufacture and sale of alcoholic beverages in America, lasted from 1920 to 1933. It began with Congress's ———————— of the Eighteenth Amendment to the Constitution in 1919. This amendment was the result of years of crusading by women's temperance groups who did not ———————— the consumption of alcohol. As a matter of fact, they were quick to ———————— drinkers, blaming them for a number of societal problems, including violence, poverty, and crime. Temperance groups would settle for nothing less than a nationwide ban on alcohol.

At first, Prohibition earned praise for significantly decreasing the number of arrests for drunkenness and reducing alcohol-related illness. However, ———————— for the law grew when it forced the manufacture and sale of liquor underground and thereby created a whole new set of problems. All throughout Prohibition, alcoholic beverages continued to be bought and sold, only now they were controlled by organized crime. No wonder, then, that by the late 1920s, an anti-Prohibition movement gained momentum. In December 1933, Congress ———————— the thirteenth anniversary of the Eighteenth Amendment by passing the Twenty-first Amendment to repeal it.

To test your mastery of the words introduced in this chapter, turn to page 209 in the back of the book.

Chapter 12

Beginnings and Endings

The Common Thread

From birth to death, life is all about beginnings and endings. Needless to say, there are many words to describe how we start and how we end or complete a project, process, or plan. This chapter introduces ten of those words.

novice	incentive
inaugural	initiate
stimulus	rudimentary
terminate	finale
wane	apex

Self-Test   Beginnings and Endings

Directions: For each italicized word, circle the letter of what you think is the correct definition.

1. *Novice* means
   a. opening.
   b. finalist.
   c. beginner.

2. *Inaugural* means
   a. first.
   b. last.
   c. closing.

3. *Stimulus* means
   a. inspire.
   b. motive.
   c. complete.

4. *Terminate* means
   a. start off.
   b. end.
   c. open up.

5. *Wane* means
   a. get bigger.
   b. start up.
   c. decrease.

6. *Incentive* means
   a. point of completion.
   b. something that encourages action.
   c. something that discourages action.

7. *Initiate* means
   a. to murder.
   b. to cause to begin.
   c. to cause to end.

8. *Rudimentary* means
   a. basic.
   b. next to last.
   c. completed.

9. *Finale* means
   a. first act.
   b. final act.
   c. first night.

10. *Apex* means
    a. starting point.
    b. high point.
    c. low point.

Turn to page 242 to correct your test. Record your grade in the self-test column on the inside front cover of your textbook. Then go on to **Words and Meanings** on pages 82–84.

Words and Meanings

Here again are the words from the self-test. Only this time, they are accompanied by their most common meanings and pointers on pronunciation.

1. novice (NŌV-ĭs)   **a.** beginner, newcomer (*n.*)

Sample Sentence Brian was a genius at computer games but a real *novice* at chess.

b. inexperienced (*adj.*)

Sample Sentence A *novice* basketball player, she nevertheless showed real talent.

MEMORY PEG   Link the *n* in *novice* to the *n* in the word *new*. A *novice* is someone who is new to a skill, field, or experience.

Common Usage   novice *at*

2. inaugural (ĭn-Ô-gyər-əl) adj.   first, occurring at the beginning

Sample Sentence The *inaugural* issue of *George* sold out, but the magazine didn't have a long run.

MEMORY PEG   You probably know the word *inauguration*, which means a "formal introduction to an office." Undoubtedly you have seen it used in reference to the ceremonies surrounding a new president as he formally takes office. Remember that an inauguration celebrates the president's "first" days in office. That connection will help you keep in mind that *inaugural* means "first," "beginning," or "introductory."

Additional Form   inaugurate

3. stimulus (STĬM-yə-ləs) n.   motive, reason for action

Sample Sentence The chance meeting with his more successful former roommate acted as a *stimulus* to his ambition, and he decided to ask for a promotion.

MEMORY PEG   In Latin, the word *stimulus* referred to a pointed stick used to prod animals to move. Think of a *stimulus* as something that prods a person or process into action.

Additional Forms   stimulate, stimulation

4. terminate (TÛR-mən-āt) v.   **a.** to end, complete, conclude

Sample Sentence They decided to *terminate* the drug study after patients began to experience life-threatening side effects.

b. to dismiss from employment

Sample Sentence They made the decision to *terminate* any employee who was accused of sexual harassment; that decision resulted in several lawsuits.

MEMORY PEG   The first four letters in *terminate* derive from the Latin word for "limit" or "boundary." The word *terminate* always carries with it the sense of time having run out or reached its limits.

Additional Forms   termination, terminator

5. wane (wān) v.   to fade, decrease, or die out

Sample Sentence   Her enthusiasm for running began to *wane* once she realized what it was doing to her knees.

> **MEMORY PEG**   When something is *waning*, it's not finished or concluded. But the end is definitely near. To remember that *wane* means "to fade or die out," keep in mind that once the moon reaches its fullest phase, it begins to *wane*, or steadily decrease in size.

6. incentive (ĭn-SĔN-tĭv) *n.*   punishment or a reward that encourages action or effort

Sample Sentence   He hated doing construction work, but the money it paid was a powerful *incentive*.

> **MEMORY PEG**   Link the word *incentive* to those things in life that personally move you to action. Is money what keeps you working as a waiter or waitress? Do you work out because you like looking fit and hate getting fat? Do you keep up your grades at school because you have your eyes on a prosperous* career? All of these things are your *incentives*.

7. initiate (ĭ-NĬSH-ē-āt)   **a.** to cause to begin, bring into being (*v.*)

Sample Sentence   It will take a new dean to *initiate* real curriculum change.

b. to introduce a person to a new field, activity, or interest (*v.*)

Sample Sentence   A long-time collector of baseball cards, he wanted to *initiate* his daughter into collecting them.

c. a beginner or novice* (*n.*)

Sample Sentence   Only the *initiates* came to the meeting on time; everyone else arrived late.

> **MEMORY PEG**   For meaning *a*, link *initiate* to *incentive* and *stimulus*. Tell yourself that with a strong *stimulus* or *incentive*, it's usually easier to *initiate* an activity you might otherwise avoid. For meaning *b*, remember that *initiation* ceremonies for fraternities and sororities "introduce" new brothers or sisters to fraternity or sorority life. For meaning *c*, remember that *novice* and *initiate* are synonyms.

8. rudimentary (rōō-də-MĔN-tə-rē) *adj.*   basic, beginning, first, earliest

Sample Sentence   She had a *rudimentary* understanding of Newton's† laws, but that was all.

> **MEMORY PEG**   The word *rudimentary* comes from the Latin word *rudis*, meaning "rough." Thus if you have a *rudimentary* understanding of something, you have only a basic or "rough" understanding. Similarly, anything in a *rudimentary* form is in its earliest or roughest form.

9. finale (fə-NĂL-ē) *n.*   **a.** end of an event or time; final moment

Sample Sentence   Czar Nicholas† did not know it at the time, but by 1916 his rule had reached its *finale*.

b. last act or close of a musical work

† Sir Isaac Newton (1642–1727): English mathematician and scientist known for his theories about gravity and light and for his three laws of motion.
† Nicholas II (1868–1918): the last czar, or ruler, of Russia before it was taken over by the communists in 1917.

Sample Sentence   The orchestra's *finale* brought the audience to its feet.

> **MEMORY PEG**   The word *final* in *finale* makes this word an easy one to remember.

10. apex (Ā-pĕks) *n.*   high point

Sample Sentence   He was supposed to balance on the ball's *apex* and lift one foot at a time. (literal)

Sample Sentence   The runner was at the *apex* of her sport when she decided to quit. (figurative)

> **MEMORY PEG**   To remember the meaning of *apex*, visualize it first in its literal meaning as the very tip or top of a hill or mountain. Then tell yourself that when you are at the *apex* of a field, career, or skill, you are in "top" form or at the "height" of your powers.

Idiom Alert

On the wane: The idiom probably comes from the phases of the moon. When the moon is waxing, it's getting larger; but when it's *on the wane*, it's decreasing. Thus you'll hear someone say, for example, that "liberal arts programs are *on the wane*," meaning they are decreasing in number.

Alpha and omega: *Alpha* and *omega* are the first and last letters in the Greek alphabet. We use the expression not to talk about the alphabet, but to indicate from beginning to end or the essential elements, for example, "In a remarkably short time, she had mastered the *alpha* and *omega* of the software."

Practice 1   Matching Words and Meanings

Directions: To match word and meaning, fill in the blanks with the appropriate letters.

1. novice	_____	a. last act
2. inaugural	_____	b. high point
3. stimulus	_____	c. basic
4. terminate	_____	d. to introduce to a field or activity
5. wane	_____	e. first
6. incentive	_____	f. end
7. initiate	_____	g. decrease
8. rudimentary	_____	h. beginner
9. finale	_____	i. motive for action
10. apex	_____	j. reward or punishment that promotes action

Practice 2   Answering True or False

Directions: To indicate if a statement is *true* or *false*, circle the correct answer.

True   False   1. If you are a *novice* at playing poker, you are probably very good at maintaining a poker face that reveals absolutely nothing.

True   False   2. Your *inaugural* day in office is likely to be your last.

True   False   3. Discovering that your clothes are too tight is often a *stimulus* to dieting.

True   False   4. Most people are delighted to have their employment *terminated*.

True   False   5. When people are first in love, their affection for one another is *waning*.

True   False   6. *Incentives* are important to achieving goals.

True   False   7. At parties, it is sometimes hard to *initiate* conversations.

True   False   8. You can get a doctorate in any field with only a *rudimentary* understanding of the subject.

True   False   9. After the *finale* of a musical, it's almost time for the intermission.

True   False   10. If you are at the *apex* of your profession, you still have a long way to go.

Practice 3   Making Sentence Sense

Directions: Fill in the blanks with the word that fits both the context and the definition in parentheses.

initiate	incentive	novice	finale	rudimentary
waned	inaugural	apex	stimulus	terminated

1. Everyone was on stage for the _____ , and when it ended, the audience was on its feet. (last act)

2. Habitually* anti-union, the new president's _____ act was to challenge the union members' right to medical coverage. (first)

3. A _____ deep-sea diver is often apprehensive* about going too deep. (inexperienced)

4. When the new head of the Red Cross tried to _____ different methods of organization and communication, she was met with reproach* on all sides. (bring into being)

5. In its most _____ form, architecture is a way of framing space. (basic)

6. For the United States, the bombing of Pearl Harbor was a _____ to entering World War II. (motive for action)

7. When the television anchorwoman was _____ for being too "old looking," she sued the station and won her job back. (dismissed)

8. When Raoul Wallenberg† sacrificed his own life to save the Jews of Hungary from certain death, his only _____ was to help those less fortunate than he. (reward or punishment that promotes action)

9. The more he talked about himself, the more her desire for his company _____ . (decreased)

10. The writer's fame was at its _____ , but his spirits were at their low point. (high point)

Practice 4   Filling in the Gaps

Directions: Fill in the blanks with one of the words from the chapter. If two words seem equally right, study the context. One word will be better than the other.

novices	**terminated**	**apex**	**incentive**	**rudimentary**
inaugural	**stimulated**	**initiated**	**wane**	**finale**

The Wright Brothers Take Flight

Few would question Wilbur and Orville Wright's claim to greatness as the inventors of the modern airplane. Yet despite the brothers' obvious claim to fame, some people think of the two brothers as gifted _____ who managed to put a plane in the air more by luck than any serious training. Yet nothing could be further from the truth. The Wright brothers did indeed have little formal training. But with their dream of flight as an _____ , the Wright brothers assiduously* learned everything there was to know about the mechanics of flight. With time and hard work, their _____ knowledge turned into a thorough understanding of how a machine might function like a bird in the air.

After a failure in family finances abruptly _____ the brothers' formal education in 1891, they tried a number of different careers. Intrepid* entrepreneurs,* they opened a bicycle repair shop and started a printing business. But already as kids, the sight of birds circling

† Raoul Wallenberg: (1912–1947?): a Swedish diplomat who single-handedly saved hundreds of Jews in World War II's final months.

in the sky had _____ their dream of building a flying machine. Even while they were repairing bicycles, they always knew that the real _____ of their career would come the day they too could soar into the air like birds.

In 1896, a much publicized newspaper article about a German glider pilot _____ their enthusiasm anew, and the two brothers went to work constructing a flying machine. They studied at night and built during the day. By 1900, they had constructed a glider. Even when an unsuccessful _____ run seemed to have written a _____ to their dreams, their determination didn't _____. Instead they abandoned plans for a glider and concentrated on building a flying machine with a propeller and an engine.

On December 14, 1903, Wilbur won the coin toss and made the first attempt at taking to the air in their new flying machine, appropriately named *Flyer*. But it stalled on takeoff. It wasn't until December 17, 1903, at 10:35 A.M. that Orville Wright successfully completed the world's first machine-powered flight.

To test your mastery of the words introduced in this chapter, turn to page 211 in the back of the book.

Chapter 13

Crime and Punishment

The Common Thread

Unfortunately, crime or wrongdoing has been a part of every society on record. Not surprisingly, then, so too has the idea of punishment. This chapter introduces you to ten words that refer to both.

felony	illicit
restitution	deterrent
misdemeanor	admonish
embezzle	penal
incarceration	rehabilitate

Self-Test — Crime and Punishment

Directions: For each italicized word, circle the letter of what you think is the correct definition.

1. *Felony* means
   a. accidental crime.
   b. minor crime.
   c. serious crime.

2. *Restitution* means
   a. compensating* for a loss.
   b. accidental death.
   c. theft of money.

3. *Misdemeanor* means
   a. drunk driving.
   b. minor crime.
   c. prison sentence.

4. *Embezzle* means
   a. steal money.
   b. lie.
   c. kill.

5. *Incarceration* means
   a. imprisonment.
   b. death by hanging.
   c. use of force.

6. *Illicit* means
   a. innocent
   b. in a series.
   c. illegal.

7. *Deterrent* means
   a. correction.
   b. discouragement.
   c. violation.

8. *Admonish* means
   a. deceive.
   b. scold.
   c. rob.

9. *Penal* means
   a. related to punishment.
   b. legal.
   c. illegal.

10. *Rehabilitate* means
    a. imprison.
    b. put to death.
    c. reform.

Turn to page 242 to correct your test. Record your grade in the self-test column on the inside front cover of your textbook. Then go on to **Words and Meanings** on pages 89–91.

Words and Meanings

Here again are the words from the self-test. Only this time, they are accompanied by their most common meanings and pointers on pronunciation.

1. felony (FĔL-ə-nē) n.   a serious crime such as murder, rape, or burglary

Sample Sentence   No one knew that the pleasant young doctor had committed a *felony* and was wanted by the police in several states.

MEMORY PEG   To remember the meaning of this word, circle the letters *felon* and write what they mean in Old French—"wicked"—across the top of the circle. Tell yourself that someone who commits a *felony* has done something society considers wicked or evil.

Additional Forms   felon, felonious
Common Usage   *commit* a felony

2. restitution (rĕs-tĭ-TŌŌ-shən) n.   compensating*, or making good for a loss or damage; making amends

Sample Sentence   Clyde felt very guilty for making his mother cry; he tried to make *restitution* by bringing her flowers.

MEMORY PEG   Link *restitution* to the first three letters in restore, because that's what people do when they make *restitution*. They try to restore or make things right. You can also link *restitution* to *compensation* from Chapter 6 because the two words are synonyms.

Common Usage   *Make* restitution

3. misdemeanor (mĭs-dĭ-MĒ-nər) n.   **a.** a crime less serious than a felony

Sample Sentence   The teenager had committed only a *misdemeanor*, but somehow he had been thrown into a cell with callous* criminals.

b. misdeed

Sample Sentence   Throughout the judge's confirmation hearing,† the committee members seemed unnecessarily concerned with the *misdemeanors* of her youth.

MEMORY PEG   Remember that a *misdemeanor* is the exact opposite of a *felony*. It's a minor crime like jaywalking. In some cases, a *misdemeanor* is not even a crime. It's just an example of silly or inappropriate behavior.

Common Usage   *commit* a misdemeanor

4. embezzle (ĕm-BĔZ-əl) v.   to steal money that has been entrusted to you

Sample Sentence   Desperate for money to maintain his extravagant* lifestyle, he decided to *embezzle* money from his own firm.

† During a confirmation hearing, the decision is made as to whether someone appointed to an office or position really is qualified enough.

> **MEMORY PEG** Tell yourself that *embezzling* involves a particular kind of theft. People who *embezzle* money have some access to or control of it. The money is in their trust, yet *embezzlers* break that trust by their actions. Consider, too, whether or not you have ever seen a movie in which *embezzlement* plays a role. Then you can attach the meaning of the word *embezzlement* to a face like that of Janet Leigh in the classic movie *Psycho*. Because of the film's success, Leigh is perhaps one of the most famous *embezzlers* in movie history.

Additional Forms   embezzler, embezzlement

5. **incarceration (ĭn-kär-sə-RĀT-shŭn)** *n.*   being shut up or confined, usually in a jail

Sample Sentence   Years of *incarceration* for a crime he didn't commit had made the old man angry and bitter.

> **MEMORY PEG** Visualize someone standing behind prison bars to remember the meaning of this word. Although *incarceration* does not have to take place in an actual prison, it usually does.

Additional Form   incarcerate

6. **illicit (ĭ-LĬS-ĭt)** *adj.*   illegal or unlawful

Sample Sentence   Unfortunately, the *illicit* trade of drugs like cocaine and marijuana is a large and lucrative* business.

> **MEMORY PEG** To remember the word *illicit*, recall that it begins with the same three letters as its synonym *illegal*. Also, think of both *felonies* and *misdemeanors* as examples of *illicit* acts.

7. **deterrent (dĭ-TÛR-ənt)** *n.*   something that prevents or discourages an action

Sample Sentence   Some people believe that being armed is a *deterrent* to burglaries and muggings.

> **MEMORY PEG** The word *deter* comes from the Latin word for "frighten." Therefore, you can remember that a *deterrent* is something that frightens someone out of carrying out a plan of action.

Additional Forms   deter, deterrence

Common Usage   *acts as a* deterrent, *serves as a* deterrent

8. **admonish (ăd-MŎN-ĭsh)** *v.*   to correct or caution critically

Sample Sentence   The conscientious inspector *admonished* the restaurant's staff for storing food items improperly.

> **MEMORY PEG** *Admonish* comes from the Latin word *monēre*, which means "to warn." So remember that *admonishing* involves warning about wrongdoing. One might, for example, *admonish* a teenager for committing a *misdemeanor* so that he does not go on to commit a *felony*.

Additional Forms   admonisher, admonishment, admonishingly

9. penal (PĒ-nəl) *adj.*   related to punishment

Sample Sentence   From the late 1700s until the 1860s, Australia served as a *penal* colony for British convicts.

> **MEMORY PEG**   *Penal* comes from the Latin word for "penalty." Keep in mind that anything having to do with the word *penal* involves some form of *penalty* or punishment for *illicit* acts.

Additional Forms   penalty, penalize

10. rehabilitate (rē-hə-BĬL-ĭ-tāt) *v.*   to reform or restore

Sample Sentence   Counseling, drug treatment programs, and educational opportunities in prisons are all designed to help *rehabilitate* the convict.

> **MEMORY PEG**   To remember this word, you might recall the informal abbreviation *rehab*, which you may have heard in conversation. The word describes a process or a place that helps change or improve behavior, as in: "He checked himself into *rehab* to overcome his addiction to prescription drugs."

Additional Form   rehabilitation

Idiom Alert

> **Poetic justice:** Justice doesn't necessarily involve prison. Where *poetic justice* is involved, the outcome of events ensures that virtue is rewarded and crime or misbehavior is not, often in an especially appropriate or unexpected way: "It was *poetic justice* that notorious* gangster Al Capone was sent to jail not for all the murders he committed, but for tax evasion."

Practice 1   Matching Words and Meanings

Directions: To match word and meaning, fill in the blanks with the appropriate letters.

1. felony	_____	a. minor crime
2. restitution	_____	b. correct or caution
3. misdemeanor	_____	c. something that discourages
4. embezzle	_____	d. reform
5. incarceration	_____	e. imprisonment
6. illicit	_____	f. serious crime
7. deterrent	_____	g. unlawful
8. admonish	_____	h. compensation*
9. penal	_____	i. steal money
10. rehabilitate	_____	j. related to punishment

Practice 2   Answering True or False

Directions: To indicate if a statement is *true* or *false*, circle the correct answer.

True   False   1. Intentionally running a red light while driving is a *felony*.

True   False   2. Criminals are not expected to make *restitution* for their crimes.

True   False   3. Kidnapping is usually a *misdemeanor*.

True   False   4. A convenience store clerk who puts a customer's money into his pocket rather than into the cash register is *embezzling*.

True   False   5. Crimes such as grand theft, assault, and forgery are usually punished by *incarceration*.

True   False   6. If you're found guilty of an *illicit* act, you may go to jail.

True   False   7. Security sensor tags on merchandise may serve as a *deterrent* to shoplifting.

True   False   8. If you *admonish* someone, you protect him by lying about his whereabouts during a crime.

True   False   9. Someone put on probation for drunk driving has to go to a *penal* institution.

True   False   10. A *rehabilitated* criminal would rob a bank.

Practice 3   Making Sentence Sense

Directions: Fill in the blanks with the word that fits both the context and the definition in parentheses.

illicit	embezzling	misdemeanors	incarceration	admonished
felony	penal	deterrent	rehabilitate	restitution

1. She went to prison when her employer discovered that she had been _____ money from the company for more than a year. (stealing money that has been entrusted to you)

2. The _____ activities of organized criminals often include drug dealing, illegal gambling, and blackmail. (illegal, unlawful)

3. For over an hour, the judge lectured the teenagers about their need to make _____ for the damage they had caused. (amends)

4. In most states, taking a gun onto the grounds of a school is a _____. (a serious crime such as murder, rape, or burglary)

5. Many ho~~~~ners install security systems as a _____ to burglars. (something that prevents ~~~~ ~~~~ges an action)

6. Shoplifting and writing bad checks are classified as _____. (misdeeds or less serious crimes)

7. The _____ of Japanese Americans during World War II is a shameful episode in America's history. (imprisonment)

8. Some judges believe that military-style boot camps can help _____ teenage criminals, teaching them about discipline and respect for authority. (reform, improve)

9. From 1934 to 1963, very violent criminals were sent to a _____ institution on Alcatraz, a remote island out in the middle of San Francisco Bay. (related to punishment)

10. After nineteen innocent people were executed as witches during the Salem witch trials of 1692, respected minister Increase Mather _____ the town's judges for their role in the tragedy. (corrected or cautioned critically)

Practice 4   Filling in the Gaps

Directions: Fill in the blanks with one of the words from the chapter. If two words seem equally right, study the context. One word will be better than the other.

| restitution | deterrent | felonies | illicit | embezzled |
| penal | misdemeanor | admonish | incarcerate | rehabilitation |

The History of the Death Penalty

For centuries, societies have made a death sentence (also known as capital punishment) part of their _____ code. Throughout Britain's history, for example, a sentence of death was common for a wide range of _____ behavior. As a matter of fact, by 1700, 222 crimes were punishable by death. Even minor violations like cutting down a tree illegally, which would be considered a _____ today, could get a man hanged or beheaded.

When British citizens came to America, they took their ideas about crime and punishment with them. In 1612, Virginia's governor demanded that both free servants and slaves make _____ with their lives if they stole chickens, traded with the Indians, or _____ money from their employers or masters. However, the colonists began to cross some of these crimes off their list out of concern that their harsh laws would discourage new settlers. So, by the late seventeenth century, a resident of New England could end up swinging from his neck if he practiced witchcraft or committed perjury by lying in a court of law. But a hundred years later, by the late 1700s, most of the colonies were reserving the death penalty for more serious _____ such as murder, burglary, and rape. One exception was North Carolina, which continued to severely punish even minor crimes until well into the 1800s. Because that state had no prison, there was no place to _____ lawbreakers; and no one was even concerned about _____. Simply eliminating the wrongdoer was much easier.

Today, the United States is the only Western nation that still executes some of its criminals. Many Americans still believe that these executions act as a _____ to homicide. Ironically, though, many European nations, including Great Britain, now criticize capital punishment for being cruel and unfair. Furthermore, these countries regularly _____ the U.S. for continuing an "uncivilized" practice.

(*Sources of information:* Michael H. Reggio, "History of the Death Penalty," in *Society's Final Solution: A History and Discussion of the Death Penalty.* Laura E. Randa, ed. Lanham, Md., University Press of America, Inc., 1997, http://www. pbs.org/wgbh/pages/frontline/shows/execution/readings/history.html.)

To test your mastery of the words introduced in this chapter, turn to page 213 in the back of the book.

Chapter 14

Lifelines

The Common Thread

This chapter is devoted to words revolving around life—having it, losing it, and regaining it. Scenes from horror films are a good source of visual associations for the words in this chapter.

vitality	animate
viable	vigor
vivacious	resuscitate
mortal	resurrection
immortal	reincarnation

Self-Test — Lifelines

Directions: For each italicized word, circle the letter of what you think is the correct definition.

1. *Vitality* means
   a. loss of life.
   b. humanity.
   c. energy.

2. *Viable* means
   a. capable of killing.
   b. barely alive.
   c. capable of living.

3. *Vivacious* means
   a. full of life.
   b. capable of death.
   c. ready to die.

4. *Mortal* means
   a. containing blood.
   b. subject to death.
   c. alive.

5. *Immortal* means
   a. early.
   b. aging.
   c. not able to die.

6. *Animate* means
   a. deaden.
   b. fill with life.
   c. make ready for death.

7. *Vigor* means
   a. energy.
   b. strictness.
   c. sickness.

8. *Resuscitate* means
   a. prepare for death.
   b. revive.
   c. leave the earth.

9. *Resurrection* means
   a. rising from the dead.
   b. burial.
   c. birth.

10. *Reincarnation* means
    a. suicide.
    b. rebirth.
    c. birth.

Turn to page 242 to correct your test. Record your grade in the self-test column on the inside front cover of your textbook. Then go on to **Words and Meanings** on pages 96–99.

Words and Meanings

Here again are the words from the self-test. Only this time, they are accompanied by their most common meanings along with pointers for pronunciation.

1. **vitality (vī-TĂL-ĭ-tē)** *n.*   energy; the capacity to live, grow, or survive

   Sample Sentence   Her long, hard battle with a chronic disease had sapped her once extraordinary *vitality.*

   | MEMORY PEG | At the heart of this word is the Latin root *vita*, meaning "life." It follows, then, that those possessed of *vitality* seem filled with life or energy. |

   Additional Forms   vital, vitalize

2. **viable (VĪ-ə-bəl)** *adj.*   capable of living or succeeding

   Sample Sentence   Working together to complete the project would be hard, but the alternative, working completely on his own, didn't seem *viable.*

   | MEMORY PEG | Like *vitality*, *viable* also comes from the Latin root *vita*, meaning "life." So, too, does the word *vitamin*. Thus, this is a good time to make a map connecting all three words: |

   ```
                         ( vita = life )
                        /       |        \
                       /        |         \
             _____       _____     _____
             vitality        viable        vitamin
              energy     capable of living   pill taken to improve life
   ```

   Additional Forms   viability, viably

3. **vivacious (vī-VĀ-shəs, vī-VĀ-shəs)** *adj.*   lively; full of energy and spirit

   Sample Sentence   Not given to small talk, President Thomas Jefferson asked the perennially* *vivacious* and convivial* Dolley Madison to be his hostess at social functions during his term in office.

   | MEMORY PEG | The word *vivacious* comes from the Latin word *vivere*, meaning "to live." Thus, people who are naturally *vivacious* know how to live. They are filled with energy and high spirits, and are not easily depressed. |

   Additional Forms   vivaciousness, vivacity

4. **mortal (MÔR-tl)**   **a.** capable of dying (*adj.*)

   Sample Sentence   Few people can readily acknowledge that they are *mortal* and will someday die.

                                         b. causing death; fatal, deadly (*adj.*)

   Sample Sentence   King Arthur's own son, Mordred, became his *mortal* enemy and killed Arthur on the battlefield. (literal)

Sample Sentence   The Yankees and the Mets are *mortal* enemies. (figurative)

c. a human, someone not godlike (*n.*)

Sample Sentence   The rest of us *mortals* could never accomplish what Michael Jordan has done on a basketball court.

> **MEMORY PEG**   To remember meaning *a*, keep in mind that, like it or not, we are all *mortal*. Sad to say, we, too, will die. Think of the second meaning of the word *mortal* as a synonym for *deadly*. One could suffer, that is, from a *mortal* wound or receive a *mortal* blow. To remember meaning *c*, keep in mind the sentence about Michael Jordan.

Additional Form   mortality

5. immortal (ĭ-MÔR-tl)   **a.** not subject to death (*adj.*)

Sample Sentence   According to Greek mythology, Zeus, Aphrodite, Poseidon, and the other gods who lived on Mount Olympus were all *immortal* beings. (literal)

Sample Sentence   In the *immortal* words of Milton Berle,† a committee is a group that keeps the minutes and loses the hours. (figurative)

b. one whose fame will never be forgotten (*n.*)

Sample Sentence   In the world of sports, Michael Jordan is an *immortal*.

> **MEMORY PEG**   The word *immortal* is formed by adding the prefix *im-*, which means "not," to the word *mortal*, which means "capable of dying." If you remember what *mortal* means, you'll recall that *immortal* means just the opposite.

Additional Forms   immortality, immortalize

6. animate (ĂN-ə-māt) *v.*   to bring to life; to give energy or interest to someone or something

Sample Sentence   The instructor tried hard to *animate* the discussion every way he could, but all his efforts failed.

> **MEMORY PEG**   *Anima* is Greek for "breath" or "soul." Thus, when you *animate* something, you give it the soul or breath it lacked and make it come or seem alive. It should come as no surprise, then, that *animation* can refer to the process of creating cartoons, in which drawings are made to appear alive.

Additional Forms   animated, animation

7. vigor (VĬG-ər) *n.*   **a.** physical or mental strength, energy, or force

Sample Sentence   The *vigor* with which he hit the ball was really amazing.

b. intensity or enthusiasm

†   Milton Berle: a comedian famous in the fifties as the King of Television.

Sample Sentence   The dancers displayed such *vigor* that the audience started to applaud even before they were finished.

> **MEMORY PEG**   On how many bottles or cans have you read the instruction "Shake *vigorously* before using"? This clearly means that you should use force—or *vigor*—as you shake; think of this phrase when you try to recall the meaning of the word.

Additional Forms   vigorous, vigorousness

8. resuscitate (rĭ-SŬS-ĭ-tāt) v.   restore consciousness or vigor, revive

Sample Sentence   After the lifeguard was able to *resuscitate* the swimmer, everyone breathed a sigh of relief. (literal)

Sample Sentence   Her son's piano lessons *resuscitated* her own interest in playing. (figurative)

> **MEMORY PEG**   To remember the literal meaning of *resuscitate*, think of the swimmer brought back to life in the first sample sentence. Whether it's used literally or figuratively, the word *resuscitate* always suggests the return of life to someone or something that seemed to be dying, dead, or falling apart.

Additional Form   resuscitation

9. resurrection (rĕz-ə-RĔK-shən) n.   **a. the act of rising from the dead or returning to life**

Sample Sentence   On Easter Sunday, Christians celebrate the *resurrection* of Jesus Christ.

b. the act of bringing back to practice or use

Sample Sentence   Oh no, don't tell me there's another *resurrection* of the musical *Annie* coming around!

> **MEMORY PEG**   One of the most common meanings for the prefix *re* in *resurrection* is "back." So tell yourself that a resurrection refers to someone or something coming "back" to life again. That return to life can be literal as in meaning *a* or figurative as in meaning *b*.

Additional Form   resurrect

10. reincarnation (rē-ən-kär-NĀ-shən) n.   rebirth or reappearance in a different form or body

Sample Sentence   Hindus believe in *reincarnation;* they believe that after death a person's spirit can return to life in a different body.

> **MEMORY PEG**   Even people who do not believe in *reincarnation* sometimes jokingly say things like "I must have been a cat in a former life." Whether they know it or not, they are talking about *reincarnation*. The word contains the Latin root *carn*, meaning "flesh." *Reincarnation* thus refers to something that reappears "in the flesh." And, no, you can't say that *reincarnation* and *resurrection* are synonyms because someone or something that has been resurrected does not assume a different form.

Additional Form   reincarnate

Common Usage   reincarnation *of*, reincarnated *as*

Idiom Alert

A charmed life: This expression means "having extremely good luck." It was first used by Shakespeare, who used it as a synonym for "magical." When we use it nowadays, we mean that the person whose life is *charmed* has exceptionally good luck: "Until his sudden and tragic death, the young reporter seemed to be leading *a charmed life*."

Practice 1   Matching Words with Meanings

Directions: To match word and meaning, fill in the blanks with the appropriate letters.

1. vitality	*j*	a. strength or force	
2. viable	*e*	b. energetic, lively	
3. vivacious	*b*	c. restore to consciousness	
4. mortal	*f*	d. not subject to death	
5. immortal	*d*	e. able to survive or succeed	
6. animate	*g*	f. capable of dying	
7. vigor	*a*	g. fill with energy or life	
8. resuscitate	*c*	h. rebirth in another form	
9. resurrection	*i*	i. rising from the dead	
10. reincarnation	*h*	j. life, energy	

Practice 2   Answering True or False

Directions: To indicate if a statement is *true* or *false,* circle the correct answer.

True ~~False~~   1. Looking bored is a sign of *vitality*.

True ~~False~~   2. *Viable* alternatives are always too complicated to succeed.

True ~~False~~   3. People lacking in *vivacity* are the most fun to have as friends.

True ~~False~~   4. Gods are always *mortal* beings.

~~True~~ False   5. Because we are not *immortal*, we have to accept the fact that we will one day die.

~~True~~ False   6. After their long winter's sleep ends, bears once again become *animated*.

True ~~False~~   7. People who pursue sports with *vigor* are half-hearted in their athletic attempts.

~~True~~ False   8. You can't *resuscitate* a corpse.

True ~~False~~   9. *Resurrection* is just another word for *dying*.

True ~~False~~   10. *Reincarnation* is just another word for *resurrection*.

Practice 3   Making Sentence Sense

Directions: Fill in the blanks with the word that fits both the context and the definition in parentheses.

mortal	animated	vitality	viable	immortality
resuscitated	resurrect	vigor	vivaciousness	reincarnation

1. In martial arts such as karate, a fighter's hands are ___mortal___ weapons that can actually kill an opponent. (deadly)

2. The film about climbing Mount Everest ___resuscitated___ his enthusiasm for high-risk sports. (restore to consciousness)

3. In his poem "Tithonus," Alfred Lord Tennyson tells the story of Tithonus, who was given ___immortality___ without eternal youth; he just got older, until he wished for death. (the inability to die)

4. Her expressionless face suddenly became ___animated___ when she talked about her dog. (filled with life)

5. The committee is looking for a ___viable___ alternative to putting police into schools, which seems too drastic a measure. (capable of succeeding)

6. The ___vivasciousness___ of the actress was so contagious it energized the entire cast. (liveliness)

7. The actor, who had not made a movie in ten years, moved back to Los Angeles to ___ressurrect___ his acting career. (bring back to life)

8. When talking about the new mayor, my grandfather shook his fist with unaccustomed ___vigor___. (strength and energy)

9. I once met a guy who thought he was the ___reincarnation___ of Napoleon.† (rebirth in a different form)

10. Even as a grandmother, she had the kind of ___vitality___ that most people lose after age thirty. (capacity to grow, energy)

---

† Napoleon Bonaparte (1769–1821): Emperor of France (1804–1814) who has had a hold on many people's imaginations ever since he died in 1821.

Practice 4   Filling in the Gaps

Directions: Fill in the blanks with one of the words from the chapter. If two words seem equally right, study the context. One word will be better than the other.

vitality	vivacious	immortal	vigorously	resurrection
viable	mortal	animated	resuscitating	reincarnated

The King of Hollywood Horror

The career of horror movie ___immortal___ Boris Karloff (1897–1967) spanned fifty years. During that time, he earned the nickname "Hollywood's King of Horror." Unquestionably, Karloff's seemingly perennial* fame rested on his performance as the monster of the horror classic *Frankenstein*.

However, Karloff's claim to horror royalty was also due, in large degree, to his title role in the 1932 film classic *The Mummy*. In the film, Karloff, playing the high priest Imhotep, is put to death by being wrapped in tape and buried alive as a living mummy. Centuries later, he is revived when archaeologists enter his tomb and bring about his ___resurrection___ by opening his coffin and reading aloud a mysterious scroll. Karloff's tape-draped corpse then goes in search of his long-lost beloved princess, who has been ___reincarnated___ as the ___vivacious___ Helen Grosvenor. Played by a striking actress named Zita Johann, the figure of Helen is an understandable magnet for her lover from the grave. At first sight, she is laughing and her face is ___animated___. But the longer Imhotep stays on the scene, the more her youthful ___vitality___ diminishes. This, of course, is precisely what her long-lost lover wants. He is determined to make Helen abandon her ___mortal___ life so that she can enter the eternal spirit world with him. He's even prepared to kill her to make sure she fulfills his idea of a "happy ending." When Helen ___vigorously___ protests that she prefers her life as a modern woman to ___resuscitating___ her life as an ancient princess, Imhotep is ready to murder her in the name of mummy love. In good Hollywood fashion, however, he is stopped in the nick of time.

Described in bare outline, the plot sounds silly. The script hardly seems a ___viable___ candidate for the status of movie classic. But one has to see the sad and soulful, yet menacing figure of Karloff to understand the movie's staying power. In his desperate attempt to keep his lost princess, Karloff is everyman unwilling to give up the love of his life. Still, the movie's most powerful moment is the unforgettable scene when Karloff is wrapped in tape until only his terror-stricken eyes are visible. Without a word, the "King of Horror" manages to convey all the mind-numbing fear of being buried alive.

To test your mastery of the words introduced in this chapter, turn to page 215 in the back of the book.

Chapter 15

On the Move

The Common Thread

Perhaps because of their pioneer past, most Americans think nothing of driving fifty miles to work or two hundred miles to go on vacation. It should come as no surprise, then, that our language has a number of words related to change and movement. Here are just ten.

junket	traverse
migrate	goad
emigrate	venturesome
trailblazer	embark
trek	flux

Self-Test | On the Move

Directions: For each italicized word, circle the letter of what you think is the correct definition.

1. *Junket* means
   a. return.
   b. trip.
   c. region.

2. *Migrate* means
   a. to fly.
   b. to go backward in time.
   c. to move from one place to another.

3. *Emigrate* means
   a. to move animals from one place to another.
   b. to move rocks.
   c. to leave one country to live in another.

4. *Trailblazer* means
   a. someone who creates new paths.
   b. someone who tracks animals.
   c. someone who starts fires.

5. *Trek* means
   a. heavy load.
   b. long path.
   c. hard journey.

6. *Traverse* means
   a. to break ground.
   b. to measure out.
   c. to travel across.

7. *Goad* means
   a. to act as a stimulus.*
   b. to be held back.
   c. to sidetrack.

8. *Venturesome* means
   a. afraid of change.
   b. ready to take risks.
   c. foolish.

9. *Embark* means
   a. to lead others.
   b. to start a trip.
   c. to end a trip.

10. *Flux* means
    a. movement.
    b. journey.
    c. signpost.

Turn to page 242 to correct your test. Record your grade in the self-test column on the inside front cover of your textbook. Then go on to **Words and Meanings** on pages 104–106.

Words and Meanings

Here again are the words from the self-test. Only this time, they are accompanied by their most common meanings and pointers on pronunciation.

1. junket (JŬNG-kĭt) *n.*   a trip or tour, often for business but also for pleasure

Sample Sentence   He had spent six weeks on a business *junket* promoting his books, and he returned home exhausted.

> **MEMORY PEG**   Link the *j* in *junket* to the *j* in *journey*, because that's what a *junket* is, a journey or a trip. You can also try using this sentence as a memory aid: "Don't pack a lot of junk to go on a *junket*."

2. migrate (MĪ-grāt) *v.*   to move from one location and settle in another

Sample Sentence   They finally made the decision to *migrate* after three years of drought and hunger,

> **MEMORY PEG**   Think of flocks of birds flying north or south depending on the time of year. That image should lock the meaning of *migrate* into your memory. It should also remind you that a migration does not have to be permanent. Migrating birds will return to the place from which they migrated, and *migrant* workers work in the same place only for a brief time before moving on.

Additional Forms   migratory, migration, migrant

Common Usage   migrate *between, to,* or *from*

3. emigrate (ĔM-ĭ-grāt) *v.*   to leave one country or region to live in another

Sample Sentence   After Fidel Castro came to power in Cuba, many wealthy Cubans *emigrated* to the United States.

> **MEMORY PEG**   Link *emigrate* to *migrate* and consider them synonyms, but only to a point. *Migrate* can refer to people or animals, but *emigrate* refers only to people. Furthermore, a *migration* is often temporary and can happen either between countries or within a country. *Emigration*, however, is more permanent and typically happens between countries.

Additional Forms   emigration, emigrant, émigré

Common Usage   emigrate *from*

4. trailblazer (TRĀL-blā-zər) *n.*   someone who identifies a new trail or direction

Sample Sentence   Christopher "Kit" Carson (1809–1868) was a guide and *trailblazer* for John C. Fremont's western expedition in the 1840s. (literal)

Sample Sentence   In the world of feminism, Betty Friedan, the author of *The Feminine Mystique,*† was a *trailblazer*. (figurative)

† *The Feminine Mystique:* Published in 1963, Friedan's book is considered a key cause of feminism's second wave that began in the mid-sixties.

> **MEMORY PEG** Keep in mind the word *blaze* in *trailblazer*. Blazes are marks left on trees or rocks by the person or group creating a trail or path that others will follow.

5. trek (trĕk)   **a.** to make a slow or hard journey, often on foot (*v.*)

Sample Sentence   Born in Fredericksburg, Virginia, James P. Beckwourth (1798–1866) escaped a life of slavery and *trekked* across the western and southern frontiers, eventually discovering a pass through the Sierra Nevada.†

b. a hard journey (*n.*)

Sample Sentence   Robert Falcon Scott's *trek* to the South Pole ended in his death.

> **MEMORY PEG** The word *trek* comes from the Dutch word *trecken*, meaning "to pull." Usually, if you *trek* someplace, you are likely to wish that someone or something were there to pull you along because the journey is so difficult.

Additional Form   trekker

Common Usage   trek *from, to, across, over*

6. traverse (trə-VÛRS, trăv-əRS) *v.*   to travel or pass across

Sample Sentence   To find shelter, the downed flier would have to *traverse* a field filled with land mines.

> **MEMORY PEG** Circle the letters *trav*, which mean "across." Tell yourself as well that the first four letters in *traverse* are the same as the first four in *travel*. Thus to *traverse* an area means "to travel across."

Additional Forms   traversal, traversable

Common Usage   traverse *a, the*

7. goad (gōd)   **a.** to drive forward or push onward, to stimulate* (*v.*)

Sample Sentence   When he was in a morose* mood, it seemed that nothing could *goad* him into action.

b. a stimulus* to action (*n.*)

Sample Sentence   His father's voice telling him he needed to do better was a constant *goad* to action.

> **MEMORY PEG** Originally *goad* referred to a long stick used for prodding animals. Think of that stick prodding a donkey to remember the meaning of *goad*.

Common Usage   goad *to* or *into*

† Now known as Beckwourth Pass and still in use today by the Union Pacific Railroad.

8. venturesome (VĔN-chər-səm) *adj.*   given to taking risks or facing danger

Sample Sentence   Among those visitors hiking in Yosemite National Park, only the most *venturesome* are willing to climb El Capitan.

> **MEMORY PEG**   Use the probably more familiar synonym *adventurous* to remember the meaning of *venturesome*. You might also link *venturesome* to intrepid* from Chapter 2. The two are very close in meaning.

Additional Forms   venture, venturous

9. embark (ĕm-BÄRK) *v.*   **a.** to set out on an undertaking that often involves complication and risk

Sample Sentence   Frances Wright† *embarked* on a tour of several states in order to spread the news about her interracial community, Nashoba.

          b. to go aboard a vessel or aircraft

Sample Sentence   The passengers were preparing to *embark* when a warning came over the loudspeaker.

> **MEMORY PEG**   The letters *bark* are a clue to the word's second meaning because they mean "boat" in Latin. However, for the first meaning, you should probably create a sentence where context gives the clue, for example, "The most *venturesome* travelers think nothing about *embarking* on a long journey."

Additional Form   embarkation
Common Usage   embark *on*

10. flux (flŭks) *n.*   **a.** constant flow, especially of fluids

Sample Sentence   The heart controls the *flux* of blood through the arteries.

          b. uninterrupted movement or constant change

Sample Sentence   My fortunes have been in *flux* now for some time, and I wish they would settle down.

> **MEMORY PEG**   Note that *flux* starts with the same two letters as its (almost) synonym, *flow*. To remember the meaning of *flux*, tell yourself that "flux is flow."

Common Usage   *in* flux

Idiom Alert

Mover and shaker: This phrase refers to a person with influence and power. The expression appeared around the mid-1850s, usually in relation to religion. But with time, it broke free from its religious context to refer to anyone with a lot of power, or clout: "Heiress Peggy Guggenheim† was a *mover and shaker* in the world of early modern art."

---

†   Frances Wright (1795–1852): Scottish-born American reformer, who lectured on women's rights, birth control, and education.
†   Peggy Guggenheim (1898–1979): an heiress who spent a good part of her fortune buying the work of unknown artists who went on to become famous.

Practice 1   Matching Words and Meanings

Directions: To match word and meaning, fill in the blanks with the appropriate letters.

1. junket   _c_   a. constant change or movement

2. migrate   _f_   b. difficult journey

3. emigrate   _d_   c. trip

4. trailblazer   _g_   d. leave one country and settle in another

5. trek   _b_   e. begin a journey

6. traverse   _j_   f. move to another location

7. goad   _i_   g. person who creates new paths or directions

8. venturesome   _h_   h. daring

9. embark   _e_   i. stimulus to action

10. flux   _a_   j. travel across

Practice 2   Answering True or False

Directions: To indicate if a statement is *true* or *false*, circle the correct answer.

True **False** 1. People who travel for business don't take *junkets*.

True False 2. Some birds *migrate* when the seasons change.

True **False** 3. *Migration* and *emigration* can always be used interchangeably.

True **False** 4. If you plan on *trailblazing* a woodsy area, you need to stay on a well-beaten path.

True **False** 5. People who enjoy a leisurely walk but hate hiking are likely to enjoy *trekking* through the woods.

True **False** 6. A person who *traverses* the United States would go from Maine to Florida.

True False 7. A young child who gobbles his lunch is probably *goaded* by hunger.

True False 8. Someone who is *venturesome* by nature might well enjoy skydiving.

True False 9. If you are ready to *embark*, the chances are good that your bags are packed.

True **False** 10. Things in *flux* are things at rest.

Practice 3   Making Sentence Sense

Directions: Fill in the blanks with the word that fits both the context and the definition in parentheses.

junkets	trek	goaded	migration	trailblazer
emigrated	traversed	embarked	venturesome	flux

1. Because they relied on buffalo for food, the Plains Indians followed the animals' _migration_ from place to place. (movement from one place to another)

2. After Hitler came to power, many German writers and scientists _emigrated_ to America. (left one country to live in another)

3. In the 1830s, trappers and fur traders _traversed_ the American wilderness in search of valuable furs. (traveled across)

4. I can't make a decision now because my prospects are still in _flux_. (constant change)

5. John Bartram (1699–1777), the father of American botany, went on numerous _junkets_ in search of rare and regional plants. (trips)

6. _Goaded_ by a misguided desire to "Americanize" the Indians of the Southwest, many early, white-run schools punished Native American students for speaking their own language. (driven)

7. In 1775, a young North Carolinian named Daniel Boone was hired to be a _trailblazer_ for a road-building crew through the Cumberland Gap. (person who creates new paths or directions)

8. The most _venturesome_ of women, writer and pilot Beryl Markham was the first female to fly solo across the Atlantic. (daring)

9. When the *Titanic*'s passengers _embarked_ on their cruise, they believed the ship was unsinkable; but as most now know, they were wrong. (started on a journey)

10. In order to find water in a desert, travelers may have to _trek_ for days on end (make a hard journey)

Practice 4   Filling in the Gaps

Directions: Fill in the blanks with one of the words from the chapter. If two words seem equally right, study the context. One word will be better than the other.

embarked	migrating	trailblazers	trek	junket
goaded	venturesome	flux	traversing	emigrants

Moving West

White settlers along the Atlantic Coast of America were originally _emigrants_ from Europe, especially England. Until 1790 or so, the vast majority of Americans lived in the East and within one hundred miles of the Atlantic Ocean. Beginning in the late eighteenth century, Americans began _migrating_ to the West. That movement from east to west was not a brief, single event. It continued for close to fifty years. By 1840, one-third of the population was living somewhere between Appalachia and the Mississippi River, and the _flux_ of people beyond the Mississippi and across the Rocky Mountains continued throughout the nineteenth century.

Although the American pioneers who made the long and difficult _trek_ west were often _goaded_ by a desire for land or riches, a few at least went in search of adventure—and maybe even a bit of fame. The American army officer Zebulon Pike (1779–1813) couldn't resist an 1806 _junket_ formed to map the Southwest. As it turned out, Pike was right to go. It was on this trip that he sighted the mountaintop entered in the history books as Pike's Peak. Two other _trailblazers_, Meriwether Lewis and William Clark, also made their way into history when they _embarked_ on a trip west to explore the vast area purchased by Thomas Jefferson in 1802.† A _venturesome_ easterner named Jedidiah Smith also couldn't resist the call of the Wild West. In 1822, he signed on to explore the upper Mississippi River. As Smith had to have known, this expedition was anything but a pleasure. In the course of this and subsequent* journeys, he almost lost his life a half dozen times; once he almost died in the angry embrace of a six-foot grizzly. But nothing could deter*

---

† Louisiana Purchase: a huge area from the Mississippi River to the Rocky Mountains that Jefferson purchased from France.

him from _____ the Mohave Desert on foot in order to explore California's San Joaquin Valley. Smith then hiked back across the Sierras and the area around the Great Salt Lake, a trip so harsh and terrifying few dared ever to try it. It's no wonder, then, that Smith and his like were revered* as legends in their own time.

To test your mastery of the words introduced in this chapter, turn to page 217 in the back of the book.

Chapter 16

Body Language

2/22/0

Test on Monday

The Common Thread

Even people who consider themselves more spiritual than physical need to know the ten words included in this chapter. All ten words describe the body—its appearance or its functions.

corporal	cardiac
brawny	ocular
emaciated	auditory
physique	respiratory
psychosomatic	cerebral

Self-Test   Body Language

Directions: For each italicized word, circle the letter of what you think is the correct definition.

1. *Corporal* means
   a. having to do with breathing.
   b. skin related.
   c. having to do with the body.

2. *Brawny* means
   a. thin and weak.
   b. strong and muscular.
   c. fat.

3. *Emaciated* means
   a. very tall.
   b. overweight.
   c. terribly thin.

4. *Physique* means
   a. build.
   b. brain.
   c. mind.

5. *Psychosomatic* means
   a. having serious physical problems.
   b. physical problems arising from the mind.
   c. a balance problem.

6. *Cardiac* means
   a. having to do with the mind.
   b. having to do with the heart.
   c. having to do with breath.

7. *Ocular* means
   a. having to do with the legs.
   b. having to do with the eyes.
   c. having to do with hearing.

8. *Auditory* means
   a. having to do with hearing.
   b. having to do with breathing.
   c. painful.

9. *Respiratory* means
   a. having to do with the mind.
   b. resting.
   c. having to do with breathing.

10. *Cerebral* means
    a. having to do with the brain.
    b. having to do with the hands.
    c. having to do with the feet.

Turn to page 242 to correct your test. Record your grade in the self-test column on the inside front cover of your textbook. Then go on to **Words and Meanings** on pages 112–114.

Words and Meanings

Here again are the words from the self-test. Only this time, they are accompanied by their most common meanings and pointers on pronunciation.

1. **corporal (KÔR-pə-rəl, KÔR-prəl) *adj.***   physical, related to the body

   Sample Sentence   Some schools still use *corporal* punishment with students who act up in class.

   | MEMORY PEG | It's not a coincidence that *corpse* and *corporal* begin with the same four letters. They have the same beginning because they both stem from the Latin word *corpus*, meaning "body." Keep that shared root in mind to remember the meaning of *corporal*. |

   Additional Form   corporeal

2. **brawny (BRÔ-nē) *adj.***   strong and muscular

   Sample Sentence   The trainer had told her that lifting heavy weights would not make her muscular, but after six weeks of training, her body was becoming *brawny*.

   | MEMORY PEG | When you think of *brawny*, imagine the build of a heavyweight boxer like Mike Tyson. Link that image to the word, and you'll remember it means "strong and muscular." |

   Additional Forms   brawn, brawniness

3. **emaciated (ĭ-MĀ-shē-āt-ĕd) *adj.***   extremely thin, skin-and-bones

   Sample Sentence   Taken prisoner by the enemy, the soldiers were poorly fed and had become *emaciated*.

   | MEMORY PEG | The letters *mac* in *emaciated* come from the Latin word *macer*, meaning "thin." However, the word *thin* is not really strong enough to serve as a synonym for *emaciated*. If you have ever seen pictures of people suffering from starvation, then you also have a visual image to attach to *emaciated*. |

   Additional Forms   emaciate, emaciation

4. **physique (fĭ-ZĒK) *n.***   build, frame, physical proportions

   Sample Sentence   He was a small man, but his bodybuilder's *physique* made him look taller than he was.

   | MEMORY PEG | The prefix *physi-* means "physical." When someone asks you about your *physique*, they are asking about your physical form or build. |

5. **psychosomatic (sī-kō-sō-MĂT-ĭk) *adj.***   concerned with the influence of the mind on the body, especially in relation to disease

   Sample Sentence   If one believes that all diseases are *psychosomatic*, then it becomes far too easy to believe in curing the body by healing the mind.

| MEMORY PEG | The prefix *psycho-* means "mind," and the root *soma* means "body." Circle the two parts of the word to better remember its meaning. |

Additional Form   psychosomatically

6. cardiac (KĂR-dē-ăk) *adj.*   relating to the heart

Sample Sentence   After being given the wrong drug, the patient went into *cardiac* arrest, and the emergency team could not get her heart pumping again.

| MEMORY PEG | The word *cardiac* comes from the Greek word *kardiakos*, as does the word *cardiologist*, which refers to the medical person who takes care of heart ailments. To remember the meaning of *cardiac*, tell yourself that a cardiologist, or heart specialist, handles *cardiac* problems. |

Additional Form   cardiology

7. ocular (ŎK-yə-lər) *adj.*   having to do with the eye

Sample Sentence   He didn't have his glasses and couldn't read the *ocular* chart; therefore, he didn't get his driver's license.

| MEMORY PEG | In Shakespeare's famous play *Othello*, the hero demands "*ocular* proof" that his wife was unfaithful. In other words, he wants proof he can *see* with his eyes. If *Othello* doesn't help you, link the word *ocular* to the image of an eye or maybe even an eye chart like those you are likely to find in doctors' offices. |

Additional Form   oculist

8. auditory (Ô-dĭ-tôr-ē) *adj.*   related to hearing

Sample Sentence   When he started having *auditory* delusions,* they knew the illness had become truly serious.

| MEMORY PEG | *Auditory* comes from the Latin word *audire*, meaning "to hear." To remember their meaning, circle the letters *aud* and write "hear" over them. You might also make a map of other words that derive from that one Latin root, for example, *audition*, *auditorium*, and *audible*. |

9. respiratory (RĔS-pər-ə-tôr-ē) *adj.*   having to do with breathing

Sample Sentence   Emphysema is a smoking-related disease that attacks the *respiratory* system; it can become so severe that the victim is unable to breathe.

| MEMORY PEG | The letters *spir* come from the Latin word *spirare*, meaning "to breathe." Try linking together *inspiration* and *respiration*. When you receive *inspiration*, you get a new breath of hope. When you engage in *respiration*, you get an actual breath of life. |

Additional Form   respiration

10. cerebral (sə-RĒ-brəl) *adj.*   **a.** related to the brain

Sample Sentence   There was, thankfully, no sign of any *cerebral* damage from the accident.

                                                    b. requiring or related to logic rather than emotions

Sample Sentence No matter how serious or emotionally painful the situation, she always took a *cerebral* approach and tried to define precisely both problem and solution.

MEMORY PEG   In this case, the English language just adopted or took over the Latin word *cerebrum*, meaning "brain." Anything related to the *cerebrum* is, thus, appropriately termed *cerebral*. If you need an image to lock this meaning into memory, imagine a mass of folded gray matter inside a human head and mentally write *cerebrum* across the folds.

Idiom Alert

The brain is the source of several idioms. Here are two:

Brain trust: a group of experts who serve as unofficial advisors. Although the expression started out in the plural form (brains trust) circa* 1910, the *s* disappeared when the phrase became popular. It was regularly applied to the group of experts surrounding Franklin Delano Roosevelt, the thirty-second president of the United States. "Although Franklin Delano Roosevelt often consulted with his *brain trust*, he much less regularly followed its advice."

Brain drain: the departure of many talented people for better pay or jobs elsewhere. The term became popular around 1960, when British scientists and scholars began coming to the United States. "Adolf Hitler's rise to power triggered a *brain drain* as scientists, artists, and scholars fled Germany for England and America."

Practice 1   Matching Words and Meanings

Directions: To match word and meaning, fill in the blanks with the appropriate letters.

1. corporal	_____	a. related to the eye
2. brawny	_____	b. having to do with the brain
3. emaciated	_____	c. physical
4. physique	_____	d. related to hearing
5. psychosomatic	_____	e. extremely thin
6. cardiac	_____	f. build or frame
7. ocular	_____	g. concerned with the mind's influence on the body
8. auditory	_____	h. strong and muscular
9. respiratory	_____	i. related to the heart
10. cerebral	_____	j. having to do with breathing

Practice 2   Answering True or False

Directions: To indicate if a statement is *true* or *false,* circle the correct answer.

True   False   1. A person suffering from *auditory* delusions will probably see things that aren't there.

True   False   2. Someone desiring *ocular* proof wants to hear facts from the people involved in the event or situation.

True   False   3. *Cardiac* problems affect the heart.

True   False   4. People who work out and eat a healthy but low-fat diet are inclined to look *emaciated.*

True   False   5. Weightlifters usually have a powerful-looking *physique.*

True   False   6. Some schools still practice *cerebral* punishment, and kids who misbehave get paddled.

True   False   7. In a *psychosomatic* illness, a problem of the mind plays itself out on the body.

True   False   8. If you believe in ghosts, you believe that the spirit can live on after the *corporal* self has passed away.

True   False   9. Double vision is a *respiratory* problem.

True   False   10. People who diet sometimes go overboard in their pursuit of a *brawny* body.

Practice 3   Making Sentence Sense

Directions: Fill in the blanks with the word that fits both the context and the definition in parentheses.

| physiques | cerebral | auditory | cardiac | emaciated |
| corporal | brawny | respiratory | psychosomatic | ocular |

1. After his heart attack, he spent a week in the _____ unit of the hospital. (having to do with the heart)

2. The smog was causing her to have terrible _____ problems. (related to breathing)

3. Many people don't realize that constant stress can cause serious _____ problems. (concerned with the influence of the mind on the body)

4. One could see the tragic effects of the months-long dry spell in the bulging stomachs and _____ bodies of the children. (extremely thin)

5. He needed a more sophisticated _____ test before his hearing aid could be fitted. (related to hearing)

6. Thanks to all those underwear ads showing well-muscled men in briefs, even little boys have begun to worry about their _____. (build or frame)

7. Some people insist that expressing emotions is crucial to mental health, but there are times when emotions need to be held in check in favor of a more _____ approach. (having to do with the brain)

8. She had a powerful _____ presence, so she had no difficulty earning the respect of her fellow soldiers. (physical)

9. The general's _____ chest showed to good effect when he put on a uniform and wore his medals. (strong and muscular)

10. By memorizing the eye chart, she hoped to pass the _____ portion of her exam. (having to do with the eye)

Practice 4   Filling in the Gaps

Directions: Fill in the blanks with one of the words from the chapter. If two words seem equally right, study the context. One word will be better than the other.

| ocular | cerebral | emaciated | brawny | physique |
| cardiac | auditory | corporal | psychosomatic | respiratory |

Mind Over Matter

Some people are quick to reject the idea of a _phychosomat_illness. The very

_____ , in particular, are often annoyed at the idea that the mind they hold in such

high esteem can play tricks on them and become an enemy. Comfortable with the _____

causes of illness, they find it hard to deal with the mental ones.

Yet, whatever the objections, it's still true that the mind can turn against the body. People

who suffer from long-term, uncontrollable stress often suffer from _____ or

_____ problems. Their hearts suddenly beat faster than normal, or their breathing

becomes difficult for no particular reason. In cases of severe depression, some people have

_____ problems. Their eyes twitch and their vision becomes blurred. Perhaps the

only area of the body not subject to mind-induced illness is the ears; _____

problems seldom have an emotional basis.

But for absolute proof of what the mind can do to the body, consider the suffering caused by anorexia, also known as the starvation disease. Those suffering from anorexia diet no matter how thin they really are, and in a matter of months, even those who started out _____ in _____ can become _____ . Yes, the human mind is capable of great achievement. But when it mounts an attack on the body, it can turn deadly. Unfortunately, there are some emotionally based illnesses for which logic has no weapons.

To test your mastery of the words introduced in this chapter, turn to page 219 in the back of the book.

Chapter 17

Words on Words

The Common Thread

If you've ever had an essay corrected and re-turned to you, then you may have seen some of the words introduced in this chapter. These words are often used to describe language. For each one, try to come up with a specific example that illustrates the word's meaning.

synopsis	verbose
abstract	verbatim
concrete	simile
glib	metaphor
succinct	cliché

Words on Words

Directions: For each italicized word, circle the letter of what you think is the correct definition.

1. *Synopsis* means
   a. brief statement.
   b. long explanation.
   c. revision.

2. *Abstract* means
   a. in theory.
   b. in practice.
   c. in denial.

3. *Concrete* means
   a. factual.
   b. having to do with theory.
   c. worn out by use.

4. *Glib* means
   a. slow-talking.
   b. colorful.
   c. superficial.

5. *Succinct* means
   a. wordy.
   b. to the point.
   c. clever.

6. *Verbose* means
   a. unoriginal.
   b. witty.
   c. wordy.

7. *Verbatim* means
   a. brief.
   b. in different words.
   c. word for word.

8. *Simile* means
   a. a comparison using *like* or *as*.
   b. an overused expression.
   c. a related thought.

9. *Metaphor* means
   a. a comparison of two similar topics.
   b. a comparison using *like* or *as*.
   c. a comparison of two seemingly unlike things.

10. *Cliché* means
    a. a colorful description.
    b. an overworked expression.
    c. a clever idea.

Turn to page 242 to correct your test. Record your grade in the self-test column on the inside front cover of your textbook. Then go on to **Words and Meanings** on pages 119–121.

Words and Meanings

Here again are the words from the self-test. Only this time, they are accompanied by their most common meanings and pointers on pronunciation.

1. synopsis (sĭ-NŎP-sĭs) *n.* | brief statement or outline of a subject, theory, or chain of events

Sample Sentence The reviewer's *synopsis* of philosopher Martha Nussbaum's† ideas badly misinterpreted Nussbaum's thought.

MEMORY PEG Link the first *s* in *synopsis* to the *s* in *summary*, which is a synonym for *synopsis*.

Additional Form synopsize

Common Usage *in* synopsis

2. abstract (ăb-STRĂKT or ĂB-străkt) | **a.** related to ideas instead of things that can be seen, felt, heard, or touched (*adj.*)

Sample Sentence Love is an *abstract* word that's hard to pin down and often misunderstood.

b. a summary statement of a text (*n.*)

Sample Sentence In addition to the paper, he had to hand in a one-page *abstract*.

MEMORY PEG To remember meaning *a* of *abstract*, think of *abstract* words like *beauty, truth, justice,* and *patriotism.* Keep in mind, too, that an *abstraction* is an idea that can be interpreted more than one way. The word *success*, for instance, is an *abstract* term. It means different things to different people. To remember meaning *b*, link *abstract* to *synopsis.* They are, indeed, synonyms.

Additional Form abstraction

3. concrete (kŏn-KRĒT, KŎN-krēt) *adj.* | related to real things that can be touched, felt, seen, or heard

Sample Sentence To avoid being misunderstood, writers often use *concrete* illustrations of *abstract* ideas, or else they risk losing their readers.

MEMORY PEG To recall the meaning of *concrete*, remember that it's an antonym for *abstract.* While *abstractions* are ideas that exist only in the mind, *concrete* things exist in the physical world; thus, we can respond to them with our senses. In other words, we can see, taste, touch, hear, or smell them.

Additional Form concreteness

4. glib (glĭb) *adj.* | smooth but insincere, slick but superficial

Sample Sentence With his *glib* tongue, Satan persuaded Eve to take a bite of the forbidden fruit.

MEMORY PEG To remember this word, think that people who are *glib* have the "gift of gab." They are able to talk with ease, without much thought or preparation, probably because they care so little about meaning. For example, a fast-talking car salesman might use *glib* speech to sell an expensive automobile.

† Martha Nussbaum (1947–): Writer, teacher, and philosopher Martha Nussbaum is the author of numerous books on literature, justice, and ethics.

Additional Form   glibness

5. succinct (sək-SĬNGKT) *adj.*   brief but clear

Sample Sentence   Ernest Hemingway's novels are written in the *succinct* style of a newspaper article.

MEMORY PEG   Unlike the *glib*, those who are *succinct* in speech or writing don't have the "gift of gab." On the contrary, they prefer to get right to the point. Imagine the most direct person you know, and use him or her to remember both word and meaning.

Additional Form   succinctness

6. verbose (vər-BŌS) *adj.*   wordy

Sample Sentence   At the dedication of the Gettysburg cemetery in 1863, Abraham Lincoln's short, 270-word address stood in stark contrast to speaker Edward Everett's *verbose*, two-hour-long speech.

MEMORY PEG   Remember that *verbose* means the opposite of *succinct*. People who are *verbose* make no effort to limit their words. As a matter of fact, they like to use as many words as possible.

Additional Form   verbosity

7. verbatim (vər-BĀ-tĭm) *adv. or adj.*   word-for-word; using the original words exactly

Sample Sentence   The court reporter prepares a *verbatim* record of every word spoken during a trial.

MEMORY PEG   The word *verbatim* comes from the Latin word *verbum*, meaning "word." Remember that a *verbatim* record always repeats the original statement word for word. If it doesn't, it can't be called *verbatim*. If you are asked to use a quote *verbatim*, paraphrasing or rewording the quote is not allowed.

8. simile (SĬM-ə-lē) *n.*   a comparison between two unlike things that uses the words *like* or *as* to reveal a hidden or unexpected similarity

Sample Sentence   Robert Burns's poem begins with the simile "O, my luve is like a red, red rose."

MEMORY PEG   You can remember the word *simile* by recalling that its sound is very close to that of the word *similar*. A *simile* is a statement that points out how two seemingly unlike things are actually "similar" or alike.

9. metaphor (MĔT-ə-fôr) *n.*   a comparison between two unlike things that reveals an unexpected similarity

Sample Sentence   We may not realize it, but we use *metaphors* every day when we refer to a "bear of a man" or a "lemon of a car."

MEMORY PEG   Like a *simile*, a *metaphor* is a statement that makes a comparison. However, a *metaphor* doesn't say that something is *like* something else; instead, it says that something *is* something else. "She is a chicken" is a *metaphor*; and "she was as scared as a chicken" is a *simile*.

Additional Form   metaphorical

10. cliché (klē-SHĀ) *n.*   an overused expression that requires little thought

Sample Sentence   His love letters were filled with *clichés* such as "you are the light of my life."

> **MEMORY PEG**   To remember what *cliché* means, think of the many *similes* and *metaphors* we use—for example, "eats like a pig," "a bear of a man," and "as easy as pie"—that have become *clichés*.

Additional Form   clichéd

Idiom Alert

To not mince words: refusing to use polite or careful language, as in: "The speaker did not *mince words:* the meeting would not continue until the members were silent." The expression dates back to the 1500s, when the word *mince* was first applied to meat. But it's not clear how the word *mince* came to apply to words.

Practice 1   Matching Words and Meanings

Directions: To match word and meaning, fill in the blanks with the appropriate letters.

1. synopsis   _b_   a. a figure of speech that compares two unlike things using *like* or *as*

2. abstract   _d_   b. outline or summary

3. concrete   _h_   c. brief and to the point

4. glib   _i_   d. related to ideas instead of things

5. succinct   _c_   e. a figure of speech that compares two unlike things to reveal an unexpected similarity

6. verbose   _f_   f. wordy

7. verbatim   _j_   g. an overused expression that requires little thought

8. simile   _a_   h. related to real, specific things

9. metaphor   _e_   i. smooth-talking, insincere

10. cliché   _g_   j. word-for-word

Practice 2   Answering True or False

Directions: To indicate if a statement is *true* or *false,* circle the correct answer.

True   False   1. A *synopsis* should record a speech word for word.

True   False   2. The word *dog* is *abstract.*

True   False   3. The word *tree* is *concrete.*

True   False   4. Situation comedies try to be deep rather than *glib.*

True   False   5. The current seven-million-word U.S. tax code, which is 1,168 pages long, is a *succinct* document.

True   False   6. Messages on postcards from vacationing friends are almost always *verbose.*

True   False   7. If you need a *verbatim* record of an interview, just make sure you change the words rather than the meaning.

True   False   8. "As cold as ice" is a *simile.*

True   False   9. "He dangled from the ladder like a monkey hanging from a branch" is an example of a *metaphor.*

True   False   10. It takes originality to compose a *cliché.*

Practice 3   Making Sentence Sense

Directions: Fill in the blanks with the word that fits both the context and the definition in parentheses.

concrete	glib	similes	clichés	synopsis
abstract	verbatim	verbose	metaphor	succinct

1. Research indicates that chimpanzees and apes can use ＿＿＿＿＿＿ words like *good* and *bad.* (related to ideas instead of things)

2. He had such a good memory he was able to give an almost ＿＿＿＿＿＿ account of the diplomat's comments. (word-for-word)

3. To ensure that Academy Award winners' speeches are as ＿＿＿＿＿＿ as possible, the show's producer limits them to forty-five seconds each. (brief and to the point)

4. In ＿＿＿＿＿＿ , the poem sounded silly and somewhat childish. (outline or summary)

5. Many comparisons of humans to animals, such as "hungry as a bear," "strong as an ox," and "mean as a snake," have become ＿＿＿＿＿＿. (overused expressions that require little thought)

6. Mark Twain's boy hero Tom Sawyer was a _____ talker who could always get

    out of a tight spot. (smooth-talking)

7. The poet Mary Oliver fills her marvelous poems with _____ descriptions of

    nature in all its danger and variety. (related to real, specific things)

8. William Shakespeare's famous "All the world's a stage" is an example of a _____ .

    (a figure of speech that compares two unlike things to reveal an unexpected similarity)

9. The _____ speaking style that earned William Jennings Bryan† both fame and

    fortune would probably not get him very far today. (wordy)

10. When Jesus said, "Behold, I sent you out as sheep in the midst of wolves. Therefore be wise as ser-

    pents and harmless as doves" (Matthew 10:16), he included three different _____

    in his instructions. (figures of speech that compare two dissimilar things using the words *like* or *as*)

Practice 4   Filling in the Gaps

Directions: Fill in the blanks with one of the words from the chapter.

verbatim	metaphors	clichés	abstractions	succinct
glib	similes	synopsis	verbose	concrete

On Being a Writer

Want to be an effective writer? If you do, keep in mind that good writers are usually not

_____ . On the contrary, they try to be as _____ as possible. They

try never to use two words when one will do. They are more likely, for example, to say "now"

instead of "at the present time" and "before" rather than "back in the past."

   Skillful writers are also careful about how they handle _____ . If they use

words like *power*, *bravery*, and *dedication*, they make sure to accompany those words with

_____ illustrations. They know that general ideas not anchored in specific details

can prove confusing and lead to a communication breakdown between author and reader.

---

†   William Jennings Bryan (1860–1925): three-time presidential candidate and staunch* Christian who fought to keep the the-
     ory of evolution out of Tennessee's schools.

General statements not followed by specific explanations can also make readers suspicious. A writer who claims "our government has lost touch with the people" without offering specific illustrations of or reasons for that claim is likely to be considered overly _____ and perhaps untrustworthy.

In addition to directness and clarity, good writers also pay attention to imagery. They try to use original _____ and _____ to make readers "see" the intended meaning more clearly. The emphasis here is on the word *original:* Writers who care about their work carefully avoid _____ . They don't want their readers to be bored by the presence of tired and overused expressions.

Lastly, writers who care about writing *never* plagiarize. Even if they offer only a _____ of someone's ideas rather than quoting them _____ , writers with experience acknowledge their sources. They know that writing is hard work and refuse to take credit for words or ideas not their own.

To test your mastery of the words introduced in this chapter, turn to page 221 in the back of the book.

Chapter 18

More Words on Words

The Common Thread

Like the words in Chapter 17, the words in this chapter describe language and how we use it. As always, try to come up with specific examples to illustrate the meanings of the ten words introduced here.

utterance	diction
enunciate	orator
gibberish	articulate
jargon	monologue
dialect	tirade

Self-Test   More Words on Words

Directions: For each italicized word, circle the letter of what you think is the correct definition.

1. *Utterance* means
   a. stuttering.
   b. spoken expression.
   c. grammatical error.

2. *Enunciate* means
   a. pronounce.
   b. whistle.
   c. scold.

3. *Gibberish* means
   a. gossip.
   b. silence.
   c. nonsense.

4. *Jargon* means
   a. special language.
   b. actors' lines in a play.
   c. accent.

5. *Dialect* means
   a. conversation between two people.
   b. argument.
   c. regional speech pattern.

6. *Diction* means
   a. voice.
   b. word choice.
   c. lecture.

7. *Orator* means
   a. teacher.
   b. public speaker.
   c. master of ceremonies.

8. *Articulate* means
   a. speak meaningless words.
   b. reciting aloud from memory.
   c. using language well.

9. *Monologue* means
   a. speech made by one person.
   b. unchanging tone of voice.
   c. vocabulary.

10. *Tirade* means
    a. word having two or more meanings.
    b. gifted at writing.
    c. long, angry speech.

Turn to page 242 to correct your test. Record your score in the self-test column on the inside front cover of your textbook. Then go on to **Words and Meanings** on pages 126–128.

Words and Meanings

Here again are the same words from the self-test. Only this time, they are accompanied by their most common meanings along with pointers for pronunciation.

1. utterance (ŬT-ər-əns) *n.*   a spoken word or statement

Sample Sentence   He had no idea that his boss, who was within earshot, had heard every one of his unkind *utterances*.

> **MEMORY PEG**   The word *utter* means "to speak," so an *utterance* is a spoken expression. Any time you use your voice to produce a sound, a word, or a sentence, you have made an *utterance*.

Additional Forms   utter, utterable, utterer

2. enunciate (ĭ-NŬN-sē-āt) *v.*   to pronounce sounds or words

Sample Sentence   When you deliver a speech, it is important to *enunciate* words clearly so the audience can understand them.

> **MEMORY PEG**   The word *enunciate* comes from a Latin word that means "to announce." If you announce something, you say it out loud. It follows, then, that *enunciate* means to pronounce, or say, aloud. As you probably guessed, you *enunciate* an *utterance*.

Additional Forms   enunciation, enunciator

Common Usage   enunciation *of*

3. gibberish (JĬB-ər-ĭsh) *n.*   words, spoken or written, that are nonsense and have no meaning

Sample Sentence   The two-year-old's statements sounded like *gibberish* to us, but his mother always understood her child.

> **MEMORY PEG**   The exact origin of the word *gibberish* is unknown, but one explanation traces its beginnings to an eleventh-century Arab named Geber, who practiced a form of magical chemistry called alchemy. To avoid getting into trouble with church officials, he invented strange terms that prevented others from understanding his work. His mysterious language (Geberish) may have given rise to the word *gibberish*. Remember Geber's story, and you'll remember *gibberish*'s meaning.

4. jargon (JÄR-gən) *n.*   **a.** nonsense or meaningless talk

Sample Sentence   I don't know anything about how a car works, so the mechanic's explanation of the problem was all *jargon* to me.

b. special words and phrases used by particular groups of people, especially in their work

Sample Sentence   When you learn to play poker, you must also learn the *jargon* associated with the game.

> **MEMORY PEG**   When it's used in the sense of meaning *a*, *jargon* is a synonym for *gibberish*, so that's one way to remember its meaning. However, *jargon* also refers to words and phrases associated with a particular profession or activity. For example, words such as *mouse*, *download*, *hyperlink*, and *RAM* are all computer *jargon*. Store these words in your memory as examples of *jargon*, and it will be easier to call up the word's meaning.

Additional Form   jargonistic

5. dialect (DĪ-ə-lĕkt) *n.*   a form of a language that differs in some words, grammar, and pronunciations from other forms of the same language

Sample Sentence   The southern *dialect* includes the expression "y'all" and pronunciations such as "cheer" for *chair*, "arn" for *iron*, and "flar" for *flower*.

> **MEMORY PEG**   The word *dialect* comes from the Latin word *dialectus*, which means "form of speech." To remember the meaning of *dialect*, imagine yourself speaking with someone from Atlanta, Boston, or New York. In each of these cities, the native-born speak a distinctive *dialect*. They share, that is, certain "forms of speech" unique to the region. You need to know, too, that a *dialect* can be spoken by members of groups not connected by region, as in "the *dialect* of science." When it's used this way, it's a synonym for *jargon*.

Additional Form   dialectal

6. diction (DĬK-shən) *n.*   **a.** the manner in which words are spoken

Sample Sentence   A teacher of a foreign language must have good diction.

b. choice of words in speaking or writing; wording

Sample Sentence   Readers of an academic research paper expect it to contain formal *diction*.

> **MEMORY PEG**   Knowing that the letters *dict* in *diction* mean "speak" should help you remember that *diction* can refer to the manner in which words are spoken, or pronounced. However, *diction* can also refer to the speaker's or writer's choice of words, which is usually *dictated* by the situation.

Additional Form   dictional

7. orator (ÔR-ə-tər) *n.*   a person who delivers a public speech; a person skilled at formal public speaking

Sample Sentence   To deliver a sermon effectively, a minister has to be a skilled *orator*.

> **MEMORY PEG**   The word *orator* contains the same Latin root as the word *oral*, which means "spoken." Tell yourself that *orators* are usually well spoken because they have delivered so many speeches. Tell yourself, too, that a good *orator* needs to enunciate* clearly.

Additional Forms   orate, oration, oratory

8. articulate (är-TĬK-yə-lĭt)   **a.** having the power to use language effectively (*adj.*)

Sample Sentence   Whatever his character flaws, President Clinton was an *articulate* speaker who understood the power of words.

b. characterized by clear, expressive language (*adj.*)

Sample Sentence   Martin Amis's witty, *articulate* essays are simply a delight to read.

c. to express in a clear and understandable form, put into words (är-TĬK-yə-lāt) (*v.*)

Sample Sentence   She knew what she wanted to say, but somehow it was hard for her to *articulate* her concerns.

> **MEMORY PEG**   To remember meanings *a*, *b*, and *c*, focus on the first three letters of the word *articulate* and tell yourself that being *articulate* (like being able to *articulate*) involves the "art" of putting thoughts into words.

Additional Forms   articulation, articulateness

9. **monologue (MŎN-ə-lôg)** *n.*   a speech made by one person

Sample Sentence   Near the end of the scene, the other characters leave the stage, and the actor is left alone to deliver his *monologue*.

> **MEMORY PEG**   You may recall that the prefix *mono-* means "one." Use your knowledge of that prefix to help you remember that a *monologue* is a speech delivered by just one person. This speech could occur in a play on the stage, in a literary work, or in a conversation, where the person delivering the *monologue* does all of the talking.

Additional Forms   monologic, monological, monologuist

10. **tirade (tī-RĀD)** *n.*   a long, angry speech

Sample Sentence   Every time I try to discuss politics with my father, he goes into a *tirade*.

> **MEMORY PEG**   To remember the meaning of *tirade*, imagine a man or woman in a fit of road rage, screaming and shouting at an offending driver. With that image, it will be hard to forget the meaning of *tirade*.

Common Usage   *launch*, *go*, or *break into* a tirade

Idiom Alert

> **Talk shop:** Around the mid-1800s it was common for shopkeepers to talk about their businesses or shops. After a while, *talking shop* became a general term used to describe conversations about work, e.g., "The husbands left the table as soon as the wives started to *talk shop*."

Practice 1   Matching Words with Meanings

Directions: To match word and meaning, fill in the blanks with the appropriate letters.

1. utterance   _____   a. public speaker

2. enunciate   _____   b. spoken or written nonsense

3. gibberish   _____   c. pronunciation or word choice

4. jargon   _____   d. good with words

5. dialect   _____   e. the specialized vocabulary of a profession

6. diction   _____   f. speech by a single person

7. orator	_____	g. pronounce words
8. articulate	_____	h. spoken word or statement
9. monologue	_____	i. type of language associated with a region
10. tirade	_____	j. long, angry speech

Practice 2   Answering True or False

Directions: To indicate if a statement is *true* or *false*, circle the correct answer.

True   False   1. A child's first *utterance* doesn't always make sense.

True   False   2. If you lose your voice, you can still *enunciate* clearly.

True   False   3. When monkeys talk, they seem to understand one another, but to us the sounds they make are *gibberish*.

True   False   4. The word *hello* is an example of *jargon*.

True   False   5. *Articulating* one's emotions is not always easy.

True   False   6. The *diction* of an advertisement aimed at teenagers is likely to be informal.

True   False   7. An *orator* typically speaks only to himself.

True   False   8. People who live in the same region are likely to speak the same *dialect*.

True   False   9. A class discussion could be described as a *monologue*.

True   False   10. Someone launching into a *tirade* always remains well-spoken.

Practice 3   Making Sentence Sense

Directions: Fill in the blanks with the word that fits both the context and the definition in parentheses.

utterances	**dialect**	**articulate**	**enunciate**	**tirade**
monologue	**gibberish**	**diction**	**orators**	**jargon**

1. E-mail messages often use an informal _____ containing slang expressions and other words from everyday speech. (word choice)

2. Politicians who are powerful _____ have an advantage over opponents who are not. (skilled public speakers)

3. Lewis Carroll's poem "Jabberwocky," which begins with the line "'Twas brillig, and the slithy toves / Did gyre and gimble in the wabe," is a good example of _____. (words that have no meaning)

4. A child's first _____ are extremely important to a parent. (spoken words)

5. The acronym† *AWOL* (*absent without leave*) is an example of military_____ .
    (special words and phrases that are used by people in a particular profession or group)

6. Before leaving office, President Richard M. Nixon† launched into a _____
    against the press, whom he considered an enemy. (long, angry speech)

7. _____, witty, and bold, Mike Malloy is the liberals' Rush Limbaugh.† (good with
    words)

8. The speaker does not _____ very clearly, so it's difficult to understand what he's
    saying. (pronounce words)

9. He ignored her attempts to share her own thoughts on the matter and continued with his
    _____ . (a speech made by one person)

10. In some regions, the local _____ contains unfamiliar words or pronounces famil-
    iar words in such a way that people from the outside have a hard time understanding the locals.
    (type of language)

Practice 4   Filling in the Gaps

Directions: Fill in the blanks with one of the words from the chapter. If two words seem equally right,
study the context. One word will be better than the other.

utterance	**oration**	**gibberish**	**tirades**	**diction**
jargon	**monologue**	**enunciate**	**dialects**	**articulate**

An Actor's Actor

British actor Sir Laurence Olivier (1907–1989) was, without a doubt, one of the greatest actors of

the twentieth century. In the ___*Jargon*___ of film and theater critics, he was an "actor's

actor" whose performances won raves even from fellow performers. Nominated twelve different

times for Academy Awards (nine of them for best actor), he won twice. Olivier also received two

---

†   Acronym: words formed from the initials of other words.
†   Richard M. Nixon: Forced to resign by the threat of impeachment, President Nixon believed that he had been hounded out
    of office by the press.
†   Rush Limbaugh and Mike Malloy are radio personalities who share a similar style but who have very different political
    leanings.

honorary Oscars. In his long career, Olivier appeared in more than 120 stage roles and nearly 60 films. Shakespeare productions were Olivier's specialty. As a matter of fact, his only best actor award was for his 1948 film version of *Hamlet*.

Laurence Olivier was blessed with dark good looks and an athletic physique.* But he knew that he could not build a distinguished acting career on those qualities alone. Thus, during his education at London's Central School of Speech Training and Dramatic Arts, he began voice training. He developed his talent for public speaking by learning the art of _Oration_. In particular, he learned to carefully _enun_ his words so that they would not sound like _jibb_ to audiences unfamiliar with the language of Shakespeare.

As an actor, Olivier was especially good at discovering the right look, walk, and speech for each character. He would work long hours with a voice coach, learning how to imitate the pronunciations and grammar of the various _dia_ appropriate to different characters. He also perfected a speech technique designed to reveal his characters' states of mind. While other actors had tended to proclaim the language of Shakespeare by letting the words roll off their tongues, Olivier used a short, clipped style of _diction_ that exposed his character's raw emotions. For example, instead of playing the cerebral* Hamlet as cool and indifferent, Olivier made every _utterance_, including several lengthy _tirades_, reveal Hamlet's pain and fury over his father's death and his mother's remarriage. As a result, it didn't matter if Olivier recited a _monologue_ or was in a dialogue, he was always wonderfully _articulate_ his words crackled with emotional fire. No wonder, then, his filmed performances are worth watching to this day.

To test your mastery of the words introduced in this chapter, turn to page 223 in the back of the book.

Chapter 19

Together and Apart

The Common Thread

The ten words in this chapter can be used to describe how people, ideas, and objects come together or break apart.

cohesive	discord
affiliation	rupture
intermingle	contention
adhere	alienate
coalesce	divisive

Self-Test   Together and Apart

Directions: For each italicized word, circle the letter of what you think is the correct definition.

1. *Cohesive* means
   a. unified.
   b. separate.
   c. argumentative.

2. *Affiliation* means
   a. a sense of separation.
   b. a sense of belonging.
   c. a sense of loss.

3. *Intermingle* means
   a. divide in the middle.
   b. mix together.
   c. weave tightly.

4. *Adhere* means
   a. separate.
   b. leave.
   c. hold fast.

5. *Coalesce* means
   a. group together.
   b. divide.
   c. unite.

6. *Discord* means
   a. combination.
   b. separation.
   c. conflict.

7. *Rupture* means
   a. union.
   b. split.
   c. combination.

8. *Contention* means
   a. unity.
   b. division.
   c. conflict.

9. *Alienate* means
   a. make hostile.
   b. include.
   c. fight over.

10. *Divisive* means
    a. encouraging agreement.
    b. bringing about unity.
    c. producing conflict.

Turn to page 242 to correct your test. Record your grade in the self-test column on the inside front cover of your textbook. Then go on to **Words and Meanings** on pages 133–135.

Words and Meanings

Here again are the words from the self-test. Only this time, they are accompanied by their most common meanings and pointers on pronunciation.

1. **cohesive (kō-HĒ-sĭv, kō-HĒ-zĭv) *adj.***   connected, consistent, united

    Sample Sentence   The different countries in the European Union† still find it difficult to agree on a *cohesive* foreign policy.

    Additional Forms   cohesiveness, cohesion, cohere, coherent

    > **MEMORY PEG**   The prefix *co-* means "together," "joint," or "mutually." It follows, then, that the word *cohesive* is used to emphasize how well people or things unite or come together.

2. **affiliation (ə-fĭl-ē-Ā-shən) *n.***   attachment, relationship; formal connection to

    Sample Sentence   The presidential candidate hotly denied any *affiliation* with a club that refused entry to women.

    > **MEMORY PEG**   Major TV networks like CBS or Fox have *affiliates* in many cities. These are local stations that get their programming from the large networks. Think of these television *affiliates* to remember that *affiliation* means "attachment," "relationship," or "connection."

    Additional Form   affiliate

    Common Usage   *have an* affiliation *with* or *to; be* affiliated *with*

3. **intermingle (ĭn-tər-MĬNG-gəl) *v.***   mix together

    Sample Sentence   The designer liked to *intermingle* colors—for example, pink, red, and orange—to create startling prints.

    > **MEMORY PEG**   The prefix *inter-* often means "among." Thus an international treaty is an agreement among several different nations. Likewise, if colors, voices, or sounds are *intermingled*, they are mixed together. Remembering the meaning of the prefix *inter-* helps you remember the meaning of *intermingle*.

    Common Usage   intermingled *with*

4. **adhere (ăd-HÎR) *n.***   stick or hold; be attached

    Sample Sentence   Before you mail a letter, make sure that the stamp firmly *adheres* to the envelope. (literal)

    Sample Sentence   Staunch* pacifists *adhere* to a belief in nonviolence. (figurative)

    > **MEMORY PEG**   Krazy Glue is an *adhesive* substance you can use to make things stick, or *adhere*, to each other. Think of what Krazy Glue does to remember the meaning of *adhere*.

    Additional Forms   adherence, adherent, adhesive, adhesion

    Common Usage   adhere and adherence *to*

5. **coalesce (kō-ə-LĔS) *v.***   fuse, unite; come together as one

---

†   Fifteen European countries, among them Germany, France, and Italy, have banded together to work as a united group.

Sample Sentence   The young recruits quickly *coalesced* into a trained fighting unit.

> **MEMORY PEG**   Keep in mind that the prefix *co-* often means "together," as it does in the word *coworkers*. Tell yourself that people or things that *coalesce* come together as one in much the same way that coworkers work together as a group.

Additional Form   coalescence

Common Usage   coalesce *into*

6. discord (DĬS-kôrd) *n.*   conflict, lack of agreement, tension

Sample Sentence   The members of the panel usually got along quite well, but the elections had caused a good deal of *discord*.

> **MEMORY PEG**   The prefix *dis-* can mean "apart." Those who experience *discord* are likely to move apart over an issue and to be less *cordial*, or friendly, with each other.

Additional Forms   discordance, discordant

7. rupture (RŬP-chər)   **a.** split, break, separation, falling-out (*n.*)

Sample Sentence   Although Joseph Lieberman and Al Gore ran together in the 2000 presidential election, there was a very public *rupture* in their relationship after the election was over.

b. to split, to break apart, to burst (*v.*)

Sample Sentence   Frozen water caused by extreme cold *ruptured* the water pipes in the basement.

> **MEMORY PEG**   *Rupture* contains the same root as *interruption*—it is, in fact, an interruption that sometimes lasts forever. Link *rupture* to *interruption* in order to remember that *rupture* means a literal or figurative break.

8. contention (kən-TĔN-shən) *n.*   disagreement, struggle, conflict, debate

Sample Sentence   In the 2000 presidential election, the result of the Florida vote was the subject of heated *contention*.

> **MEMORY PEG**   A good way to remember the meaning of *contention* is to link it to the word *contender*, as in "the contenders in the Miss America pageant" or "heavyweight boxing contenders." If you have *contention*, you have *contenders* competing for or fighting over something.

Additional Form   contentious

9. alienate (ĀL-yə-nāt, Ā-lē-ə-nāt) *v.*   to cause to become unfriendly, hostile, or unresponsive

Sample Sentence   Initially, the voters supported the governor's tax plan, but his decision to triple property taxes quickly *alienated* even his supporters.

> **MEMORY PEG**   An *alien* is a person living in a foreign country. It can also be a creature from outer space (as in the *Alien* movies). Remember, then, that if you *alienate* someone, you cause them to behave like an unfriendly *alien*, or stranger.

Additional Forms   alien, alienation

10. divisive (də-VĪ-sĭv) *adj.*   causing argument, tension, or disagreement

Sample Sentence   The role of women in military combat continues to be a *divisive* issue.

> **MEMORY PEG**   If you *divide* a number, you break it into smaller numbers. Something that is *divisive* has a similar effect: It breaks into pieces agreements or understandings that may have existed before. Or, to put it another way: *Divisive* people or issues produce *divisions*.

Additional Form   divisiveness

Idiom Alert

Piece together: Although this phrase (circa* 1500) began as a reference to scraps of cloth, it took on a more figurative meaning over time and began referring to the art of figuring things out a little at a time until a larger picture emerges: "Bit by bit, the biographer was able to *piece together* the mystery of the young man's childhood."

Practice 1   Matching Words and Meanings

Directions: To match word and meaning, fill in the blanks with the appropriate letters.

1. cohesive	_____	a. conflict, lack of agreement
2. affiliation	_____	b. causing conflict
3. intermingle	_____	c. disagreement
4. adhere	_____	d. connected
5. coalesce	_____	e. mix together
6. discord	_____	f. attachment or relationship
7. rupture	_____	g. break
8. contention	_____	h. to make hostile or unresponsive
9. alienate	_____	i. come together as one
10. divisive	_____	j. stick or hold

Practice 2   Answering True or False

Directions: To indicate if a statement is *true* or *false*, circle the correct answer.

True   False   1. Bad relationships are characterized by a great amount of *cohesiveness*.

True   False   2. If you have an *affiliation* with an organized religion, you probably don't believe in God.

True   False   3. Mixers are parties where people are supposed to *intermingle*.

True   False   4. Cheaters are people who *adhere* to the rules of a game.

True   False   5. Things that *coalesce* are falling apart.

True   False   6. Research shows that marriages with a lot of *discord* last the longest.

True   False   7. Nothing can *rupture* a friendship like a shared sense of humor.

True   False   8. An agreement is a form of *contention*.

True   False   9. Most people aren't *alienated* by a waiter whose fingernails are dirty.

True   False   10. Abortion is a *divisive* issue in the United States.

Practice 3   Making Sentence Sense

Directions: Fill in the blanks with the word that fits both the context and the definition in parentheses.

cohesive	intermingled	discord	contention	alienated
affiliation	adhere	rupture	coalesce	divisive

1. Try as they might, the members couldn't seem to _____ into an effective group. (to come together as one)

2. The religious leader _____ his followers when he took a second wife. (made hostile or unresponsive)

3. John Adams's long-time _____ with the Federalist party did not save him from being attacked by one of the party's most prominent members, Alexander Hamilton. (attachment or relationship)

4. After World War II ended, the major source of _____ among the Allies was how to divide up the territory of the defeated enemies. (disagreement or conflict)

5. The snakes _____ so well with the leaves of the tree, it was impossible to tell where the snakes left off and the tree began. (mixed together)

6. During the 1960s and early 1970s, the Vietnam War was the most _____ issue facing the nation. (causing conflict)

7. The leadership's heavy-handed actions led to much _____ within the union. (disagreement or conflict)

8. After the president discovered that the former press secretary had betrayed his confidence, the _____ between the two was complete. (break)

9. Written in extreme haste, the reporter's sentences were not as _____ as they should have been, making the chain of events hard to follow. (connected)

10. People who join the military must be willing to _____ to its rules and regulations. (stick or hold)

Practice 4   Filling in the Gaps

Directions: Fill in the blanks with one of the words from the chapter.

cohesion	discord	divisive	affiliation	contention
alienation	coalesce	rupture	adhering	intermingled

Quarreling Over the Pledge of Allegiance

When Baptist minister Francis Bellamy composed the Pledge of Allegiance in 1892, he had a definite purpose in mind. Aware that different ethnic groups in the United States were

_____ yet often at odds, Bellamy hoped the pledge would encourage those groups

to put aside their differences and _____ into a unified nation. He wanted the men,

women, and children who recited the pledge to feel an _____ with the United

States and its democratic ideals. Since Bellamy also wanted the pledge to be used by other naions

_____ to similar principles, he did not mention the United States by name.

Unfortunately, Bellamy's refusal to specifically name the United States caused significant

_____ over time, and the pledge itself often proved to be a source of

_____ rather than _____.

Bellamy's original Pledge of Allegiance read: "I pledge allegiance to my flag and the republic

for which it stands: one nation indivisible, with liberty and justice for all." Then, in 1923, a

_____ opened between Bellamy and the National Flag Conference when members

changed the words from "my flag" to "the flag of the United States of America." Bellamy hated the

change and protested, but his objection was ignored. The new wording stayed.

In 1954, Congress's addition of the words "under God" became another source of heated conflict

as atheists insisted that the phrase produced in them a profound sense of _____. As nonbelievers, they were angered by a Pledge of Allegiance that forced faith upon them. In addition to the atheists, some of the faithful were also displeased. They argued that reciting the pledge on a regular basis could be a mind-numbing exercise that undermined serious religious belief.

Another controversy broke out in 2002 when the U.S. Court of Appeals for the 9th Circuit ruled that reciting the pledge in public schools was unconstitutional because it blurred the separation of church and state. Needless to say, the decision proved _____ , sparking so much violent disagreement that a union of political and religious groups took out public ads proclaiming the need to keep the pledge in the schools. Michael Newdow, who had brought the issue before the courts, even received several death threats.

To test your mastery of the words introduced in this chapter, turn to page 225 in the back of the book.

Chapter 20

Getting Mad and Making Up

The Common Thread

It's human nature for people to get mad at one another. Fortunately, it's also human nature for people to make up. In this chapter you'll look at words that describe both activities. As often as you can, link the ten words to your own experiences of getting mad and making up.

bellicose	affront
bicker	pacify
animosity	concede
vanquish	amicable
altercation	rapport

Self-Test / Getting Mad and Making Up

Directions: For each italicized word, circle the letter of what you think is the correct definition.

1. *Bellicose* means
   a. ready to fight.
   b. unnecessarily unkind.
   c. outspoken.

2. *Bicker* means
   a. calm down.
   b. quarrel.
   c. make up.

3. *Animosity* means
   a. hatred.
   b. friendship.
   c. battle.

4. *Vanquish* means
   a. outnumber.
   b. defeat.
   c. challenge.

5. *Altercation* means
   a. peace.
   b. argument.
   c. dislike.

6. *Affront* means
   a. interference.
   b. advice.
   c. insult.

7. *Pacify* means
   a. challenge.
   b. calm.
   c. irritate.

8. *Concede* means
   a. give in or accept.
   b. irritate.
   c. badly defeat.

9. *Amicable* means
   a. neutral.
   b. friendly.
   c. hostile.

10. *Rapport* means
    a. contradiction.
    b. attack or insult.
    c. feeling of trust.

Turn to page 242 to correct your test. Record your grade in the self-test column on the inside front cover of your textbook. Then go on to **Words and Meanings** on pages 140–142.

Words and Meanings

Here again are the words from the self-test. Only this time, they are accompanied by their most common meanings and pointers on pronunciation.

1. **bellicose (BĔL-ĭ-kōs) *adj.***   aggressive, ready to fight

   Sample Sentence   After President Truman learned that the United States had successfully exploded an atomic bomb, he grew much more *bellicose* in his dealings with the Russians.

   MEMORY PEG   *Bellicose* derives from *bellum*, the Latin word for "war." You may have come across this word in the phrase "antebellum South," which refers to the South before the Civil War. If you keep in mind that *bellum* means "war," you're likely to remember that someone who is *bellicose* is ready to go to war.

2. **bicker (BĬK-ər) *v.***   to engage in a petty or silly quarrel

   Sample Sentence   No president and first lady want to be seen *bickering* in public.

   MEMORY PEG   Most of us know couples who seem to fight a lot over small things. Think of these *bickering* couples, and you will remember what *bicker* means.

   Additional Form   bickerer
   Common Usage   bicker *about* or *over*

3. **animosity (ăn-ə-MŎS-ĭ-tē) *n.***   hatred, bitterness, hostility

   Sample Sentence   Any personal *animosity* has to be put aside when people work together toward a common goal.

   MEMORY PEG   People who "fight like animals" really go at it. To remember the meaning of *animosity*, link the word in your mind to a picture of two animals—for example, two pit bulls—fighting fiercely with each other, and you will remember that *animosity* means "hostility" or "hatred."

4. **vanquish (VĂNG-kwĭsh, VĂN-kwĭsh) *v.***   defeat soundly; overcome completely

   Sample Sentence   *Vanquished* in World War II, Germany lost a sizable portion of its area; the rest was divided into two different countries and remained so for more than forty years.

   MEMORY PEG   Movie action heroes, as played by actors such as Vin Diesel, are not content with just winning in the end. They want to smash everything in their way to smithereens and completely destroy their enemies. Link the word *vanquish* to an image of someone like Vin Diesel or Arnold Schwarzenegger who's determined to *vanquish*, or completely defeat, a foe.

   Additional Forms   vanquisher, vanquishment

5. **altercation (ôl-tər-KĀ-shən) *n.***   heated argument, fight, or controversy

   Sample Sentence   Certain parts of the president's budget proposal led to a heated *altercation* in Congress.

   MEMORY PEG   Link the word *altercation* to the word *bellicose*. Tell yourself that people who are *bellicose* frequently get into *altercations*.

Common Usage   *get into an* altercation

6. affront (ə-FRŬNT)   **a.** insult (*n.*)

Sample Sentence   The Iraqi dictator Saddam Hussein would execute anyone he thought guilty of a personal *affront*.

b. anger, insult, annoy (*v.*)

Sample Sentence   *Affronted* when Sir Thomas More would not admit that his divorce was acceptable to the church, King Henry VIII had More beheaded.

> **MEMORY PEG**   *Affront* contains the Latin root *front*, which means "face." That root is used directly in a phrase like the "front of a building," meaning the building's face. It also occurs in *confront*, meaning "coming face-to-face with someone or something." An *affront* is a stronger form of confrontation, one that annoys or insults a person. To *affront* someone is to "get in someone's face" in order to be insulting.

7. pacify (PĂS-ə-fī) *v.*   calm, soothe, smooth over

Sample Sentence   The contractor had to *pacify* his client because expenses were way over budget.

> **MEMORY PEG**   The letters *pac* come from the Latin word for "peace." (The Spanish word for peace, *paz*, derives from the same Latin word.) It makes sense, then, that the rubber nipple parents use to make peaceful, or *pacify*, a crying baby is called a *pacifier*. Keep that image of the child with a *pacifier* in mind to remember both word and meaning.

Additional Forms   pacification, pacifier

8. concede (kən-SĒD) *v.*   to acknowledge the truth of something, often reluctantly; to give in or yield

Sample Sentence   His argument was fueled by emotion and no amount of logic could make him *concede* that he was dead wrong.

> **MEMORY PEG**   Think of how an election has to end. Once all the votes are counted, someone has to *concede*, or give in. The loser has to acknowledge that he or she has lost.

Additional Form   concession

Common Usage   *to make a* concession

9. amicable (ĂM-ĭ-kə-bəl) *adj.*   friendly, peaceful, in good humor

Sample Sentence   Despite their prior quarrels, they managed to separate in an *amicable* divorce.

> **MEMORY PEG**   The word *amicable* comes from *amicus*, the Latin word for "friend." The Spanish word *amigo* (as in the movie *The Three Amigos*) derives from the same Latin word. Picture anything that is *amicable* as if it were done between amigos, or friends.

Additional Form   amicability

10. rapport (ră-PÔR) *n.*   trust; emotional or intellectual understanding

Sample Sentence   After working together for years, the two had developed a great *rapport* and were often able to communicate without words.

> **MEMORY PEG** Think of someone with whom you are completely comfortable and ready to discuss everything that comes to your mind. Then tell yourself that you have an excellent *rapport* with that person.

Common Usage   *share* or *have* a rapport *with*

Idiom Alert

Bone of contention: A *bone of contention* is the issue of disagreement people quarrel or bicker over, for example, "In the baseball strike, a salary cap was the *bone of contention* for both players and owners."

Practice 1   Matching Words and Meanings

Directions: To match word and meaning, fill in the blanks with the appropriate letters.

1. bellicose	_____	a.	friendly, peaceful
2. bicker	_____	b.	heated argument
3. animosity	_____	c.	calm or soothe
4. vanquish	_____	d.	a sense of understanding
5. altercation	_____	e.	eager to fight
6. affront	_____	f.	solidly defeat
7. pacify	_____	g.	extreme dislike
8. concede	_____	h.	disagree over petty things
9. amicable	_____	i.	yield or give in
10. rapport	_____	j.	insult

Practice 2   Answering True or False

Directions: To indicate if a statement is *true* or *false*, circle the correct answer.

True   **False**   1. If there's *animosity* between two people, they are unlikely to become friends.

True   **False**   2. Being *vanquished* means being a winner.

True   **False**   3. Nobody ever minds making a *concession*.

True   **False**   4. A feeling of *rapport* among coworkers makes for a good working situation.

True   **False**   5. *Bickering* is just another word for *fighting*.

True   **False**   6. We all like personal *affronts* as long as they come from our enemies.

True   **False**   7. *Bellicose* nations always use diplomacy to solve their disagreements.

True   **False**   8. People who are not angry don't need to be *pacified*.

True   False   9. The goal of a good relationship is to avoid *amicable* remarks.

True   False   10. In an *altercation* over property lines, neighbors mutually agree on the borders.

Practice 3   Making Sentence Sense

Directions: Fill in the blanks with the word that fits both the context and the definition in parentheses.

| bellicose | vanquished | conceded | amicable | bickering |
| animosity | pacify | rapport | altercation | affront |

1. It came as a complete surprise when the underdogs _____ their opponents by a score of 45 to 6. (soundly defeated)

2. There was a time when wealthy men thought that a personal _____ was cause for a duel. (insult)

3. Nothing could _____ the angry shareholders once they discovered the accounting fraud. (calm, soothe)

4. There was nothing _____ about the way the two fighters talked about each other at the press conference. (friendly, peaceful)

5. _____ by nature, he managed to get into a fight even with those he loved best. (inclined or eager to fight)

6. The two business partners were constantly _____ ; unfortunately, their arguments caused discord* among their employees. (quarrelling)

7. After much persuasion, he _____ to letting his daughter go on the overnight outing. (yield or give in)

8. Even after the contract was signed, there remained _____ between management and the union. (hostility)

9. The American colonists' _____ with England over taxes led to the Boston Tea Party, in which 200 colonists dressed as Native Americans dumped 342 chests of tea into Boston Harbor. (heated argument)

10. Studies show that middle children often become successful managers because they have learned strategies for creating a positive _____ with all kinds of people. (a sense of understanding)

Practice 4   Filling in the Gaps

Directions: Fill in the blanks with one of the words in the chapter. If two words seem equally right, study the context. One word will be better than the other.

vanquish	pacify	bickering	concessions	rapport
affront	amicable	altercations	animosities	bellicose

Managing Conflict

Busy managers don't want to waste time trying to _____ those _____ employees who are willing to let their personal _____ disturb the workplace. As a matter of fact, a growing number of managers expect the employees themselves to make _____ , resolve their conflicts, and develop the appropriate _____ necessary to a peaceful and productive workplace. For that reason, many companies offer courses in how to manage conflict. The course teaches employees a few basic steps for handling minor disagreements and even nasty _____ .

    The first and most basic step is to analyze the situation in order to decide if there is a real basis for disagreement. Analysis and discussion often reveal that employees are not so far apart as they might have appeared. Employees who are willing to stop being pointlessly _____ can often find an _____ solution that gives all involved the feeling they have been understood. Conflict management can be very effective. In fact, it seems to fail with only two personality types. It's not terribly successful with people who take any suggestion that they are not completely in the right as a personal _____ . Conflict management is also likely to fail with those who want to totally _____ anyone holding an opposing point of view. Such people aren't looking for a peaceful solution. They prefer defeating any and all opponents that appear in their path.

To test your mastery of the words introduced in this chapter, turn to page 227 in the back of the book.

Friends and Enemies

The Common Thread

Chapter 21 supplies words to describe friendship and the bonds that create it. However, it also focuses on enemies and how we make them. Use that contrast to make connections among the words.

peer	affinity
alter ego	animus
collaborator	enmity
congenial	adversarial
fraternal	confidant

Self-Test Friends and Enemies

Directions: For each italicized word, circle the letter of what you think is the correct definition.

1. *Peer* means
   a. enemy.
   b. equal.
   c. brother.

2. *Alter ego* means
   a. second self.
   b. coworker.
   c. rival.

3. *Collaborator* means
   a. coworker.
   b. competitor.
   c. good friend.

4. *Congenial* means
   a. similar.
   b. friendly.
   c. conflicting.

5. *Fraternal* means
   a. outgoing.
   b. in agreement.
   c. brotherly.

6. *Affinity* means
   a. natural attraction.
   b. strong dislike.
   c. cooperation.

7. *Animus* means
   a. sense of competition.
   b. friendship.
   c. feeling of ill will.

8. *Enmity* means
   a. relationship.
   b. hatred.
   c. fondness.

9. *Adversarial* means
   a. affectionate.
   b. bonded together.
   c. hostile.

10. *Confidant* means
    a. close friend.
    b. casual acquaintance.
    c. harsh critic.

Turn to page 242 to correct your test. Record your grade in the self-test column on the inside front cover of your textbook. Then go on to **Words and Meanings** on pages 146–148.

Words and Meanings

Here again are the words from the self-test. Only this time, they are accompanied by their most common meanings and pointers on pronunciation.

1. peer (pîr) *n.*   person equal in rank, class, or age

Sample Sentence   Teenagers tend to prefer the company of their *peers* to that of their parents.

> **MEMORY PEG**   When you see the word *peer*, remember that people who are equal in standing can *peer* into each other's eyes, so to speak, because they are on the same level.

2. alter ego (ÔL-tər Ē-gō, Ĕ-gō) *n.*   **a.** another side of oneself; a second self

Sample Sentence   Clark Kent is Superman's rather ordinary *alter ego*.

                                                        b. an intimate friend or constant companion

Sample Sentence   When I was growing up, my twin sister was my *alter ego;* we did everything together.

> **MEMORY PEG**   The word *alter* comes from a Latin word meaning "other." The word *ego* comes from the Latin word meaning "I" or "self." Thus *alter ego* means "other self." In meaning *a*, the "other self" is the opposite side of the same personality. In meaning *b*, the phrase refers to a second person with a similar personality. To keep these different meanings of *alter ego* clear in your head, tell yourself that *alter ego* can refer to an "other self" who might be different or the same.

3. collaborator (kə-LĂB-ə-rāt-tər) *n.*   **a.** person who works toward a shared goal with one or more other people

Sample Sentence   The two scientists' research was very similar, and they decided to join forces and become *collaborators*.

                                                        b. person who turns against his or her own country and works with the enemy

Sample Sentence   In World War II France, members of the Vichy government† were considered *collaborators* because they did what the Germans told them to do.

> **MEMORY PEG**   The prefix *co-* means "together." Thus, for example, *coauthors* write a book together. Notice, too, that the word *collaborator* contains the word *labor*. Put the prefix and root word together to remember that *collaborators* are people who labor together in order to get a job done. To remember meaning *b*, tell yourself that *collaborators* can work together with the enemy rather than with their country.

Additional Forms   collaborate, collaboration, collaborative

4. congenial (kən-JĒN-yəl) *adj.*   friendly; easy to get along with

Sample Sentence   She was new to the group, but its *congenial* members put her at ease and made her feel welcome.

---

†   Vichy government: Vichy, a city in central France, was home to a French government considered a tool of the Nazis.

| MEMORY PEG | You may have heard that the contestants in a beauty pageant vote for one girl who wins the title "Miss Congeniality." The winner of this title is well liked by the other girls for her agreeable personality. Keep Miss Congeniality in mind to remember that the word *congenial* means "pleasant and good-natured." |

Additional Form   congeniality

5. fraternal (frə-TÛR-nəl) *adj.*   devoted, loyal, brotherly

Sample Sentence   While serving together during a war, soldiers tend to develop a *fraternal* affection for one another.

| MEMORY PEG | You probably already know that a *fraternity* is a social organization for male college students. Students in a *fraternity* pledge to be as devoted to one another as brothers. Keep *fraternity* brothers in mind to remember that the word *fraternal* means "loyal to another person in a brotherly way." |

Additional Forms   fraternity, fraternize, fraternalism

6. affinity (ə-FĬN-ĭ-tē) *n.*   a natural attraction or feeling of kinship

Sample Sentence   The close *affinity* among the family members prevented any of them from moving away from their hometown.

| MEMORY PEG | When you see the word *affinity*, think of the word *affection*. Two people who have an *affinity* feel a natural *affection* for each other. You probably have *affinity* with at least one special relative or at least one close friend. And yes, people with an *affinity* for one another are likely to have a natural rapport.* |

Common Usage   affinity *with, between, among; to have an* affinity *for*

7. animus (ĂN-ə-məs) *n.*   feeling of ill will

Sample Sentence   The *animus* and disdain* that had marked the personal and political relationship of Aaron Burr and Alexander Hamilton finally erupted into a deadly duel that cost Hamilton his life.

| MEMORY PEG | The Latin word *anima* means "soul" or "feeling." Keep in mind, then, that someone who feels *animus* has a "soul" possessed by anger, even hatred. You can also link *animus* to animate* from Chapter 14 and tell yourself that anyone feeling *animus* is animated by ill will or hatred. |

Common Usage   *to feel* or *have* animus

8. confidant (KŎN-fĭ-dănt) *n.*   person to whom one tells secrets

Sample Sentence   In Shakespeare's play *Othello,* the character of Iago constantly dissembles*; he pretends to be Othello's friend and *confidant.*

| MEMORY PEG | Think of the word *confide* to remember the definition of *confidant:* "someone in whom you can safely confide." |

9. enmity (ĔN-mĭ-tē) *n.*   deep, often mutual hatred

Sample Sentence   The *enmity* between the two was so great that they could not cross paths without getting into a fistfight.

> **MEMORY PEG** The word *enmity* sounds a lot like the word *enemy*. Use the similarity in sound to remember that our enemies are likely to arouse *enmity*, or "hatred." Also, remember that *enmity* is an antonym for *affinity* and a synonym for *animus*.

10. adversarial (ăd-vər-SÂR-ē-əl) *adj.*   involving disagreement or opposition; hostile

Sample Sentence   The *adversarial* relationship between Romeo's and Juliet's parents forced the two young lovers to keep their romance a secret.

> **MEMORY PEG** The word *adversary* is a synonym for the word *enemy*. So, if you have an *adversarial* relationship with someone, you relate to each other as enemies. As you probably guessed, those who are *adversarial* have no *affinity* for one another.

Additional Forms   adversary, adverse

Idiom Alert

Friend in high places: This expression dates back to circa* 1400. This was a time when having *a friend in high places*, or in the royal court, could do one a lot of good. Nowadays, the idiom suggests that a friend with an important position can often make unpleasant difficulties go away. "Thanks to a *friend in high places*, the young man's speeding tickets did not result in the loss of his license."

Practice 1   Matching Words and Meanings

Directions: To match word and meaning, fill in the blanks with the appropriate letters.

1. peer	_____	a. coworker
2. alter ego	_____	b. equal
3. collaborator	_____	c. natural bond
4. congenial	_____	d. feeling of ill will
5. fraternal	_____	e. a person to whom one can confide
6. affinity	_____	f. second self
7. animus	_____	g. like a brother
8. enmity	_____	h. involving opposition or disagreement
9. adversarial	_____	i. deep, often mutual hatred
10. confidant	_____	j. easy to get along with

Practice 2   Answering True or False

Directions: To indicate if a statement is *true* or *false*, circle the correct answer.

True   False   1. A third-grade student and her teacher are *peers*.

True   False   2. It's not unusual for a best friend to be an *alter ego*.

True   False   3. Wilbur and Orville Wright, the inventors of the airplane, were *collaborators*.

True   False   4. A *congenial* person usually has a lot of enemies.

True   False   5. Two men who have *fraternal* feelings for each other are probably not on speaking terms.

True   False   6. Love is a type of *affinity*.

True   False   7. Two people who feel *animus* toward each other are likely to argue.

True   False   8. At a wedding ceremony, the bride and groom usually display their *enmity* for each other.

True   False   9. If you have *adversarial* feelings toward someone, you enjoy spending time with that person.

True   False   10. In times of trouble, it usually helps to have a *confidant*.

Practice 3   Making Sentence Sense

Directions: Fill in the blanks with the word that fits both the context and the definition in parentheses.

affinity	confidant	peers	congenial	animus
fraternal	alter ego	adversarial	collaborate	enmity

1. In Robert Louis Stevenson's famous novel *The Strange Case of Dr. Jekyll and Mr. Hyde*, Mr. Hyde is good Dr. Jekyll's evil _____ . (another side of oneself)

2. Her husband was not just her friend but also her _____ . (person to whom one can tell secrets)

3. Over the years, an initial dislike between the two associates developed into a deep-seated _____ . (mutual hatred)

4. In America's justice system, people who are on trial for a crime are judged by a jury of their _____ . (people who are equal in rank, class, or age)

5. The company likes to hire _____ people to work in the customer service department. (friendly and easy to get along with)

6. Despite the divorce, neither husband nor wife felt any _____ . (strong feeling of ill will)

7. Most Americans say they dislike _____ political campaigns in which the opponents attack each other's character and actions. (involving disagreement or opposition)

8. A venture is a temporary agreement between two or more companies that _____ to produce a product or service. (work together to achieve a common goal)

9. People who believe in astrology think that certain signs of the zodiac have an _____ for one another. (a natural attraction)

10. Organizations such as the Brotherhood of American Workmen and the Boy Scouts of America are clubs that promote _____ bonds among members. (loyal and brotherly)

Practice 4   Filling in the Gaps

Directions: Fill in the blanks with one of the words from the chapter.

fraternal	peers	adversaries	affinity	animus
confidants	congenial	alter ego	collaboration	enmity

Jefferson and Adams, Friends and Enemies

John Adams and Thomas Jefferson, the second and third presidents of the United States, were initially personal and political allies. In later years, however, political disagreements caused a mutual _____ that made them _____ , and all _____ stopped.

Although Adams was the older of the two, the two were political _____ when they first met in 1775. Both were serving as members of the Continental Congress, which met to redefine America's relationship with England. In many ways, Adams functioned as Jefferson's _____ . Quick and forceful, Adams would openly express the passions that the far more reticent* Jefferson kept inside. As different sides of the same independent coin, the two men felt a natural _____ for each other that made them close and caring _____ with a natural rapport.* Their _____ feelings only grew stronger from their shared work on the Declaration of Independence. Then, in 1784, they were both sent to France as diplomats, which gave them a chance to share many _____ hours sampling French wine and food.

Unfortunately, politics, which brought them together in the first place, eventually became a source of animosity.* Neither man could forgive the other's affiliation* with a rival party. Jefferson, the staunch* Republican,† could not tolerate Adams's belief in Federalism,† and vice versa. Tensions came to a head when Adams became president. All the while feigning* friendship, Jefferson would furtively* criticize his old friend, and by the time Adams left office, there was an _____ between the two that lasted for years until—at last—a friend persuaded them to make peace. The two remained friends until they died on the same day of the same year, July 4, 1826.

> **To test your mastery of the words introduced in this chapter, turn to page 229 in the back of the book.**

---

† Republican: not to be confused with today's Republican Party, which was founded much later. Jefferson's party was, in fact, the forerunner of today's *Democratic* Party.
† Federalism: belief in the importance of a centralized government.

Chapter 22

Talking of Love and Marriage

The Common Thread

In the United States at least, falling in love and getting married go hand in hand.† For that reason, it makes sense to combine and connect the words associated with both events.

ardor	lovelorn
amorous	betrothal
erotic	nubile
platonic	nuptial
infatuation	conjugal

Self-Test   Talking of Love and Marriage

Directions: For each italicized word, circle the letter of what you think is the correct definition.

1. *Ardor* means
   a. love of marriage.
   b. lost love.
   c. passion.

2. *Amorous* means
   a. desirable.
   b. engaged.
   c. passionate.

3. *Erotic* means
   a. mental.
   b. spiritual.
   c. sexual.

4. *Platonic* means
   a. having to do with sexual love.
   b. having to do with spiritual love.
   c. lonely.

5. *Infatuation* refers to a
   a. distrust of romantic love.
   b. loss of love.
   c. feeling of being wildly in love.

6. *Lovelorn* means
   a. abandoned by love.
   b. being in love.
   c. hatred of love.

7. *Betrothal* means
   a. marriage.
   b. engagement.
   c. divorce.

8. *Nubile* means
   a. sadness after love.
   b. ready to divorce.
   c. ready to be married.

9. *Nuptial* means
   a. notice of engagement.
   b. having sex appeal.
   c. marriage ceremony.

10. *Conjugal* means
    a. related to marriage.
    b. after marriage.
    c. before marriage.

Turn to page 242 to correct your test. Record your grade in the self-test column on the inside front cover of your textbook. Then go on to **Words and Meanings** on pages 153–155.

† In several European countries, marriage is on the decline as more people live together without being married.

Words and Meanings

Here again are the words from the self-test. Only this time, they are accompanied by their most common meanings and pointers on pronunciation.

1. ardor (ĂR-dər) n.   passion; intense feelings for a person or pursuit

Sample Sentence   In his *ardor* for the Egyptian queen Cleopatra, Julius Caesar didn't notice that his enemies were plotting against him.

> **MEMORY PEG**   The first three letters of *ardor* are the remains of the Latin word *ardēre*, meaning "to burn." So when you think of *ardor*, think of someone burning with passion.

Additional Form   ardent

Common Usage   ardor *for*

2. amorous (ĂM-ər-əs) adj.   passionate; in pursuit of love and romance

Sample Sentence   He tried to hint at his *amorous* mood by humming love songs, but his wife was too intent on her steak to notice.

> **MEMORY PEG**   The root *amor* means "love," and the suffix *-ous* means "full of." So, an *amorous* person is full of loving feelings and shows it.

Additional Form   amorousness

3. erotic (ĭ-RŎT-ĭk) adj.   having to do with sexual love

Sample Sentence   The bookseller insisted he was selling *erotic* literature, but the police labeled the magazine pornography.

> **MEMORY PEG**   The word *erotic* comes from *Eros*, the Greek god of sexual love. The Greeks commonly depicted Eros as a handsome man of athletic build, but the Romans turned him into a boy-god with a bow and arrow. Whatever version of the god you choose to remember, always link Eros to *erotic*, or sexual love.

Additional Forms   erotically, eroticism, erotica

4. platonic (plə-TŎN-ĭk) adj.   describing spiritual rather than physical love or desire

Sample Sentence   According to Greek myth, Phaedra, the wife of Theseus, fell passionately in love with her stepson; but his love for her was purely *platonic*, and he rejected her advances.

> **MEMORY PEG**   No, the ancient Greek philosopher Plato did not coin the word, but he did see sexual desire as only a steppingstone to a higher, more spiritual love. Over time, people began describing intellectual or spiritual love as "purely platonic." Thus *platonic* love became the antonym for *erotic* love.

Additional Form   platonically

Common Usage   platonic *love, relationships,* or *feelings*

5. infatuation (ĭn-făch-ōō-Ā-shən) n.   the feeling of being madly in love, usually without any sound or reliable basis

Sample Sentence   Biffy the Clown openly displayed his *infatuation* for the trapeze artist, but she didn't seem to know he was alive.

> **MEMORY PEG**   The word *infatuation* comes from the Latin word *fatuus,* meaning "silly." And silliness is pretty much the point of the word *infatuation,* which strongly suggests that our passionate feelings should not be taken too seriously. However, just try telling that to someone experiencing an *infatuation:* The chances are good he or she won't listen to a word you say.

Additional Form   infatuated

Common Usage   infatuation *for,* infatuated *by* or *with*

6. lovelorn (LŬV-lôrn) *adj.*   loveless; abandoned by a lover

Sample Sentence   The bar was filled with the obviously *lovelorn,* who kept on playing Roy Orbison's "Only the Lonely" over and over again.

> **MEMORY PEG**   The word *lorn* means "having lost" or "being without." Circle that word-within-a-word to remember that the *lovelorn* have, temporarily at least, lost all hope of love.

7. betrothal (bĭ-TRŌ-thəl, bĭ-TRÔ-thəl) *n.*   an engagement; a promise to marry

Sample Sentence   After her *betrothal* and marriage to Prince Rainier of Monaco, actress Grace Kelly never made another movie, despite some very lucrative* offers.

> **MEMORY PEG**   At the center of this word is another word, *troth,* meaning "faith" or "faithfulness." Think of *betrothal,* then, as a pledge of faith that a marriage will take place.

Additional Form   betrothed

Common Usage   betrothed *to*

8. nubile (NOO-bĭl, NOO-bĭl) *adj.*   **a.** ready to get married, of a marriageable age (used normally for young women)

Sample Sentence   In some parts of the world, girls are considered *nubile* at the age of thirteen.

b. sexy or attractive (used normally for young women)

Sample Sentence   After divorcing his wife of twenty-five years, the wealthy entrepreneur* dated a number of *nubile* young women.

> **MEMORY PEG**   Circle the letters *nubil* and remember their Latin origin, *nubilis,* which means "suitable for marriage." In the first sense, *nubile* means "suitable for marriage" by reason of age. In the second sense, it means "suitable for marriage" by reason of attractiveness. In both cases, the word is normally used to describe young women.

9. nuptial (NŬP-shəl, NŬP-chəl)   **a.** relating to marriage or the wedding ceremony (*adj.*)

Sample Sentence   The bride made it clear that all *nuptial* arrangements were to be handled by the groom because she had too much work to do.

b. the marriage ceremony (often plural) (*n.*)

Sample Sentence   Excited about their daughter's impending* *nuptials,* the parents could think of little else.

> **MEMORY PEG**   Like *nubile,* the word *nuptial* comes from the Latin word meaning "suitable for marriage." Try thinking of the *nuptial* as a formal ceremony for the *nubile.* It officially allows those suitable for marriage to tie the knot.

10. conjugal (KÔN-jə-gəl) *adj.*   relating to marriage

Sample Sentence   The court found that both husband and wife had denied the other all *conjugal* rights.

> **MEMORY PEG**   Keep in mind the phrase "*conjugal* rights," which refers to the rights associated with marriage, especially the rights of companionship and sexual relations.

Idiom Alert

A marriage of true minds or **marriage of the minds:** A phrase from Shakespeare, it refers to complete agreement between two like-minded people. "Whatever the friends' artistic differences, on the subject of politics, it was a *marriage of the minds.*"

Practice 1   Matching Words and Meanings

Directions: To match word and meaning, fill in the blanks with the appropriate letters.

1. ardor	_____	a. abandoned by love
2. amorous	_____	b. of marriageable age
3. erotic	_____	c. feeling of being madly in love
4. platonic	_____	d. relating to marriage
5. infatuation	_____	e. passion
6. lovelorn	_____	f. romantic, passionate
7. betrothal	_____	g. sexual
8. nubile	_____	h. spiritual
9. nuptial	_____	i. relating to the wedding ceremony
10. conjugal	_____	j. engagement

Practice 2   Answering True or False

Directions: To indicate if a statement is *true* or *false*, circle the correct answer.

True   False   1. The famed lovers Romeo and Juliet were filled with *ardor* for one another.

True   False   2. On Valentine's Day, people express their *amorous* feelings for one another.

True   False   3. An *erotic* relationship is more about the spirit than the body.

True   False   4. It's sometimes hard to tell the difference between *platonic* literature and pornography.

True   False   5. It's generally agreed that *infatuation* is a sound basis for a marriage.

True   False   6. Valentine's Day can be a difficult holiday for the *lovelorn*.

True   False   7. A marriage usually follows a *betrothal*.

True   False   8. The word *nubile* is usually applied to both sexes.

True   False   9. Many women still wear white at their *nuptials*.

True   False   10. A young girl ready for marriage is called *conjugal*.

Practice 3   Making Sentence Sense

Directions: Fill in the blanks with the word that fits both the context and the definition in parentheses.

infatuation	conjugal	betrothal	platonic	lovelorn
erotic	ardor	amorous	nuptials	nubile

1. Anne Rice, best-selling author of books about vampires, also pens _____ novels under two pseudonyms.* (related to sexual love)

2. Famous for his _____ pursuit of women, movie star Warren Beatty finally settled down and became a family man. (passionate)

3. When in the grip of an _____, most of us are inclined to make fools of ourselves. (the feeling of being intensely in love, often without any sound basis)

4. The angry husband claimed that he had been habitually* denied his _____ rights. (related to marriage)

5. As their upcoming _____ got closer, she became more and more nervous about living her life as part of a couple. (marriage ceremony)

6. The relationship between prima ballerina Suzanne Farrell and her teacher, George Balanchine, was purely _____. (spiritual)

7. Filled with _____ for Wallis Simpson, a woman not of royal blood, King Edward VIII of England willingly gave up his throne to marry her. (passion)

8. The _____ of Prince Charles and Lady Diana Spencer was a cause for great celebration, but the marriage did not work out. (engagement)

9. _____ young pop stars come and go, but Madonna somehow survives and prospers.* (attractive and sexy)

10. It's probably better to be _____ than unhappily married. (abandoned by a lover)

Practice 4   Filling in the Gaps

Directions: Fill in the blanks with one of the words from the chapter. *Note:* Here, too, some of the words are interchangeable. Just choose one that fits the context.

platonic	erotic	amorous	ardor	lovelorn
betrothal	conjugal	nuptials	nubile	infatuation

A Message for Valentine's Day

In a Valentine's Day essay titled "The Love Bloat," writer Andrew Sullivan warns about the danger of confusing _____ with love. According to Sullivan, Americans, in particular, tend to marry on the basis of _____ attraction and forget the importance of more _____ connections. Ridiculing the idea that _____ feelings are all that counts in a marriage or long-term relationship, Sullivan insists that even the _____ should think less about physical _____ and more about mental companionship.

Yet, unfortunately, Mr. Sullivan's wisdom will probably go ignored. It will be drowned in a flood of Hollywood movies and greeting cards that suggest the opposite approach to love and marriage. Does your heart beat faster at the sight of some _____ young woman you met at a party last night? Does your stomach flutter in the presence of a glib* but handsome young man you bumped into while grocery shopping? If so, say Hollywood and Hallmark, then you are probably experiencing love at first sight and should start thinking about a quick _____ and an appropriate date for your impending* _____ .

Despite the evidence of _____ difficulties all around us—three out of four marriages end in divorce—we continue to believe that passionate romance is a sound basis for marriage, even when the foundation for a lasting friendship is notably* absent.

To test your mastery of the words introduced in this chapter, turn to page 231 in the back of the book.

Words with a Story

The Common Thread

In Chapter 23, each word has a story associated with it. Learn the stories, and the meanings will follow.

stereotype	maudlin
odyssey	cynic
chauvinist	sabotage
ostracize	nemesis
bedlam	mentor

Self-Test — Words with a Story

Directions: For each italicized word, circle the letter of what you think is the correct definition.

1. *Stereotype* means
   a. an overused political expression.
   b. an oversimplified idea about a group of people.
   c. a fancy speech.

2. *Odyssey* means
   a. longing for freedom.
   b. hopeless search.
   c. adventurous journey.

3. *Chauvinist* means
   a. a person who hates others for no apparent reason.
   b. a person who believes his or her country or group is superior.
   c. heroic figure.

4. *Ostracize* means
   a. to exclude from a group.
   b. to hypnotize by mind control.
   c. thinking in simplistic terms.

5. *Bedlam* means
   a. noisy confusion.
   b. passion.
   c. living space.

6. *Maudlin* means
   a. violent.
   b. passionately angry.
   c. overly sentimental.

7. *Cynic* means
   a. a person who loves people.
   b. a person who distrusts the motives of others.
   c. a person who likes to be with people.

8. *Sabotage* means
   a. travel by sled.
   b. damage to enemy property.
   c. old-fashioned underwear.

9. *Nemesis* means
   a. source of strength.
   b. conclusion.
   c. source of failure.

10. *Mentor* means
    a. dangerous companion.
    b. wise friend and teacher.
    c. military leader.

Turn to page 242 to correct your test. Record your grade in the self-test column on the inside front cover of your textbook. Then go on to **Words and Meanings** on pages 160–162.

Words and Meanings

Here again are the words from the self-test. Only this time, they are accompanied by their most common meanings and pointers on pronunciation.

1. **stereotype (STĚR-ē-ə-tīp)**   **a.** an oversimplified idea or image of a group (*n.*)

   Sample Sentence   Early silent movies generally relied on *stereotypes* instead of complex characters: They featured evil villains, stalwart* heroes, and pure-hearted heroines.

   b. to describe by using an oversimplified idea or image (*v.*)

   Sample Sentence   Although she meant to be fair, the speaker on women's rights was inclined to *stereotype* men.

   > **MEMORY PEG**   Originally, a *stereotype* was a metal plate used for printing. Anything printed with a *stereotype* came out exactly the same—there was no variation. Over time, the word *stereotype* came to mean a way of thinking that denied or disregarded differences. It also came to have a negative connotation. To remember what *stereotype* means, just think of a metal plate turning out cookie-cutter descriptions of reality, for example, "women are emotional"; "men are logical"; "Italians are passionate"; "Germans are cold."

   Additional Form   stereotypical

2. **odyssey (ŎD-ĭ-sē) *n.***   **a.** a long journey where many adventures occur

   Sample Sentence   The hunter's *odyssey* in the wilderness had made him physically stronger but not much wiser.

   b. an intellectual or spiritual search

   Sample Sentence   His studies in Tibet had taken him on an *odyssey* of discovery that forever changed his life.

   > **MEMORY PEG**   According to legend, Odysseus, a Greek king, spent ten years wandering after the Trojan War ended. During that time, he and his men had many extraordinary adventures, including being turned into pigs by a famed witch. However, he managed to escape the swinish spell and return home. Thanks to Odysseus' travels, an *odyssey* now refers to a long, adventurous journey that can take place in either reality or fantasy.

3. **chauvinist (SHŌ-və-nĭst) *n.***   someone who believes that the country or group to which he or she belongs is superior to all others

   Sample Sentence   Although he tried to hide it, the French chef was a complete *chauvinist* on the subject of food; to him, only French food was really worth eating.

   > **MEMORY PEG**   Nicolas Chauvin served under Napoleon, whom he openly worshiped. Chauvin's obvious admiration for Napoleon became a public joke. Over time, Chauvin's name was used to describe someone who firmly believes that his or her group or country is superior to all others. To remember the meaning of *chauvinist*, then, just think of Nicolas Chauvin's boasting about Napoleon.

Additional Forms   chauvinistic, chauvinistically, chauvinism

4. ostracize (ŎS-trə-sīz) v.   to exclude or banish from a group

Sample Sentence   A completely social being, the writer was destroyed when her friends chose to *ostracize* her for writing a tell-all book.

> **MEMORY PEG**   When the ancient Greeks thought someone should be *ostracized* or banished, they wrote the person's name on an *ostrakon*, or oyster shell. Think of the oyster shell to remember that *ostracize* means "banish" or "exclude." You can also link *ostracize* to its more well-known synonym "blackball."

5. bedlam (BĔD-ləm) n.   a place or situation filled with noise or confusion

Sample Sentence   There was complete *bedlam* in the classroom after the teacher was called out for an emergency.

> **MEMORY PEG**   In the fifteenth century, the Hospital of St. Mary of Bethlehem, a hospital for the poor in London, was used to house the mentally disturbed. Because so little care was given to the inmates, the hospital was a place of wild confusion. Consequently, over time the name Bethlehem became a synonym for disorder. Common usage, however, eventually shortened *Bethlehem* to *bedlam*. That mispronunciation became part of the language. To remember the meaning of *bedlam*, visualize the scene of disorder that was Bethlehem hospital.

Common Usage   *was* or *is* bedlam

6. maudlin (MÔD-lĭn) adj.   excessively emotional or sentimental

Sample Sentence   If you don't have pets yourself, you may not understand people who grieve for a dead animal; instead, you may view their misery as silly and *maudlin*.

> **MEMORY PEG**   In the Bible, the prostitute reformed by Jesus is called Mary Magdalene (often pronounced like *maudlin*). In paintings, Mary Magdalene is often shown red eyed and weeping. Thus with time her name became linked to excessive emotion. In fact, it became associated with the easy tears that often accompany drunkenness. Think of someone who, after one too many beers, starts weeping over a long-lost high school sweetheart. That's a good description of someone being *maudlin*.

7. cynic (SĬN-ĭk) n.   a person convinced that all people are motivated by selfishness

Sample Sentence   *Cynics* need to ignore all historical evidence of self-sacrifice; if they don't, it's hard for them to maintain that selfishness is the key to human nature.

> **MEMORY PEG**   Originally, the Cynics were a group of philosophers in ancient Greece who believed that virtue and self-control were the highest human qualities. Yet according to the Cynics, few human beings seemed to display either virtue or self-control. Quite the contrary, the Cynical view was that selfishness motivated humanity. In time, the school of philosophy disappeared. However, the word *cynic* remained to describe someone with little or no faith in human goodness.

Additional Forms   cynical, cynicism

8. sabotage (SĂB-ə-täzh)   a. an action aimed at weakening an enemy or opponent by damaging property or interrupting enemy operations (*n.*)

Sample Sentence   It was not clear if the explosion at the factory was an accident or *sabotage*.

> **b.** to damage property or interrupt an operation in order to weaken an enemy or opponent (*v.*)

Sample Sentence   The underground fighters decided it was time to *sabotage* the railroad used to transport the enemy troops they were fighting.

> **MEMORY PEG**   Stories about the origin of *sabotage* differ. But all agree that it contains the French word *sabot*, meaning "wooden shoe" or "clog." In one story, enraged farmhands destroyed the fields of the landowner they were working for with their *sabots*, thus committing a clear act of *sabotage*. In your mind, picture furious workers trampling a field of wheat with their clogs or *sabots*, and you will remember what *sabotage* means.

Additional Form   saboteur

9. nemesis (NĔM-ĭ-sĭs) *n.*

> a source of failure, harm, or ruin, often in the form of an obstacle or opponent that can't be overcome

Sample Sentence   When it comes to video products, Sony has long been Matsushita's *nemesis* and has consistently outsold the latter company.

> **MEMORY PEG**   According to Greek myth, Nemesis was the goddess of justice. It was her job to hunt down anyone who broke the law and see to it that the person was severely punished. Think of your *nemesis* as a bloodhound set on tracking you down to bring you bad luck.

10. mentor (MĔN-tôr, MĔN-tər)

> **a.** a trusted friend, counselor, or guide (*n.*)

Sample Sentence   Thomas Jefferson was James Madison's *mentor*, but over time the two reversed roles, and Madison became Jefferson's most trusted adviser.

> **b.** to advise or teach (*v.*)

Sample Sentence   New teachers often need a senior colleague to *mentor* them.

> **MEMORY PEG**   In *The Odyssey* (See *odyssey*, above), Mentor is the teacher of Odysseus' son. When Pallas Athena, the goddess of wisdom, wants to help Odysseus' family, she takes the form of Mentor so that no one will know of her presence. Thus the word *mentor* entered the language and came to mean "an adviser." To anchor the word in your memory, associate it with someone who was or is your *mentor* in some area of life.

Idiom Alert

> **Play, raise, or wreak havoc:** disrupt, damage or destroy something. The word *havoc* was once a command for invaders to steal and kill. But in the nineteenth century, the word became associated more with the destruction of objects than of people. It also became synonymous with confusion or disorganization, as in: "The sabotage* by undercover agents *wreaked havoc* with the drug smugglers."

Practice 1   Matching Words and Meanings

Directions: To match word and meaning, fill in the blanks with the appropriate letters.

1. stereotype   _____   a. one who believes his own gender, group, or kind is superior

2. odyssey   _____   b. overly weepy and sentimental

3. chauvinist   _____   c. an oversimplified idea or image of a group

4. ostracize   _____   d. a source of harm or ruin

5. bedlam   _____   e. a person who believes all people are motivated by selfishness

6. maudlin   _____   f. a wise and trusted counselor or teacher

7. cynic   _____   g. to exclude

8. sabotage   _____   h. a long journey during which significant or danger-ous events occur

9. nemesis   _____   i. a noisy place of confusion

10. mentor   _____   j. damage to enemy property or operations

Practice 2   Answering True or False

Directions: To indicate if a statement is *true* or *false*, circle the correct answer.

True   False   1. People who think in *stereotypes* don't fully understand that no two people are completely alike.

True   False   2. An *odyssey* can take place only on a boat.

True   False   3. A *chauvinist* believes that all people are equal in importance.

True   False   4. *Ostracism* is always an expression of goodwill.

True   False   5. A place of *bedlam* is orderly, efficient, and productive.

True   False   6. *Maudlin* movies are usually tearjerkers designed to make the audience weepy and sentimental.

True   False   7. A *cynic* firmly believes in the goodness of all humankind.

True   False   8. *Sabotage* is a special form of spying.

True   False   9. A president's broken promise about tax increases can prove to be his *nemesis*.

True   False   10. Your best friend can also be your *mentor*.

Practice 3   Making Sentence Sense

Directions: Fill in the blanks with the word that fits both the context and the definition in parentheses.

nemesis	ostracized	odyssey	stereotypes	bedlam
cynical	mentors	maudlin	sabotage	chauvinists

1. After his _____ throughout South America, he better understood the dangers threatening the rain forest. (a long journey with many adventures)

2. One of the most famous acts of _____ in history occurred in 1812 when the Russians set Moscow, their own capital, on fire in order to drive out the occupying French troops. (damage to enemy operations)

3. The song's _____ lyrics annoyed him; still, listening to it brought tears to his eyes. (tearfully sentimental)

4. Before his fiancée arrived on the scene, he had been _____ about romance, but falling in love completely transformed his attitude. (believing that all people are motivated by selfishness)

5. Because of his odd clothing and weird behavior, the student was _____ by his classmates. (excluded or banished from others)

6. Most _____ about men and women have little or no basis in reality. (oversimplified idea or image of a group)

7. Laziness is often the _____ of achievement. (a source of harm or ruin)

8. The kindergartners refused to obey the substitute, and when the principal entered the room, she found a scene of complete _____. (a place or situation in noisy uproar and confusion)

9. Animal rights activists insist that many humans are _____ where animals are concerned. (people who believe in the superiority of their country or group)

10. Some successful individuals pass on the wisdom they've gained through experience by becoming _____ to those just starting their careers. (wise and trusted counselors or teachers)

Practice 4   Filling in the Gaps

Directions: Fill in the blanks with one of the words from the chapter. If two words seem equally right, study the context. One word will be better than the other.

bedlam	odyssey	nemesis
mentor	sabotage	cynical

1. **King Arthur and Camelot**

   There are many legends about King Arthur and his royal court known as Camelot. Many of those legends involve the pursuit of the Holy Grail—the cup Christ was believed to have used at the Last Supper. In most versions, Arthur or one of his knights goes on a long _____ in search of the grail. The stories tell of the various schemes hatched by the forces of evil to _____ the knights' quest.

   Several versions of Arthur's story also include the figure of Merlin the magician, Arthur's _____ and friend. Merlin helps Arthur in his battle against his evil _____, Mordred, who is—depending on which version you read—Arthur's half-brother, son, nephew, or alter ego.* Arthur has faith in humanity's basic goodness, but Mordred is far more _____. Convinced that human selfishness can be exploited to evil ends, he sets out to destroy Arthur and Camelot out of pure animus.* Because he hates and envies Arthur, Mordred encourages a love affair between Guinevere, Arthur's queen, and his favorite knight, the handsome Lancelot. In most versions of the story, Mordred is successful at turning the gracious and orderly Camelot into _____ with Arthur dead, Guinevere in a convent, and the quest for the Holy Grail abandoned.

stereotypes	ostracized
maudlin	chauvinistic

2. **Why Are Soap Operas Popular?**

   Soap operas have been with us since radio was the main source of family entertainment. But for those of us who aren't fans, it's hard to understand why soap operas are still around. It can't be the _____ storylines. How many beautiful young people can die of a brain tumor while the rest of the cast weeps and wails? Is it soap operas' heavy reliance on comforting, if

simple-minded, _____ about love and marriage? After all, if you watch the

longest-running soap operas, you'd be convinced that every woman dreams of having a big white

wedding and then a baby. In soap opera land, men are no longer as obviously _____

as they were portrayed in an earlier era. Yet they still have a terrible time recognizing or commu-

nicating their feelings. As one might expect, horrible misunderstandings are always occurring

because some smart guy can't figure out his emotional state of mind. In what also appears to be a

complete break with the real world, almost everybody in a soap opera spends a good portion of

the day pursuing a love affair. Nobody ever seems to have a serious professional goal like becom-

ing a teacher or holding political office. In fact, any soap opera that focused on characters

obsessed more by work than love would probably be _____ by soap opera

addicts, who seem to like their daytime dramas removed from reality.

To test your mastery of the words introduced in this chapter, turn to page 233 in the back of the book.

Chapter 24

Speaking of Government

The Common Thread

Read a newspaper or magazine article about the government, and you are bound to find one or more of the words in this chapter. Use that to your advantage by linking as many words as possible to real people or events.

legislation	conservative
filibuster	tariff
constituent	electoral
lobby	judicial
liberal	subsidy

Self-Test   Speaking of Government

Directions: For each italicized word, circle the letter of what you think is the correct definition.

1. *Legislation* means
   a. judgment.
   b. government.
   c. lawmaking.

2. *Filibuster* means
   a. long speech used as protest.
   b. disagreement among judges.
   c. legal dispute.

3. *Constituent* means
   a. a member of a group.
   b. a vote counted in an election.
   c. a law.

4. *Lobby* means
   a. big government.
   b. a group trying to influence lawmakers.
   c. a government official.

5. *Liberal* means
   a. someone who supports change and the role of government.
   b. someone who favors tradition and individual self-reliance.
   c. someone who does not believe in any form of government.

6. *Conservative* means
   a. someone who likes change and supports big government.
   b. someone who supports tradition and mistrusts big government.
   c. someone who believes people do not need any government.

7. *Tariff* means
   a. traffic ticket.
   b. group of voters.
   c. tax on imports or exports.

8. *Electoral* means
   a. related to the presidency.
   b. related to voting.
   c. related to the justice system.

9. *Judicial* means
   a. related to voting.
   b. related to the courts of law.
   c. mistrustful of government.

10. *Subsidy* means
    a. supporter of government spending.
    b. challenge to the law.
    c. financial aid.

Turn to page 243 to correct your test. Record your grade in the self-test column on the inside front cover of your textbook. Then go on to **Words and Meanings** below.

Words and Meanings

Here again are the words from the self-test. Only this time, they are accompanied by their most common meanings and pointers on pronunciation.

1. **legislation (lĕj-ĭ-SLĀ-shən)** *n.*   **a.** the act of passing laws by lawmakers

   Sample Sentence   New *legislation* can begin in either the U.S. House of Representatives or the U.S. Senate, but both groups must pass the law before it goes to the president for final approval.

   b. a law or group of laws passed by lawmakers

   Sample Sentence   *Legislation* restricting the sale of liquor was once much stricter than it is today.

   MEMORY PEG   The Latin root *leg* does not refer to the legs you walk on. Rather, it means "law." Thus, a *legislature* is the group of elected officials that makes laws. *Legislation* refers to making laws or to the laws created, and something is *legal* because *legislation* makes it so.

   Additional Forms   legislator, legislate, legislative, legislature

2. **filibuster (FĬL-ə-bŭs-tər)**   **a.** an action, such as a long speech, that delays or prevents the passage of a new law (*n.*)

   Sample Sentence   During World War I, eleven members of the U.S. Senate used a *filibuster* to block President Wilson's law allowing the arming of U.S. merchant ships.

   b. use long speeches or other actions to delay or prevent the passage of a new law (*v.*)

   Sample Sentence   Senators are still allowed to *filibuster* voting on a law they don't like.

   MEMORY PEG   When you see the word *filibuster*, picture in your mind a senator delivering a rambling, long-winded speech.

3. **constituents (kən-STĬCH-oo-ənts)** *n.*   members of a group represented by an elected official

   Sample Sentence   Before the vote on the new prescription drug law, many of the congresswoman's retired *constituents* called her office and wrote letters urging her to support it.

   MEMORY PEG   Visualize one of your senators surrounded by a group of people from your home state. Each member of the group carries a sign saying, "I'm a *constituent*."

   Additional Form   constituency

4. **lobby (LŎB-ē)**   **a.** a group of people trying to influence lawmakers to support a specific cause (*n.*)

Sample Sentence   The tobacco *lobby* is always urging lawmakers to vote against higher cigarette taxes.

b. to influence lawmakers to support a specific cause (*v.*)

Sample Sentence   Environmental groups have been *lobbying* Congress for stronger antipollution laws.

MEMORY PEG   To remember the meaning of the word *lobby*, recall its other definition: "a hall, foyer, or waiting room inside a building's entrance." In the seventeenth century, people with special interests would gather in the *lobby* of a government building and wait. When lawmakers arrived, *lobbyists* would plead their cases, trying to convince the lawmakers to vote in a certain way. Thus the word *lobby* came to refer to influencing elected officials.

Additional Form   lobbyist

5. **liberal (LĬB-ər-əl, LĬB-rəl)**   **a.** favoring change in social policy and supporting government involvement (*adj.*)

Sample Sentence   The Democratic Party is the more *liberal* of the two political parties; its members have faith in government as a positive force for change.

b. a person who favors change in social policy and supports government involvement (*n.*)

Sample Sentence   *Liberals* in the civil rights movement and in feminist organizations have been responsible for significant changes in American society.

MEMORY PEG   The word *liberal* comes from the Latin word *liber*, meaning "free." Remember, then, that *liberals* are likely to be "free" of the past and not so ready to revere* tradition. *Liberals* also believe that the government can make positive changes in society, and they readily use government revenues* for social programs.

Additional Form   liberalism

6. **conservative (kən-SÛR-və-tĭv)**   **a.** favoring traditional views and values and opposing government control (*adj.*)

Sample Sentence   The staunch* *conservative* Supreme Court Chief Justice William Rehnquist is an avid* tennis player and painter.

b. a person who favors traditional views and values, and opposes government control (*n.*)

Sample Sentence   *Conservatives* are usually opposed to the concept* of using tax increases to create new government programs.

MEMORY PEG   As you probably guessed, *conservative* is the antonym of *liberal*. *Conservatives* believe that the past offers a precedent* for the future, and they pay homage* to tradition. They also believe that individuals, rather than governments, are best suited to making positive changes in society.

Additional Form   conservatism

7. tariff (TĂR-ĭf) *n.*   a government tax on goods that enter or leave the country

Sample Sentence   When the government lowered the *tariff* on foreign automobiles, including those by Honda and Toyota, dealers were able to reduce car prices.

MEMORY PEG   It was the English government's *tariff* on tea sent to the American colonies that inspired the famous Boston Tea Party in 1773. So to remember the meaning of the word *tariff*, think of the Boston Tea Party, when patriots disguised as Native Americans threw British tea into Boston Harbor.

8. electoral (ĭ-LĔK-tər-əl) *adj.*   relating to voters or elections

Sample Sentence   Many people believe that the *electoral* college† is an archaic* system that has outlived its usefulness.

MEMORY PEG   You probably noticed right away that the word *electoral* contains the word *elect*. To *elect* means "to select by vote." Use your knowledge of that word as a memory peg for *electoral*, which means "related to voters or voting."

Additional Forms   elector, electorate

9. judicial (jōō-DĬSH-əl) *adj.*   **a.** related to courts of law or dispensing of justice

Sample Sentence   Trial by jury is an important part of the *judicial* system in this country.

b. decided by a court of law

Sample Sentence   The Supreme Court's *judicial* decision in the 2000 election was the subject of much debate.

MEMORY PEG   Link the first letters in *judicial* to the first three letters in *judge*. You are bound to remember that *judicial* always has something to do with the courts.

10. subsidy (SŬB-sĭ-dē) *n.*   money given to support someone or something

Sample Sentence   Farmers receive *subsidies* to help them stay in business.

MEMORY PEG   *Subsidy* comes from the Latin word *subsidium,* meaning "support." Remember that a *subsidy* is used to support something, usually a person or activity that would struggle financially without assistance. Financial aid for students, such as the Pell Grant, is one kind of government *subsidy*. Although the government is a source of *subsidies*, so, too, are parents. Many a frustrated one has been heard to say, "Do you expect me to *subsidize* you for the rest of your life?" Remembering that question can help you hold onto the word's meaning.

Additional Forms   subsidize, subsidizer

---

†   The U.S. electoral college grants each state a certain number of electoral votes. The presidential candidate who gets the majority of electoral votes wins even if he did not get the most votes overall.

Idiom Alert

Vote down: to defeat a candidate or piece of legislation. The expression, an old one, was first recorded in the seventeenth century. "The legislation was *voted down* by a large majority."

Vote with one's feet: to show disapproval by leaving, as in: "The residents *voted with their feet* and left the state when taxes went up."

Practice 1   Matching Words and Meanings

Directions: To match word and meaning, fill in the blanks with the appropriate letters.

1. legislation	_____	a. laws
2. filibuster	_____	b. believer in tradition and self-reliance
3. constituent	_____	c. related to the courts
4. lobby	_____	d. citizen represented by a lawmaker
5. liberal	_____	e. long speech meant to delay or prevent passage of a law
6. conservative	_____	f. import or export tax
7. tariff	_____	g. group trying to influence lawmakers
8. electoral	_____	h. believer in social change and government intervention
9. judicial	_____	i. financial assistance
10. subsidy	_____	j. voting related

Practice 2   Answering True or False

Directions: To indicate if a statement is *true* or *false*, circle the correct answer.

True   False   1. *Legislation* can make a thing or an activity illegal.

True   False   2. If the U.S. Senators want a law to pass, they will *filibuster* it.

True   False   3. The word *constituent* is a synonym for the word *lawmaker*.

True   False   4. *Lobbyists* ignore lawmakers and take their case straight to the American people.

True   False   5. A *liberal* would be likely to support the creation of new government programs.

True   False   6. A *conservative* would be unlikely to agree that the Constitution needs to be revised.

True   False   7. Buyers of imported goods are always happy if a *tariff* is added to the selling price.

True   False   8. People who want to become members of Congress must participate in an *electoral* race.

True   False   9. A *judicial* decision will have no effect on the courts, but it will affect the economy.

True   False   10. Farmers who receive money for growing or *not* growing particular crops are getting a *subsidy*.

Practice 3   Making Sentence Sense

Directions: Fill in the blanks with the word that fits both the context and the definition in parentheses.

liberals	conservatives	judicial	filibuster	electoral
lobbies	constituents	subsidy	legislation	tariffs

1. The first _____ happened in 1854 when a group of senators tried to talk the

    Kansas-Nebraska† Act of 1854 to death. (actions, such as long speeches, that delay or prevent the

    passage of a new law)

2. Many _____ argue against government welfare programs, claiming they make

    people less self-reliant. (favoring traditional views and values and opposing government control)

3. The National Rifle Association _____ lawmakers to protect gun owners' rights.

    (to influence lawmakers to support a specific cause)

4. Following the congressman's reprehensible* involvement in the scandal, his _____

    threw him out of office when he came up for reelection. (members of a group represented by an

    elected official)

5. The North American Free Trade Agreement (NAFTA) did away with _____ on

    products entering the United States from Canada and Mexico. (taxes on goods that enter or leave

    the country)

6. To fund their research, scientists can apply for a government _____ or a private

    endowment.* (money given to support someone or something)

7. Many _____ believe that the government should take charge of health care in the

    United States. (favoring change in social policy and supporting government involvement)

8. _____ is the main duty of Congress. (making laws)

9. The _____ college is made up of representatives from each state, who make the final

    decision on who won the election for U.S. president and vice president. (relating to voters or elections)

10. Democracies must keep the _____ system free from political influence and cor-

    ruption. (related to the courts of law)

† Kansas-Nebraska Act: The U.S. Congress established Kansas and Nebraska as territories and allowed Kansas to maintain the
  institution of slavery.

Practice 4   Filling in the Gaps

Directions: Fill in the blanks with one of the words from the chapter. If two words seem equally right, study the context. One word will be better than the other.

judicial	conservative	constituents	electoral	legislation
liberal	filibuster	tariffs	lobby	subsidies

The Influence of Special Interest Groups

A *special interest group* is any organization that seeks to influence public policy. Groups such as the American Medical Association, the National Association for the Advancement of Colored People (NAACP), the American Farm Bureau, and the AFL-CIO† labor organization affect government by supporting certain candidates for office during the _____ process. They also diligently _____ elected officials, trying to persuade them to vote either for or against certain pieces of _____ .

There are two kinds of interest groups. The first represents the *interests of institutions* such as companies, trade associations, or local governments. For example, the American Cotton Manufacturers Institute represents southern textile mills. This group works hard to get the federal government to pass laws that will result in better sales of American-made textiles. They argue for keeping in place the _____ that raise the price of foreign competitors' goods.

The second kind of group represents *membership interests*. People become members of groups to protect and advance their specific desires and goals. For example, interest groups that speak for veterans or farmers encourage the government to financially support their members with _____ . Not surprisingly, interest groups are often criticized for using their resources, especially their money, for selfish ends. In many cases, for instance, they have influenced senators to _____ laws the groups oppose, even if those laws would benefit a majority of American citizens. Yet, currently at least, this kind of lobbying is perfectly legal and not subject to any _____ restraint.

† AFL-CIO: Originally two separate unions, the American Federation of Labor and the Congress of Industrial Organizations were fused into one labor union.

While many interest groups focus on the specific needs of certain people, others claim to work not just for the _____ of a specific state but for the common good of the country. The Christian Coalition, for example, pursues a _____ agenda by supporting laws that uphold traditional religious and family values. Another group, the American Civil Liberties Union, pursues a _____ agenda defending freedom of speech. Both call themselves public interest groups. Both claim to work for the common good. However, they have very different views of what that common good is.

To test your mastery of the words introduced in this chapter, turn to page 235 in the back of the book.

Fiery Words

The Common Thread

Whether it's the literal heat of a blazing fire or the figurative warmth of a heated argument, the words in the chapter have something to do with heat. Use that common thread to create connections between and among the words.

acrid	irate
acrimony	kindle
incensed	ignite
molten	inflammable
caustic	fervent

Self-Test   Fiery Words

Directions: For each italicized word, circle the letter of what you think is the correct definition.

1. *Acrid* means
   a. smell.
   b. bitter.
   c. fiery.

2. *Acrimony* means
   a. fire.
   b. passion.
   c. bitterness.

3. *Incensed* means
   a. smoky.
   b. furious.
   c. irritated.

4. *Molten* means
   a. enraged.
   b. melted.
   c. ablaze.

5. *Caustic* means
   a. aflame.
   b. cruel.
   c. sarcastic.

6. *Irate* means
   a. outraged
   b. flaming.
   c. melted by heat.

7. *Kindle* means
   a. barbecue.
   b. start a fire.
   c. extinguish a fire.

8. *Ignite* means
   a. burn up.
   b. burn out.
   c. light up.

9. *Inflammable* means
   a. incapable of burning.
   b. capable of burning.
   c. heating to boiling.

10. *Fervent* means
    a. burned out.
    b. emotionally intense.
    c. in a fury.

Turn to page 243 to correct your test. Record your grade in the self-test column on the inside front cover of your textbook. Then go on to **Words and Meanings** on pages 176–178.

Words and Meanings

Here again are the words from the self-test. Only this time, they are accompanied by their most common meanings and pointers on pronunciation.

1. acrid (ĂK-rĭd) *adj.*   **a.** sharp or bitter in taste or smell

Sample Sentence   The *acrid* smoke made the firefighters cough.

                                                 b. harsh, bitter, or mean in temper, manner, or tone

Sample Sentence   His supervisor's *acrid* smile signaled that the meeting would not be pleasant.

MEMORY PEG   To remember meaning *a*, use a concrete* example. Link the word *acrid* to the bitter taste of cough medicine or the smell of burning trash. To remember meaning *b*, keep in mind that *acrid* comes from the Latin word *acer*, meaning "sharp." Thus an *acrid* tone is a sharp and unpleasant one.

Additional Forms   acridity, acridness

2. acrimony (ĂK-rə-mō-nē) *n.*   strong or bitter dislike, especially with respect to speech or behavior

Sample Sentence   When the estate was divided, there was so much *acrimony* between the heirs that they even fought over the ashtrays.

MEMORY PEG   *Acrimony* also comes from *acer*, meaning "sharp." Circle the letters *ac* and tell yourself that someone filled with *acrimony* has sharp or bitter feelings toward a person or group.

Additional Forms   acrimonious, acrimoniousness

3. incensed (ĭn-SĔNST) *adj.*   furious

Sample Sentence   The driver was so *incensed* by the slow speed of the truck ahead that he began shouting and waving his fist.

MEMORY PEG   *Incensed* is derived from the Latin *incendere*, meaning "to set on fire." When you *incense* somebody, you haven't just made them mad, you've made them so furious they are figuratively aflame. Thus you wouldn't say that a mother was *incensed* at her little boy because the child wouldn't eat his mashed potatoes. That's cause only for annoyance or irritation. *Incensed* is the word you might use to describe how some drivers respond when in a spasm of road rage.

Common Usage   incensed *by* or *at*

4. molten (MŌL-tən) *adj.*   **a.** made liquid by heat; melted

Sample Sentence   The intense heat had turned the steel beams into *molten* pools of metal.

                                                 b. brilliantly glowing from or as if from intense heat

Sample Sentence   The vampire's eyes were pools of *molten* fury.

| MEMORY PEG | For the first definition, link the word *molten* to *melted*, which contains four of the same letters. For the second, think of a Halloween pumpkin aglow from a lit candle. |

5. caustic (KÔ-stĭk) *adj.*   **a.** sarcastic, cutting

Sample Sentence   Unfortunately, she has the kind of *caustic* humor that can cause hard feelings.

b. capable of burning or dissolving by chemical action

Sample Sentence   Just one drop of the *caustic* fluid will burn through two layers of skin.

| MEMORY PEG | To remember the meaning of *caustic*, visualize a large brown bottle labeled "Caustic Chemical" in large print, with "Warning: Can cause serious burns" underneath in smaller print. The bottle image will link you directly to meaning *b* for *caustic*. To create a connection to meaning *a* as well, tell yourself that *caustic*, or sarcastic, comments can produce a slow burn. |

6. irate (ī-RĀT) *adj.*   **a.** enraged, furious

Sample Sentence   The Secretary of Defense was openly *irate* about the publication of his supposedly secret memo.

b. caused or occasioned by anger

Sample Sentence   The Senate switchboard was flooded with *irate* phone calls about the new tariff.*

| MEMORY PEG | Circle the letters *ira* in *irate*. Over the circle, write the word *fury* because that's what the letters mean in Latin. It might also help to remember the word *ire*, which means "fury." That way you can more easily remember *irate* and its meaning, "full of fury." |

Additional Form   irateness

7. kindle (KĬN-dl) *v.*   **a.** to build, set, or fuel a fire

Sample Sentence   Because of the heavy rains, she couldn't *kindle* a campfire.

b. to arouse an emotion

Sample Sentence   The very sight of a baby *kindled* his paternal feelings.

| MEMORY PEG | For meaning *a*, visualize people throwing sticks of wood in a big pile in order to *kindle* a bonfire. For meaning *b*, remember that *kindle* comes from a similar-sounding Middle English word, meaning "to give birth to." Thus you can *kindle*, or give birth to, emotions. |

Additional Form   kindling

8. ignite (ĭg-NĪT) *v.*   **a.** to cause to burn

Sample Sentence   The boy had used matches to *ignite* the fire that burned down a row of houses. (literal)

Sample Sentence   Just the sight of his new wife *ignited* his ardor.* (figurative)

b. to begin to burn

Sample Sentence   Once the gas *ignited*, the explosion was instantaneous.

c. to light up

Sample Sentence   After they lit a torch to *ignite* the cave, the researchers could hear but still not see the bats that surrounded them.

> **MEMORY PEG**   The letters *igni* come from *ignis*, the Latin word for "fire." When you think of the word *ignite*, visualize someone lighting a candle with a match. The match gives you meaning *a* because it causes the candle to burn. The candle itself gives you the other two meanings because it is (1) beginning to burn and (2) lighting up its surroundings.

9. **inflammable (ĭn-FLĂM-ə-bəl) *adj.***   **a.** easily ignited; capable of catching fire

Sample Sentence   Although the truck carried a highly *inflammable* liquid, it carried no warning sign.

b. quickly aroused to strong emotion

Sample Sentence   My friend has such an *inflammable* temper, the slightest imagined affront* sends him into a fury.

> **MEMORY PEG**   Keep in mind that many people misunderstand this word. From the letters *flam*, they figure out that *inflammable* has something to do with fire. But then they mistakenly assume that *in-* means "not." They forget that *in-* can also mean "in" or "into." Thus something *inflammable* is capable of being ignited into flame.

Additional Form   inflammatory

10. **fervent (FÛR-vənt) *adj.***   emotionally intense

Sample Sentence   A pious* young woman, Joan of Arc had a *fervent* belief in God that could not be shaken.

> **MEMORY PEG**   *Fervent* comes from the Latin word *fervere*, meaning "to boil," and that's exactly how you should think about *fervent* feelings or emotions. They are at the boiling point. And yes, avid* from Chapter 3 is a good synonym for *fervent*.

Additional Form   fervency

Idiom Alert

Baptism of or by fire: In the early days of Christianity, this expression referred to the salvation, or deliverance from evil, achieved by believers who were killed because of their faith. By the nineteenth century, it was used to refer to a soldier's first experience with gunfire. Nowadays, it refers to any difficult first encounter. "The young cadet had survived her inaugural* *baptism by fire:* She had gotten through her first day of basic training."

Practice 1   Matching Words and Meanings

Directions: To match word and meaning, fill in the blanks with the appropriate letters.

1. acrid	_____	a. made liquid by heat
2. acrimony	_____	b. sharp or bitter
3. incensed	_____	c. very angry
4. molten	_____	d. to light up
5. caustic	_____	e. furious
6. irate	_____	f. easily catching on fire
7. kindle	_____	g. sarcastic
8. ignite	_____	h. strong dislike
9. inflammable	_____	i. emotionally intense
10. fervent	_____	j. to build or arouse

Practice 2   Answering True or False

Directions: To indicate if a statement is *true* or *false*, circle the correct answer.

True   False   1. Perfume with an *acrid* scent is usually considered sexy by both men and women.

True   False   2. If a relationship is *acrimonious*, you can be sure that the people involved are deeply infatuated.*

True   False   3. An *incensed* dog can really scare you.

True   False   4. You don't need heat to make metal *molten*.

True   False   5. A man who wants to impress a woman with the ardor* of his feelings will write her *caustic* love letters.

True   False   6. *Irate* and *incensed* are synonyms.

True   False   7. Toasted marshmallows taste better if cooked on a fire that hasn't been *kindled*.

True   False   8. A lamp can *ignite* a room.

True   False   9. A truck loaded with hot chili peppers will usually carry the label *inflammable*.

True   False   10. A *fervent* liquid can cause terrible burns if spilled on the skin.

Practice 3   Making Sentence Sense

Directions: Fill in the blanks with the word that fits both the context and the definition in parentheses.

inflammable	acrimony	irate	kindled	molten
acrid	caustic	fervent	incensed	ignite

1. When the two candidates appear on stage together, the _____ between them is obvious: They can't stop bickering. (bad feeling)

2. Pewter candlesticks and dinnerware are made by pouring _____ tin mixed with copper into molds that are then left so the metals can harden. (melted by heat)

3. The union members became _____ when they heard that the company had furtively* hired strikebreakers. (outraged)

4. After the fire was over, they couldn't get the _____ smell of smoke out of the rugs. (bitter)

5. Once they had _____ a fire and were warm again, the campers' mood improved and they grew more amicable* with one another. (to build a fire)

6. The words she said were pleasant enough, but the _____ tone made them seem rude and insulting. (sarcastic)

7. The gas burner would not _____ because the pilot light was out. (start to burn)

8. When the thief spotted the diamonds, his eyes took on a _____ look of desire. (intensely passionate)

9. When the reporter seemed to chide* the comedian for his lewd* humor, the entertainer became _____ and ended the interview. (furious)

10. After the Office of Consumer Affairs announced the pajamas were _____ , sales decreased by half. (capable of burning)

Practice 4   Filling in the Gaps

Directions: Fill in the blanks with one of the words from the chapter. *Note:* Here, too, some of the words are interchangeable. Just make sure to use a word that fits the context.

caustically	kindle	acrid	molten	inflammable
acrimony	ignited	incensed	irate	fervently

An American Tragedy

The most famous duel in American history occurred on July 11, 1804, when Alexander Hamilton and Aaron Burr, two powerful players in America's young government, met to settle a long-standing feud once and for all. Feelings of personal _____ had emerged years earlier as their respective political parties struggled for control of the new republic. Burr, a Republican,† and Hamilton, a Federalist,† clashed many times. Each man had made _____ comments about the other as both sought to advance their careers along with their party's objectives. While serving as senator, Burr had openly and often _____ criticized Hamilton's financial proposals. For his part, Hamilton had, in public and private, _____ denounced Burr as a man without character or principle. However, the event that _____ the deadly duel came when a letter in the *Albany Register* reported that Hamilton had publicly expressed his personal contempt for Burr's lack of integrity* and disreputable* character. Always possessed of a highly _____ temper, Burr was _____ and demanded that Hamilton deny making any such statement. Hamilton, apparently not recognizing how _____ Burr was, insisted that the public comments were too vague to disavow. For Burr, who was now _____ with fury, this was the final insult. As a result, the two men ended up on a hot July day on the grounds of Weehawken, New Jersey, where Burr mortally* wounded Hamilton, who died the next day.

† Republican: The Republican Party as we know it today was organized in 1854 to oppose the extension of slavery. In the early nineteenth century, the term "Republican" referred to a person who wanted power to reside more in the people than in the government.
† Federalist: political party founded in 1787 to advocate a strong central government.

Although there was evidence that Burr was deeply saddened by what he had done, newspaper accounts of the duel did not record his distress. Instead, they suggested that Burr was blasé,* even callous,* about the tragic incident. Consequently, the accounts served mainly to _____ the flames of public opinion against him. As a result, Burr had to lie low until public feeling against him became less passionate.

(*Source of information:* Joseph J. Ellis, *Founding Brothers: The Revolutionary Generation.* New York: Knopf, 2001, pp. 22–47.)

To test your mastery of the words introduced in this chapter, turn to page 237 in the back of the book.

Chapter 26

The Language of Humor

The Common Thread

This chapter introduces you to words likely to pop up whenever wit and humor are the subject of discussion. Use that common thread to make connections between the different kinds of humor described.

quip	parody
punch line	bawdy
facetious	prank
irony	banter
slapstick	gleeful

The Language of Humor

Directions: For each italicized word, circle the letter of what you think is the correct definition.

1. *Quip* means
   a. funny rhyme.
   b. clever remark.
   c. long-winded joke.

2. *Punch line* means
   a. the opening line of a funny story.
   b. the point of a joke.
   c. funny story.

3. *Facetious* means
   a. having a double meaning.
   b. humorous or playful.
   c. high-spirited and noisy.

4. *Irony* means
   a. saying something serious in a comical way.
   b. saying the opposite of what's meant.
   c. making jokes at others' expense.

5. *Slapstick* means
   a. sophisticated humor.
   b. unsophisticated, often physical humor.
   c. humor that involves clowns.

6. *Parody* means
   a. old-fashioned joke.
   b. political cartoon.
   c. exaggerated imitation.

7. *Bawdy* means
   a. wildly funny.
   b. harsh and wounding.
   c. humorously vulgar.

8. *Prank* means
   a. a popular joke.
   b. a funny story.
   c. a practical joke.

9. *Banter* means
   a. playful conversation.
   b. clever sayings.
   c. insulting humor.

10. *Gleeful* means
    a. joyful.
    b. quick-witted.
    c. extremely funny.

Turn to page 243 to correct your test. Record your grade in the self-test column on the inside front cover of your textbook. Then go on to **Words and Meanings** on pages 184–186.

Words and Meanings

Here again are the words from the self-test. Only this time, they are accompanied by their most common meanings and pointers on pronunciation.

1. quip (kwĭp)   **a.** a clever, witty remark (*n.*)

Sample Sentence   When Drew Barrymore whipped off her shirt on television, even the always-ready-with-a-*quip* David Letterman was shocked into silence.

                                                    b. to make a clever, witty remark (*v.*)

Sample Sentence   When famed writer and wit Dorothy Parker heard that the oh-so-boring Calvin Coolidge† was dead, she immediately *quipped*, "How can you tell?"

MEMORY PEG   Try personalizing the meaning of the word *quip*. Link it to someone who is quick to come up with a funny remark for any occasion. Think of that person as a *quipster*—someone always ready with a quick and funny comment.

2. punch line (pŭnch līn) *n.*   the point of a joke

Sample Sentence   The audience waited expectantly for the *punch line*, but the comedian was so nervous, she couldn't remember what it was.

MEMORY PEG   Search your memory for a specific example of a *punch line*. Take, for example, the following joke: "A grasshopper walks into a bar. The bartender looks him over and says, 'You know, we have a drink named after you.' The grasshopper responds, 'Why in the world would anyone name a drink Bob?'" In this joke, the final question is the *punch line* because there's actually a well-known drink called a grasshopper.

3. facetious (fə-SĒ-shəs) *adj.*   playful, humorous, or funny

Sample Sentence   The student thought she was being *facetious*, but the instructor considered her remarks insolent.*

MEMORY PEG   Link the *f* in *facetious* to the *f* in "funny" because that's what people are trying to be when they make a *facetious* comment. They are trying to be funny or humorous.

Additional Form   facetiousness

4. irony (Ī-rə-nē) *n.*   **a.** saying the exact opposite of what is really meant

Sample Sentence   The instructor looked at the pile of papers and said, with obvious *irony*, "Oh joy, another weekend correcting papers."

                                                    b. a difference between what is expected and what actually occurs

Sample Sentence   Given that the French were supposed to dislike American fast food, it was pure *irony* to see so many McDonald's signs in Paris.

---

†   Calvin Coolidge (1872–1933): the thirtieth president of the United States (1923–1929), who led the country into a deep economic slump that became known as the Great Depression.

| MEMORY PEG | When you think of *irony*, concentrate on the word *opposite* because that's the key word in meaning *a*. When we use *irony*, we say the opposite of what we mean. When we experience the *irony* of meaning *b*, we witness the opposite of what we expect. |

Additional Forms   ironic, ironically

5. slapstick (SLĂP-stĭk)

a. the kind of comedy that gets laughs from practical jokes and fake fighting (*n.*)

Sample Sentence   The parents may have been bored, but the kids adored the clown's *slapstick*.

b. going for laughs by using practical jokes and fake fighting (*adj.*)

Sample Sentence   *Slapstick* humor was a staple of early movies and television.

| MEMORY PEG | In nineteenth-century America, variety shows often featured clowns who chased and slapped each other with fake paddles. The paddles were called "slapsticks." Those routines with *slapsticks* were so popular their name eventually referred to any loud, knockabout comic act. To remember what *slapstick* means, visualize circus clowns chasing one another around while tooting horns and hitting each other with fake bats or paddles. |

6. parody (PĂR-ə-dē)

a. an exaggerated imitation of someone or something done with the intention of being funny (*n.*)

Sample Sentence   The comedian Chevy Chase became famous for his *parody* of the less-than-graceful President Gerald Ford. For example, Chase would pretend to fall off the desk he was sitting on just as he was about to give a speech.

b. to imitate using heavy exaggeration (*v.*)

Sample Sentence   The actress *parodied* the erotic* dance routines favored by singer Christina Aguilera.

c. a very poor or weak imitation (*n.*)

Sample Sentence   In that *parody* of a trial, justice will never be served.

| MEMORY PEG | Celebrities, novels, and songs are often the subjects of *parodies*. For years, household adviser Martha Stewart was *parodied* on the television show *Saturday Night Live*. In the *parodies*, a Martha look-alike would offer exaggerated versions of Stewart's real-life advice about running a home. The Martha *parody* might, for example, counsel homemakers to raise their own cattle if they wanted to eat fresh meat. To remember the meaning of a *parody*, think of those *Saturday Night Live* routines that imitated Gerald Ford or Martha Stewart. |

Common Usage   a parody *of*

7. bawdy (BÔ-dē) *adj.*   humorously crude or vulgar

Sample Sentence   In the sixties, comedian Lenny Bruce's *bawdy* routines got him in trouble with the law.

> **MEMORY PEG**   You'll probably remember the meaning of *bawdy* once you know that it comes from the English word *bawd*, meaning "prostitute." Although at one time *bawdy* meant "like a prostitute," it now refers to any humor that makes sex part of the joke. And yes, the word *lewd** is a synonym for *bawdy*.

Additional Forms   bawdiness, bawdily

8. prank (prăngk) *n.*   a mischievous trick or practical joke

Sample Sentence   Although the tradition is becoming passé*, you can expect kids to engage in a *prank* or two on Halloween.

> **MEMORY PEG**   Like the word *trick*, the word *prank* has one syllable and five letters. It also ends in a *k*. But more importantly, the two words are synonyms for one another. Just keep in mind that a *prank*, unlike a trick, is always intended to be harmless.

Additional Form   prankster

9. banter (BĂN-tər)   **a.** good-humored, playful conversation (*n.*)

Sample Sentence   The party's convivial* *banter* turned acrimonious* when the subject of gun control came up.

                                          b. to make pleasant, humorous conversation (*v.*)

Sample Sentence   It's usual now for local news shows to have anchors who *banter* with each other between reports or with the weather person.

> **MEMORY PEG**   To personalize this definition, imagine sitting with your best friend. The two of you are joking with one another about past times you've shared. Although you are openly teasing one another, there is no hint of sarcasm or caustic* humor. In other words, when you *banter* with someone, no one gets hurt.

Additional Form   banterer

10. gleeful (GLĒ-fəl) *adj.*   full of joy or delight

Sample Sentence   The child's *gleeful* laughter echoed throughout the house.

> **MEMORY PEG**   Think of experiences that make you *gleeful*—dancing to your favorite song, riding a roller coaster, running with your dog, or winning at basketball. When you want to remember the meaning of *gleeful*, think of how these experiences make you feel.

Additional Forms   glee, gleefulness

 Idiom Alert

> **Gallows humor:** The origin is unknown. However, it's likely that more than one person stepping on the gallows tried to hide their terror by making a joke. From those desperate jokes, the phrase probably entered our language. "With only a few months left to live, *gallows humor* was his means of fighting moroseness* and depression."

Practice 1   Matching Words and Meanings

Directions: To match word and meaning, fill in the blanks with the appropriate letters.

1. quip _____ a. an exaggerated imitation

2. punch line _____ b. playfully humorous

3. facetious _____ c. humorously vulgar

4. irony _____ d. full of joy

5. slapstick _____ e. saying the opposite of what's meant

6. parody _____ f. the point of a joke

7. bawdy _____ g. crude physical humor

8. prank _____ h. a clever remark

9. banter _____ i. harmless trick

10. gleeful _____ j. playful conversation

Practice 2   Answering True or False

Directions: To indicate if a statement is *true* or *false,* circle the correct answer.

True   False   1. Most comedians don't like *quips* because they take too long to tell.

True   False   2. Without a *punch line,* jokes fall flat.

True   False   3. A *facetious* comment is always meant to wound.

True   False   4. *Ironic* humor doesn't rely on double meanings to be funny.

True   False   5. You need to be thoughtful and sophisticated to enjoy *slapstick* humor.

True   False   6. A *parody* relies on exaggeration for effect.

True   False   7. A *bawdy* joke is appropriate in any situation.

True   False   8. Whoopee cushions† are ideal for use in *pranks*.

True   False   9. Most old friends like to engage in *banter*.

True   False   10. Winning the lottery would make most people *gleeful*.

†   Whoopee cushion: a pillow that makes an embarrassing noise when someone sits on it.

Practice 3   Making Sentence Sense

Directions: Fill in the blanks with the word that fits both the context and the definition in parentheses.

prank	slapstick	quips	gleeful	banter
irony	parody	facetiousness	bawdy	punch line

1. _____ at the thought of her first party, the vivacious* little girl practically danced up the stairs. (joyful or delighted)

2. After her affair with the president was made public, the nubile* young woman became the subject of _____ jokes on late-night television. (vulgarly sexual)

3. To prove that they are just plain folks, political candidates often try to engage in good-natured _____ with the press. (pleasant conversation)

4. After a while, her cousin's _____ got on her nerves because she didn't get any of his jokes. (playful humor)

5. A writer who uses _____ to make a point runs the risk of being misinterpreted if the reader takes the statements at face value, ignoring the author's intent. (saying the opposite of what's meant)

6. The students' supposedly funny _____ ended with all twelve of them getting arrested and charged with a misdemeanor.* (practical joke)

7. Meant to be a _____ , the movie *Scream* purposely exaggerated the typical elements of horror films. (exaggerated imitation)

8. In the early days of moviemaking, _____ comedies were popular, and audiences enjoyed seeing fake fights, car crashes, and other catastrophes. (going for laughs by using practical jokes)

9. The stand-up comedian's _____ were so quick and clever, audiences had a hard time keeping up. (clever remarks)

10. She loved to tell jokes, but somehow she always ruined the _____ . (point of a joke)

Practice 4   Filling in the Gaps

Directions: Fill in the blanks with one of the words from the chapter. *Note:* Here, too, some of the words are interchangeable. Just choose one that fits the context.

parodies	irony	banter	facetious	gleeful
punch line	quips	slapstick	bawdiness	pranks

The King and Queen of Television Comedy

In television's infancy, comedy was crucial. Along with live drama, comedy shows ensured television's popularity and expanded its viewing audience. Yet comedy on early television was very different from the comedy we know today. The comedians who made the television a household necessity didn't employ the cutting sarcasm of Bill Maher. Nor did they rely on the X-rated ———————————— of comics like Chris Rock or Eddie Murphy. Although a trail-blazing* talk show host like Jack Paar might employ the subtle tool of ————————————, most of the early comedians specialized in ————————————. They sat on whoopee cushions, got hit with cream pies, and just generally relied on ————————————, goofy ———————————— that their audience seemed to adore.

But of all the early television comedians, it was Milton Berle and Lucille Ball who captured America's heart. Berle, known as the King of Television, was never the master of verbal wit. Quick and clever ———————————— were not his specialty. But Americans tuned in anyway in the hope that "Uncle Miltie" would do one of his famous ————————————, such as his wonderfully exaggerated imitation of Latin entertainer Carmen Miranda. Like Miranda, Berle would appear on stage shaking his hips and wearing a basket of bananas on his head. When he did, his jokes did not need a ————————————. His appearance alone was enough to get the audience howling.

Although the ———————————— ———————————— between Lucille Ball and real-life husband Desi Arnaz was part of what made *I Love Lucy* a long-running hit, it was the actress's physical humor that made the audience tune in week after week. Whether she was pressing juicy grapes with her feet in a failed attempt to make wine, stuffing candy in her mouth to keep up with a fast-moving assembly line, or employing an obvious ruse* to win a spot on a talent show, Lucy's elastic face and hopeless incompetence won the audience's heart, and Americans watched her show for almost a decade.

To test your mastery of the words introduced in this chapter, turn to page 239 in the back of the book.

Mastery Test / **Chapter 2:** Character Comments

Directions: Define the italicized word in each of the following sentences.

1. *Obstinate* by nature, he never knew when to quit.

   In this sentence, *obstinate* means _____ .

2. An *assiduous* note taker, she filled page after page with her cramped handwriting.

   In this sentence, *assiduous* means _____ .

3. Despite the many dangers, the *intrepid* explorers were determined to keep going forward.

   In this sentence, *intrepid* means _____ .

4. Successful salespeople are often *extroverted*.

   In this sentence, *extroverted* means _____ .

5. His *callous* criticism of her painting hurt her feelings.

   In this sentence, *callous* means _____ .

6. Always *altruistic* in times of crisis, he dropped what he was doing and rushed out to help the victims of the explosion.

   In this sentence, *altruistic* means _____ .

7. He is coming down with the flu, so he is feeling *lethargic*.

   In this sentence, *lethargic* means _____ .

8. Because she is *introverted*, she prefers spending her evenings home alone.

   In this sentence, *introverted* means _____ .

9. Because of her *insolent* remark, the child was sent to her room.

   In this sentence, *insolent* means _____ .

10. Unlike his nervous competitors, he seemed *blasé* about winning the game.

    In this sentence, *blasé* means _____ .

> When you get your test back, record the grade in the mastery test column on the inside front cover of your textbook.

Mastery Test / **Chapter 3:** More Character Comments

Directions: Define the italicized word in each of the following sentences.

1. She hates violence of any kind, so she is a *staunch* supporter of antiwar organizations.

    In this sentence, *staunch* means _____ .

2. He was such an *avid* runner that he ran even in the rain.

    In this sentence, *avid* means _____ .

3. Only *credulous* people would believe the company's claim that one can lose ten pounds in two days.

    In this sentence, *credulous* means _____ .

4. A truly *proficient* driver rarely causes accidents.

    In this sentence, *proficient* means _____ .

5. The medication lifted his spirits and made him much less *morose*.

    In this sentence, *morose* means _____ .

6. She is so *pretentious* that she goes to the grocery store in a limousine.

    In this sentence, *pretentious* means _____ .

7. Their grandmother was a *staid* woman who had no tolerance for loud, ill-mannered children.

    In this sentence, *staid* means _____ .

8. The senator was a *pious* hypocrite who accused others of the very sins he himself committed.

    In this sentence, *pious* means _____ .

9. The new instructor is *reticent* about his personal life, so we don't know much about him.

    In this sentence, *reticent* means _____ .

10. At their wedding reception, the bride and groom were surrounded by a *convivial* group of well-wishers.

    In this sentence, *convivial* means _____ .

> **When you get your test back, record the grade in the mastery test column on the inside front cover of your textbook.**

Chapter 4: Words for Thought

Directions: Define the italicized word in each of the following sentences.

1. To write a research paper, students must *synthesize* ideas and information from different sources.

   In this sentence, *synthesize* means _____ .

2. The accused was *apprehensive* about the jury's verdict.

   In this sentence, *apprehensive* means _____ .

3. She was so *engrossed* in her work she forgot her appointment.

   In this sentence, *engrossed* means _____ .

4. He believes that there must be a *rational* explanation for the mysterious lights in the sky.

   In this sentence, *rational* means _____ .

5. If someone does you a favor, there's no need to *ponder* why; just graciously accept it.

   In this sentence, *ponder* means _____ .

6. The results of the very first experiment proved that her *hypothesis* was incorrect.

   In this sentence, *hypothesis* means _____ .

7. The stock's price rose on nothing but sheer *conjecture*.

   In this sentence, *conjecture* means _____ .

8. He is under the *delusion* that he can move to Hollywood and instantly become a star.

   In this sentence, *delusion* means _____ .

9. In Hollywood, the term "high *concept*" applies to scripts based on a single, and usually simple, idea.

   In this sentence, *concept* means _____ .

10. Her long walks to work gave her plenty of time for *introspection*.

    In this sentence, *introspection* means _____ .

> When you get your test back, record the grade in the mastery test column on the inside front cover of your textbook.

Mastery Test **Chapter 5:** Honorable and Dishonorable Mention

Directions: Define the italicized word in each of the following sentences.

1. Most Americans *revere* George Washington as the father of our country.

   In this sentence, *revere* means _____ .

2. On Veterans Day, we pay *homage* to the people who have fought for our freedom.

   In this sentence, *homage* means _____ .

3. *Stalwart* bodyguards formed a protective ring around the president.

   In this sentence, *stalwart* means _____ .

4. Thomas Jefferson believed that founding the University of Virginia was one of his most *notable* achievements.

   In this sentence, *notable* means _____ .

5. She proved her *integrity* by refusing to accept the bribe.

   In this sentence, *integrity* means _____ .

6. He is *notorious* for breaking hearts.

   In this sentence, *notorious* means _____ .

7. The mayor is under investigation for her *reprehensible* financial dealings.

   In this sentence, *reprehensible* means _____ .

8. The teacher was fired for his *disreputable* conduct.

   In this sentence, *disreputable* means _____ .

9. The bicyclist's *lewd* gesture shocked her.

   In this sentence, *lewd* means _____ .

10. She thought up a *devious* plan for robbing the heavily guarded casino.

    In this sentence, *devious* means _____ .

When you get your test back, record the grade in the mastery test column on the inside front cover of your textbook.

Mastery Test **Chapter 6:** Money Talk

Directions: Define the italicized word in each of the following sentences.

1. The depressed economy is turning my grandmother into a *frugal* spender.

   In this sentence, *frugal* means _____ .

2. Her boss's *extravagant* purchases led her to believe that he was rich.

   In this sentence, *extravagant* means _____ .

3. The quarterback signed a very *lucrative* contract.

   In this sentence, *lucrative* means _____ .

4. She is giving up her job at the company to become an *entrepreneur*.

   In this sentence, *entrepreneur* means _____ .

5. If our employer's *revenue* does not increase, we will not get a pay raise this year.

   In this sentence, *revenue* means _____ .

6. Many an immigrant hopes to *prosper* in America.

   In this sentence, *prosper* means _____ .

7. The jury awarded her two million dollars as *compensation* for her pain and suffering.

   In this sentence, *compensation* means _____ .

8. If he didn't work a second job, there would be a *deficit* in his monthly budget.

   In this sentence, *deficit* means _____ .

9. The oil *cartel* has agreed that it must again raise the price on barrels of oil.

   In this sentence, *cartel* means _____ .

10. The wealthy businessman plans to *endow* the school with the funds for a brand-new library.

   In this sentence, *endow* means _____ .

When you get your test back, record the grade in the mastery test column on the inside front cover of your textbook.

| Mastery Test | **Chapter 7:** Timely Words |

Directions: Define the italicized word in each of the following sentences.

1. As she wrote her autobiography, she realized that in *retrospect* her childhood had been a very happy one.

   In this sentence, *retrospect* means _____ .

2. The judge's decision set an important *precedent* for future cases.

   In this sentence, *precedent* means _____ .

3. The company and its workers cannot agree, so a strike is *imminent*.

   In this sentence, *imminent* means _____ .

4. To arrive at the same time, they *synchronized* their watches.

   In this sentence, *synchronized* means _____ .

5. The area is overcrowded, and traffic jams are a *perennial* fact of daily life.

   In this sentence, *perennial* means _____ .

6. He is recovering and will return to the office eventually, but we must hire a temporary worker in the *interim*.

   In this sentence, *interim* means _____ .

7. He failed the bar exam on his first attempt, and *subsequent* attempts were no more successful.

   In this sentence, *subsequent* means _____ .

8. Many people plan to exercise but then *procrastinate* about getting started.

   In this sentence, *procrastinate* means _____ .

9. She wants her son to phone every week, but he calls only *sporadically*.

   In this sentence, *sporadically* means _____ .

10. Because it happened *concurrently* with her divorce, her father's death was doubly devastating.

    In this sentence, *concurrently* means _____ .

> When you get your test back, record the grade in the mastery test column on the inside front cover of your textbook.

Mastery Test   **Chapter 8:** More Timely Words

Directions: Define the italicized word in each of the following sentences.

1. Fashion magazines declare which trends are in style and which ones are *passé*.

   In this sentence, *passé* means _____ .

2. The year 2000 began both a new decade and a new *millennium*.

   In this sentence, *millennium* means _____ .

3. The dog's growls warned him of the *impending* danger.

   In this sentence, *impending* means _____ .

4. The antiques expert said the vase was made *circa* 1870.

   In this sentence, *circa* means _____ .

5. The very first video game, PONG, now seems *archaic* in comparison to today's video games.

   In this sentence, *archaic* means _____ .

6. We analyzed the process and broke it down into a series of five *sequential* steps.

   In this sentence, *sequential* means _____ .

7. She planned to renovate her kitchen to make it look more *contemporary*.

   In this sentence, *contemporary* means _____ .

8. Beach volleyball had only *provisional* status during the 1996 and 2000 Olympic Games, but now it is a medal sport in the competition.

   In this sentence, *provisional* means _____ .

9. Cyclist Lance Armstrong has won the Tour de France† for five *consecutive* years.

   In this sentence, *consecutive* means _____ .

10. A *habitual* womanizer, the senator destroyed both his career and his marriage.

   In this sentence, *habitual* means _____ .

†   Tour de France: the most prestigious cycling race in the world.

When you get your test back, record the grade in the mastery test column on the inside front cover of your textbook.

Mastery Test / **Chapter 9**: Keeping Secrets

Directions: Define the italicized word in each of the following sentences.

1. When it comes to *espionage* novels, John le Carré's *The Spy Who Came in from the Cold* has no equal.

   In this sentence, *espionage* means _____ .

2. When she stumbled upon the lovers' secret, she was swept up into the *intrigue*.

   In this sentence, *intrigue* means _____ .

3. She is supposed to be dieting, but she keeps a *covert* stash of candy bars in her closet.

   In this sentence, *covert* means _____ .

4. Under the *guise* of being altruistic,* he donated money only to lower his tax bill.

   In this sentence, *guise* means _____ .

5. When he is engaging in disreputable* activities, he uses a *pseudonym*.

   In this sentence, *pseudonym* means _____ .

6. They exchanged *furtive* glances, so she knew that they were up to something.

   In this sentence, *furtive* means _____ .

7. The thief tore the house apart looking for a *cache* of jewels.

   In this sentence, *cache* means _____ .

8. When it comes to *dissembling,* no one can match Shakespeare's Richard III, who wept uncontrol-lably at the funerals of those he murdered.

   In this sentence, *dissembling* means _____ .

9. The thief's *stealthy* movements did not protect him from the alarm's sensors, and the siren went off five minutes after he entered the room.

   In this sentence, *stealthy* means _____ .

10. Something is wrong with my computer, but I don't understand the *cryptic* message on the screen.

    In this sentence, *cryptic* means _____ .

> **When you get your test back, record the grade in the mastery test column on the inside front cover of your textbook.**

Mastery Test / **Chapter 10:** Hiding Out

Directions: Define the italicized word in each of the following sentences.

1. The stray cats *skulk* around our garbage can looking for food.

   In this sentence, *skulk* means _____.

2. Movie stars often go *incognito* to avoid being mobbed by adoring fans.

   In this sentence, *incognito* means _____.

3. He didn't have a *duplicitous* bone in his body; thus he always said exactly what he felt.

   In this sentence, *duplicitous* means _____.

4. Everyone knew their marriage was a *sham;* they were staying together solely for the sake of the children.

   In this sentence, *sham* means _____.

5. If the prisoners were to escape, they needed a *ruse* to distract the guard's attention.

   In this sentence, *ruse* means _____.

6. The young women were accused of being witches, who held *clandestine* meetings in the woods at night.

   In this sentence, *clandestine* means _____.

7. The intrepid* detective tracked the serial killer to his *lair*.

   In this sentence, *lair* means _____.

8. The pond was so *secluded* that few people knew it was there.

   In this sentence, *secluded* means _____.

9. Toward the end of his life, millionaire inventor and businessman Howard Hughes became a *recluse* who was afraid of being around people.

   In this sentence, *recluse* means _____.

10. Although he *feigned* reverence* for his father, the young prince was secretly plotting to take over as king.

   In this sentence, *feigned* means _____.

> When you get your test back, record the grade in the mastery test column on the inside front cover of your textbook.

Mastery Test / Chapter 11: Expressions of Approval and Disapproval

Directions: Define the italicized word in each of the following sentences.

1. The coach *reproached* the player for his insolent* comment to the referee.

   In this sentence, *reproached* means _____ .

2. We must *denounce* such callous* attempts to violate human rights.

   In this sentence, *denounce* means _____ .

3. The teacher *chided* the student for disrupting the class.

   In this sentence, *chided* means _____ .

4. Many people feel *disdain* for those who have inherited their wealth rather than working for it.

   In this sentence, *disdain* means _____ .

5. Although she likes to fish, she won't touch worms because she has such a strong *aversion* to them.

   In this sentence, *aversion* means _____ .

6. The governor urged the lawmakers to *sanction* his plan for a tax increase on cigarettes.

   In this sentence, *sanction* means _____ .

7. A stalwart* *proponent* of the death penalty, the judge had handed out several death sentences.

   In this sentence, *proponent* means _____ .

8. The actor Charlton Heston has long *advocated* the individual's right to own a gun.

   In this sentence, *advocated* means _____ .

9. To be added to the U.S. Constitution, an amendment must be *ratified* by three-fourths of the states.

   In this sentence, the word *ratified* means _____ .

10. The Vietnam War Memorial was built to *commemorate* the men and women who died in the Vietnam War.

    In this sentence, *commemorate* means _____ .

> When you get your test back, record the grade in the mastery test column on the inside front cover of your textbook.

Mastery Test / **Chapter 12:** Beginnings and Endings

Directions: Define the italicized word in each of the following sentences.

1. A *novice* at bowling, she nevertheless kept on getting strikes.†

   In this sentence, *novice* means _____ .

2. The pilot's *inaugural* solo flight had gone badly, and he was sure he would be cut from the program.

   In this sentence, *inaugural* means _____ .

3. Give your dog a treat every time it responds correctly to the *stimulus* of a command.

   In this sentence, *stimulus* means _____ .

4. If you *terminate* your lease early, your security deposit will not be refunded.

   In this sentence, *terminate* means _____ .

5. During the second hour of the lecture, the students became lethargic* and their attention began to *wane*.

   In this sentence, *wane* means _____ .

6. In the early stages of his career, his father's approval had been his main *incentive* for success.

   In this sentence, *incentive* means _____ .

7. He smiled at her in the hopes of *initiating* a conversation, but she looked right through him.

   In this sentence, *initiating* means _____ .

8. Many adults possess only *rudimentary* knowledge of history.

   In this sentence, *rudimentary* means _____ .

9. Right after the *finale*, the entire cast of the show returned to the stage to take a bow.

   In this sentence, *finale* means _____ .

10. Winning a gold medal was the *apex* of her dreams.

    In this sentence, *apex* means _____ .

† strikes: All ten pins go down at once.

When you get your test back, record the grade in the mastery test column on the inside front cover of your textbook.

Mastery Test   **Chapter 13:** Crime and Punishment

Directions: Define the italicized word in each of the following sentences.

1. Rape is a *felony*.

   In this sentence, *felony* means _____ .

2. For the crime of homicide, there is no way to make *restitution*.

   In this sentence, *restitution* means _____ .

3. In retrospect,* a more proficient* lawyer could have gotten the charge reduced to a *misdemeanor*.

   In this sentence, *misdemeanor* means _____ .

4. The cashier began to *embezzle* small amounts of the store's revenue* from the cash register.

   In this sentence, *embezzle* means _____ .

5. Long *incarceration* as a prisoner of war had left her pale and sickly looking.

   In this sentence, *incarceration* means _____ .

6. Undercover police officers are working to terminate* the drug trade and other *illicit* activities.

   In this sentence, *illicit* means _____ .

7. Burglar alarms function as an effective *deterrent* to crime.

   In this sentence, *deterrent* means _____ .

8. The officer decided to *admonish* the young driver instead of giving him a ticket.

   In this sentence, *admonish* means _____ .

9. According to Texas's *penal* code, the sentence for a convicted murderer is either life in prison or the death penalty.

   In this sentence, *penal* means _____ .

10. If we want to *rehabilitate* criminals, we must do more than just send them to prison.

    In this sentence, *rehabilitate* means _____ .

> When you get your test back, record the grade in the mastery test column on the inside front cover of your textbook.

Mastery Test / **Chapter 14**: Lifelines

Directions: Define the italicized word in each of the following sentences.

1. Battling cancer has drained all of his *vitality*.

   In this sentence, *vitality* means _____ .

2. Only *viable* hearts and lungs can be used in organ transplants.

   In this sentence, *viable* means _____ .

3. An afternoon with a *vivacious* friend will lift your spirits.

   In this sentence, *vivacious* means _____ .

4. The emperor died of a *mortal* wound to his chest.

   In this sentence, *mortal* means _____ .

5. Risking his life every day, he behaves as though he is *immortal*.

   In this sentence, *immortal* means _____ .

6. Trisha's smile *animates* her whole face.

   In this sentence, *animates* means _____ .

7. He dances with *vigor*, so he is dripping with sweat when he finishes.

   In this sentence, *vigor* means _____ .

8. This time his spirits were so low not even his wife's giggle could *resuscitate* them.

   In this sentence, *resuscitate* means _____ .

9. The owner of the crumbling old building had to decide whether to tear it down or *resurrect* it.

   In this sentence, *resurrect* means _____ .

10. The plot revolves around an obstinate* and disreputable* old man who dies and is *reincarnated* as a nun.

    In this sentence, *reincarnated* means _____ .

When you get your test back, record the grade in the mastery test column on the inside front cover of your textbook.

Mastery Test **Chapter 15:** On the Move

Directions: Define the italicized word in each of the following sentences.

1. He met his wife-to-be on a sales *junket* to Hawaii.

   In this sentence, *junket* means _____ .

2. Every fall, the birds begin their *migration* to a winter home in the south.

   In this sentence, *migration* means _____ .

3. The ancestors of many Americans *emigrated* from England.

   In this sentence, *emigrated* means _____ .

4. If you're not familiar with the woods, it's dangerous to try to be a *trailblazer*.

   In this sentence, *trailblazer* means _____ .

5. He is in training for his impending* *trek* across Australia.

   In this sentence, *trek* means _____ .

6. You can *traverse* the whole country by air in five hours.

   In this sentence, *traverse* means _____ .

7. The horse was *goaded* into action by the sound of the whistle.

   In this sentence, *goaded* means _____ .

8. Astronauts have to be both *venturesome* and stalwart.*

   In this sentence, *venturesome* means _____ .

9. She tended to get seasick, so she was reluctant to *embark*.

   In this sentence, *embark* means _____ .

10. At the shore, the tides are always in *flux*.

    In this sentence, *flux* means _____ .

> When you get your test back, record the grade in the mastery test column on the inside front cover of your textbook.

Directions: Define the italicized word in each of the following sentences.

1. *Corporal* decorations, such as tattoos and body piercings, are fashionable now.

   In this sentence, *corporal* means _____ .

2. The *brawny* lifeguard carried the woman to the first-aid station.

   In this sentence, *brawny* means _____ .

3. Too many contemporary* fashion models tend to look *emaciated* and unhealthy.

   In this sentence, *emaciated* means _____ .

4. She had the muscular *physique* of a bodybuilder.

   In this sentence, *physique* means _____ .

5. Counseling may help him discover the cause of his *psychosomatic* illnesses.

   In this sentence, *psychosomatic* means _____ .

6. Chest pain is one warning sign of a *cardiac* malfunction.

   In this sentence, *cardiac* means _____ .

7. Her allergy to the eye drops caused the *ocular* swelling.

   In this sentence, *ocular* means _____ .

8. Hearing aids can improve *auditory* performance.

   In this sentence, *auditory* means _____ .

9. Wearing a gas mask protects the *respiratory* system from deadly fumes.

   In this sentence, *respiratory* means _____ .

10. Chess is a *cerebral* game.

    In this sentence, *cerebral* means _____ .

When you get your test back, record the grade in the mastery test column on the inside front cover of your textbook.

Mastery Test / **Chapter 17:** Words on Words

Directions: Define the italicized word in each of the following sentences.

1. At the end of the lecture, the instructor asked for a brief *synopsis* of the play.

   In this sentence, *synopsis* means _____ .

2. The word "prosperous" is an *abstract* term with many different interpretations.

   In this sentence, *abstract* means _____ .

3. *Concrete* words create mental images in readers' minds.

   In this sentence, *concrete* means _____ .

4. If you believe those *glib* promises, you're more gullible than I thought.

   In this sentence, *glib* means _____ .

5. Abraham Lincoln delivered his *succinct* but poetic Gettysburg Address in about two minutes.

   In this sentence, *succinct* means _____ .

6. The *verbose* speaker put everyone to sleep.

   In this sentence, *verbose* means _____ .

7. The secretary could not record the speech *verbatim*.

   In this sentence, *verbatim* means _____ .

8. His love letters were filled with *similes* such as "your skin is like satin" and "your eyes sparkle like diamonds."

   In this sentence, *similes* means _____ .

9. In her poetry, a battlefield is a common *metaphor* for love.

   In this sentence, *metaphor* means _____ .

10. Expressions such as "neat as a pin" and "quiet as a mouse" have become *clichés*.

    In this sentence, *clichés* means _____ .

When you get your test back, record the grade in the mastery test column on the inside front cover of your textbook.

Mastery Test / **Chapter 18:** More Words on Words

Directions: Define the italicized word in each of the following sentences.

1. No sooner were the words out of his mouth than he wanted to take back an *utterance* bound to hurt.

   In this sentence, *utterance* means _____ .

2. Often, small children cannot *enunciate* the "th" sound.

   In this sentence, *enunciate* means _____ .

3. When a song is played backwards, the lyrics sound like *gibberish*.

   In this sentence, *gibberish* means _____ .

4. In the *jargon* of golf, a "slice" means hitting the ball so badly that it curves instead of flying straight.

   In this sentence, *jargon* means _____ .

5. The actress learned to speak in a British *dialect* to play the role of the Englishwoman.

   In this sentence, *dialect* means _____ .

6. Although the words "physician," "doctor," and "doc" are all synonyms, their level of *diction* differs.

   In this sentence, *diction* means _____ .

7. He is a gifted *orator*, so we're looking forward to hearing his speech.

   In this sentence, *orator* means _____ .

8. Action heroes don't need to be *articulate*.

   In this sentence, *articulate* means _____ .

9. The stand-up comedian's *monologue* made the audience roar with laughter.

   In this sentence, *monologue* means _____ .

10. The disk jockey launched into a *tirade* against the music industry.

   In this sentence, *tirade* means _____ .

> When you get your test back, record the grade in the mastery test column on the inside front cover of your textbook.

Mastery Test   **Chapter 19:** Together and Apart

Directions: Define the italicized word in each of the following sentences.

1. In a *cohesive* paragraph, all sentences are clearly related to one another.

   In this sentence, *cohesive* means _____.

2. An *affiliation* with a professional organization will enhance your résumé.

   In this sentence, *affiliation* means _____.

3. America is called a "melting pot" because it's a country where people of different races and cultures *intermingle*.

   In this sentence, *intermingle* means _____.

4. My parents always *adhere* to the rules and would never exceed a speed limit.

   In this sentence, *adhere* means _____.

5. The two groups' goals and activities are similar, so they really should *coalesce* into a single unit.

   In this sentence, *coalesce* means _____.

6. The organization was plagued by *discord*.

   In this sentence, *discord* means _____.

7. The unequal terms of his will caused a *rupture* between his two grandchildren.

   In this sentence, *rupture* means _____.

8. The death penalty is a habitual* matter of *contention* between its proponents* and opponents.

   In this sentence, *contention* means _____.

9. The president's insistence on war will *alienate* those who advocate* a peaceful solution.

   In this sentence, *alienate* means _____.

10. The Vietnam War was a *divisive* issue that caused protestors to denounce* the American government.

    In this sentence, *divisive* means _____.

> When you get your test back, record the grade in the mastery test column on the inside front cover of your textbook.

Mastery Test **Chapter 20:** Getting Mad and Making Up

Directions: Define the italicized word in each of the following sentences.

1. The prime minister's *bellicose* speech was meant to frighten the opposition.

   In this sentence, *bellicose* means _____ .

2. The two roommates have opposite personalities, so they *bicker* constantly.

   In this sentence, *bicker* means _____ .

3. Dave feels *animosity* toward his ex-wife.

   In this sentence, *animosity* means _____ .

4. In the karate trials, she easily *vanquished* her opponents.

   In this sentence, *vanquished* means _____ .

5. The ruling families have been feuding for so long no one even remembers the original *altercation.*

   In this sentence, *altercation* means _____ .

6. His sexist utterances* were an *affront* to the women present.

   In this sentence, *affront* means _____ .

7. He tried to *pacify* the angry men by promising to increase their compensation.*

   In this sentence, *pacify* means _____ .

8. If only one side would *concede,* we might be able to resolve our difficulties.

   In this sentence, *concede* means _____ .

9. Despite the seriousness of their disagreement, the two leaders managed to reach an *amicable* settlement.

   In this sentence, *amicable* means _____ .

10. From the very first day of class, the teacher tried to build a *rapport* with his students.

    In this sentence, *rapport* means _____ .

When you get your test back, record the grade in the mastery test column on the inside front cover of your textbook.

Mastery Test **Chapter 21:** Friends and Enemies

Directions: Define the italicized word in each of the following sentences.

1. His parents are apprehensive* because he is not reading as well as his *peers* are.

   In this sentence, *peers* means _____ .

2. Sometimes introverts* need extroverts* to play the role of *alter ego*.

   In this sentence, *alter ego* means _____ .

3. When the two researchers became *collaborators,* they shared information and moved closer to an

   imminent* breakthrough.

   In this sentence, *collaborators* means _____ .

4. Most people are more productive if they work in a *congenial* atmosphere.

   In this sentence, *congenial* means _____ .

5. The two brothers' *fraternal* rivalry habitually* erupted into fistfights.

   In this sentence, *fraternal* means _____ .

6. Humans tend to feel an *affinity* for intelligent animals like dolphins and chimpanzees.

   In this sentence, *affinity* means _____ .

7. In the interim* between interviews, the *animus* between the actress and her leading man grew more obvious.

   In this sentence, *animus* means _____ .

8. The ancient *enmity* between the two nations has instigated several wars.

   In this sentence, *enmity* means _____ .

9. Environmentalists and industrialists frequently have an *adversarial* relationship.

   In this sentence, *adversarial* means _____ .

10. All throughout high school, her twin sister had been her loyal *confidant*.

   In this sentence, *confidant* means _____ .

When you get your test back, record the grade in the mastery test column on the inside front cover of your textbook.

Mastery Test / Chapter 22: Talking of Love and Marriage

Directions: Define the italicized word in each of the following sentences.

1. The lovers' *ardor* for one another prevents them from thinking rationally.*

   In this sentence, *ardor* means _____ .

2. They kept their *amorous* relationship a secret, but their friends still suspected that the two were

   meeting clandestinely.*

   In this sentence, *amorous* means _____ .

3. When his mother knocked, the boy furtively* stashed the cache* of *erotic* photos in a drawer.

   In this sentence, *erotic* means _____ .

4. People think the two are romantically involved, but they insist that their relationship is just *platonic*.

   In this sentence, *platonic* means _____ .

5. Like many adolescent boys, he was easily *infatuated*.

   In this sentence, *infatuated* means _____ .

6. The advice columnist receives many letters from the *lovelorn*.

   In this sentence, *lovelorn* means _____ .

7. She gave him back the engagement ring when they agreed to terminate* their *betrothal*.

   In this sentence, *betrothal* means _____ .

8. The beaches were filled with *nubile* girls in bikinis.

   In this sentence, *nubile* means _____ .

9. After their *nuptials*, they embarked* upon a honeymoon cruise.

   In this sentence, *nuptials* means _____ .

10. A married couple's quarrels over money often disrupt their *conjugal* happiness.

    In this sentence, *conjugal* means _____ .

> When you get your test back, record the grade in the mastery test col-
> umn on the inside front cover of your textbook.

Mastery Test / **Chapter 23:** Words with a Story

Directions: Define the italicized word in each of the following sentences.

1. He fit perfectly the *stereotype* of the glib,* fast-talking Hollywood agent who would never pass up a
   lucrative* deal.

   In this sentence, *stereotype* means _____ .

2. Adam's year-long trek* across Europe was an *odyssey* of discovery.

   In this sentence, *odyssey* means _____ .

3. A notorious* *chauvinist*, he refused to hire women for top management positions.

   In this sentence, *chauvinist* means _____ .

4. Those who collaborated* with the enemy found themselves *ostracized* by their neighbors.

   In this sentence, *ostracized* means _____ .

5. The building was on fire, and the scene was *bedlam* as everyone fled toward the exits.

   In this sentence, *bedlam* means _____ .

6. How did these *maudlin* songs about love and loss ever become hits?

   In this sentence, *maudlin* means _____ .

7. Nelson is a covert* *cynic*, who secretly believes that women marry for money, not love.

   In this sentence, *cynic* means _____ .

8. Angry at being terminated,* the engineer tried to *sabotage* the building's completion.

   In this sentence, *sabotage* means _____ .

9. The champion is nervous about facing his old *nemesis* in the upcoming fight.

   In this sentence, *nemesis* means _____ .

10. In her award acceptance speech, she credited her *mentor* for goading* her on whenever she wanted to quit.

    In this sentence, *mentor* means _____ .

> **When you get your test back, record the grade in the mastery test column on the inside front cover of your textbook.**

Mastery Test / **Chapter 24**: Speaking of Government

Directions: Define the italicized word in each of the following sentences.

1. Some airline pilots advocate* new *legislation* that would allow them to carry guns to protect themselves.

   In this sentence, *legislation* means _____ .

2. Democratic senators have threatened a *filibuster* to prevent the passage of the bill.

   In this sentence, *filibuster* means _____ .

3. The congresswoman was never so engrossed* in her work that she couldn't find time to listen to her *constituents*.

   In this sentence, *constituents* means _____ .

4. *Lobbyists* for small business owners are asking lawmakers for more tax breaks.

   In this sentence, *lobbyists* means _____ .

5. *Liberals* weren't exactly reticent* when it came to denouncing* the cuts in welfare spending.

   In this sentence, *liberal* means _____ .

6. He is a staunch* *conservative* who has always argued in favor of lowering taxes.

   In this sentence, *conservative* means _____ .

7. High *tariffs* on imported fruits and vegetables provide the U.S. government with revenue.*

   In this sentence, *tariff* means _____ .

8. If your name is not on the official *electoral* roll, you will not be able to cast a vote.

   In this sentence, *electoral* means _____ .

9. The U.S. Supreme Court is part of the *judicial* branch of government.

   In this sentence, *judicial* means _____ .

10. The researchers will not be able to continue their work without a government *subsidy*.

    In this sentence, *subsidy* means _____ .

When you get your test back, record the grade in the mastery test column on the inside front cover of your textbook.

Chapter 25: Fiery Words

Directions: Define the italicized word in each of the following sentences.

1. Her *acrid* tone of voice betrayed her feelings of resentment.

   In this sentence, *acrid* means _____ .

2. The *acrimony* between them may even lead to an altercation.*

   In this sentence, *acrimony* means _____ .

3. She was *incensed* when she discovered that her duplicitous* accountant had been embezzling

   money from her.

   In this sentence, *incensed* means _____ .

4. *Molten* sand that has been struck by lightning turns to glass as it cools.

   In this sentence, *molten* means _____ .

5. He alienates* people with his cerebral* and *caustic* humor.

   In this sentence, *caustic* means _____ .

6. The town's citizens are *irate* about what they consider to be an extravagant* increase in property taxes.

   In this sentence, *irate* means _____ .

7. In the hopes of *kindling* her enthusiasm, he described the joy and excitement of flying.

   In this sentence, *kindling* means _____ .

8. The school board's decision has *ignited* parents' fury.

   In this sentence, *ignited* means _____ .

9. Gasoline is a highly *inflammable* liquid, so don't smoke while you fill your tank.

   In this sentence, *inflammable* means _____ .

10. In his decidedly amorous* love letter, he expressed his *fervent* desire.

   In this sentence, *fervent* means _____ .

When you get your test back, record the grade in the mastery test column on the inside front cover of your textbook.

Mastery Test / Chapter 26: The Language of Humor

Directions: Define the italicized word in each of the following sentences.

1. His *quips* were so cerebral* she had to ponder* them carefully to get the point.

   In this sentence, *quips* means _____ .

2. She didn't laugh at his joke because she didn't understand the *punch line*.

   In this sentence, *punch line* means _____ .

3. His *facetious* comment about her clothes was unintentionally cruel.

   In this sentence, *facetious* means _____ .

4. There was no mistaking the *irony* in her voice when she said that she loves going to the dentist.

   In this sentence, *irony* means _____ .

5. Much of the so-called violence in children's cartoons is just *slapstick* comedy.

   In this sentence, *slapstick* means _____ .

6. Their comedy skit is a *parody* of the popular television show "Who Wants to Be a Millionaire?"

   In this sentence, *parody* means _____ .

7. She reached the apex* of embarrassment when her husband began telling *bawdy* jokes to their guests.

   In this sentence, *bawdy* means _____ .

8. When the frog leaped out of the teacher's desk drawer, she demanded to know who was responsible for the *prank*.

   In this sentence, *prank* means _____ .

9. Between takes, the two actors engaged in congenial* *banter*.

   In this sentence, *banter* means _____ .

10. He was *gleeful* when he realized that his lottery ticket was a winner.

    In this sentence, *gleeful* means _____ .

> When you get your test back, record the grade in the mastery test column on the inside front cover of your textbook.

Self-Test   Answer Key

Chapter 2: Character Comments

1. c	6. b
2. a	7. c
3. a	8. c
4. b	9. a
5. c	10. b

Chapter 3: More Character Comments

1. a	6. c
2. c	7. b
3. b	8. b
4. a	9. a
5. a	10. c

Chapter 4: Words for Thought

1. a	6. a
2. b	7. a
3. b	8. a
4. c	9. b
5. a	10. a

Chapter 5: Honorable and Dishonorable Mention

1. b	6. c
2. c	7. c
3. a	8. c
4. c	9. b
5. a	10. b

Chapter 6: Money Talk

1. b	6. b
2. a	7. b
3. a	8. b
4. c	9. b
5. b	10. a

Chapter 7: Timely

1. b	
2. a	
3. c	8.
4. b	9. a
5. c	10. c

Chapter 8: More Timely Words

1. b	6. b
2. b	7. c
3. c	8. a
4. c	9. c
5. b	10. a

Chapter 9: Keeping Secrets

1. b	6. a
2. a	7. a
3. b	8. c
4. b	9. b
5. b	10. b

Chapter 10: Hiding Out

1. c	6. c
2. a	7. c
3. b	8. b
4. c	9. c
5. c	10. c

Chapter 11: Expressions of Approval and Disapproval

1. b	6. c
2. a	7. b
3. c	8. b
4. a	9. c
5. a	10. c

Chapter 12: Beginnings and Endings

1. c	6. b
2. a	7. b
3. b	8. a
4. b	9. b
5. c	10. b

Chapter 13: Crime and Punishment

1. c	6. c
2. a	7. b
3. b	8. b
4. a	9. a
5. a	10. c

Chapter 14: Lifelines

1. c	6. b
2. c	7. a
3. a	8. b
4. b	9. a
5. c	10. b

Chapter 15: On the Move

1. b	6. c
2. c	7. a
3. c	8. b
4. a	9. b
5. c	10. a

Chapter 16: Body Language

1. c	6. b
2. b	7. b
3. c	8. a
4. a	9. c
5. b	10. a

Chapter 17: Words on Words

1. a	6. c
2. a	7. c
3. a	8. a
4. c	9. c
5. b	10. b

Chapter 18: More Words on Words

1. b	6. b
2. a	7. b
3. c	8. c
4. a	9. a
5. c	10. c

Chapter 19: Together and Apart

1. a	6. c
2. b	7. b
3. b	8. c
4. c	9. a
5. c	10. c

Chapter 20: Getting Mad and Making Up

1. a	6. c
2. b	7. b
3. a	8. a
4. b	9. b
5. b	10. c

Chapter 21: Friends and Enemies

1. b	6. a
2. a	7. c
3. a	8. b
4. b	9. c
5. c	10. a

Chapter 22: Talking of Love and Marriage

1. c	6. a
2. c	7. b
3. c	8. c
4. b	9. c
5. c	10. a

Chapter 23: Words with a Story

1. b	6. c
2. c	7. b
3. b	8. b
4. a	9. c
5. a	10. b

Chapter 24: Speaking of Government

1. c	6. b
2. a	7. c
3. a	8. b
4. b	9. b
5. a	10. c

Chapter 25: Fiery Words

1. b	6. a
2. c	7. b
3. b	8. c
4. b	9. b
5. c	10. b

Chapter 26: The Language of Humor

1. b	6. c
2. b	7. c
3. b	8. c
4. b	9. a
5. b	10. a

Index

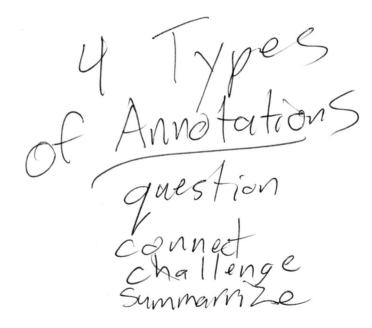

4 Types
of Annotations
question
connect
challenge
Summarrize